What people are saying about:
Marketing Singers

"Where was Mark Stoddard when I was 23?? His new book should quite simply be required reading for all singers/musicians."

"This material is SO desperately needed. THANK YOU for putting it down for us. Thank you for giving us singers permission to feel okay about "selling ourselves"...!

"Your writing style is just as direct and engaging as your speaking style. I had no idea you had SO MUCH history! What a life you've led. You are truly an inspiration—both in person and on paper."   **Andrea Huber**
International Star of Opera, Germany

"His precepts are exactly what my participants need. I saw their eyes light up as they heard and learned skills that have never been offered them before... His lectures are filled with solid advice, strong skills, positive attitudes for business and life and he sprinkles the entire lecture with witty anecdotes, funny stories and a sense of happiness that is infectious."   **Dr. Thomas King**
American Institute of Music (AIMS), Graz, Austria

"Within two weeks of using Mark Stoddard's strategies I was invited to make my Carnegie Hall debut. This is a groundbreaking book. Stoddard's obvious love and enthusiasm for each classical singer and their art form fill the book. Marketing Singers (early edition) puts effective tools for a successful singing career directly in the hands of the artist. Stoddard serves up bite-sized marketing nuggets even a raw beginner can quickly use to increase their audience and their singing income. And he does it in an entertaining way. Marketing Singers is jam-packed."

Linda Priebe
Opera Performer, Founder of Arrivi Artist Marketing, Washington, D.C.

"Your book is the most readable book on business I've come across. I zip through the pages with complete comprehension and feel inspired rather than depleted by the idea of putting the ideas into action."

Elizabeth Harmetz
Opera Performer and Entrepreneur, California

"I read your book from front to back in two days. I could not put it down. Everything seems so much clearer now and the book laid out very specific actions that I can take to market myself in an appropriate manner."

Maria Elena Armijo
Opera Singer, New Mexico

Marketing Singers
— *A Performer's Guide to Artfully Making Money*

3rd Edition Copyright 2016 Mark J. Stoddard
All rights reserved.
Printed in the U.S.A.
ISBN: 978-0-615-74331-8

Cover design by Elizabeth Stoddard, Marketing Artists, LLC.
Editing by Lisa Jackson

Other books by Mark J. Stoddard
available at www.marketingartists.com

Non-Fiction Business
The Power of 117 – Gorilla Marketing
Developing a Real Estate Investment Business
110 Businesses Any Teen Can Start
Handbook for Exploring Russia
Handbook for Exploring China
Seven Steps to Success for the Entrepreneur – Creating a Business Plan
Seven Steps to Success for the Entrepreneur – The Marketer
Seven Steps to Success for the Entrepreneur – The Leader
Seven Steps to Success for the Entrepreneur – The Executive
Seven Steps to Success for the Entrepreneur – The Financier
Seven Steps to Success for the Entrepreneur – The Negotiator

Non-Fiction Biography
How Gramps Became a World War II Hero
My Spiritual Odyssey

Fiction
Strangers in Nauvoo -- A full length musical
An English Toffee in American Molars – a comedy in One Act
Twice Told Tales -- A collection of short stories and poems

Marketing Singers

– A Performer's Guide to Artfully Making Money

3rd Edition

by

Mark J. Stoddard

Can you find the dog in this picture? Once you find it, you'll never look at this picture and NOT see it. That is much the same way you'll find marketing. Once you've understood the principles taught in this book, you'll never view marketing your art the same way. It will be an opportunity to expand your talent.

Marketing Singers
– A Performer's Guide to Artfully
Making Money

Table of Contents

8

SECTION III   **VENUES, NEGOTIATING, CREATE A CONCERT, WHAT TO DO NEXT**

Section I

Developing a Marketing Mindset

Key Marketing Principles

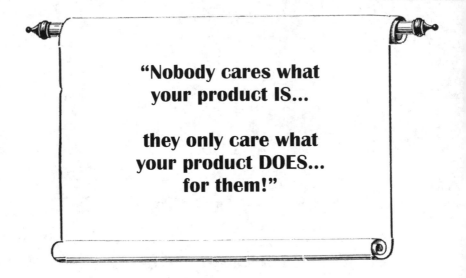

"Nobody cares what
your product IS...

they only care what
your product DOES...
for them!"

Chapter 1

Overview and Warning

No amount of good marketing advice can improve a bad product. Marketing only gets the musician a chance to play, a singer a chance to sing. After that, it is, in the words of Rossini, "Voce, voce, voce." In the case of a singer, the product is "voice." Regardless of the art form, only three things get you where the great stars are: perform, perform, perform.

But how can a musician get that many jobs? That is what this book is about – getting musicians jobs. Performances. Lots of them. They are the same principles every successful business leader knows. The same principles every entrepreneur must practice to see his or her new business or product become successful. While in this book I focus on musicians – mostly singers – the principles are the same for everyone in every business. Do understand that business means simply a situation in which someone has a product or service that another person will find value. One person trades what they have of value for what the other person has of value. That's just business.

This book is designed to help singer and musician who:

1. Is determined to make a stage career survive and prosper until he or she is ready for the main stage.

2. Just wants to perform regularly and get paid for it.

3. Is unsure about where to use his or her talents, and needs the experiences necessary to make that decision.

4. Has succeeded on-stage, make transition to new career avenues.

In all such cases, the performer must know how to:

1. Gauge the market place and evaluate possibilities.

2. Examine his products and skills, and know the audience who would want them.

3. Determine when, if and how to get a manager; and how to make sure the manager is doing what he needs to do to properly promote the performer.

4. Negotiate the proper value.

5. Create paid job opportunities that lead to additional paid work, meanwhile providing the performer with experience and skills necessary to be ready for the greatest stage challenges.

6. Create written, visual and other messages to alert potential clients, customers and benefactors of the singer's talents and skills, and how these people will be benefited by associating with the singer.

7. Keep all the above rolling while still finding time for rehearsals, vocal studies, family and personal time.

It's only fair to know as much as possible about people giving you advice. Are they really qualified to provide life-changing information, or do they merely preach the latest fad? Because I wrote this book (no ghost writer) it's fair to ask, "Who is he and what about his experiences should compel me to read his marketing advice for performers?"

First of all, know that I am NOT a musician; not a classical singer. I have never sung in an opera, nor play the piano and will never do so on purpose. While I love great music, great performers and great talent, my own talent is empowering musicians to earn more money and find greater enjoyment in their profession. If you need help with your art form, get a coach or teacher. If you want to earn more money or find more musical jobs, go to someone who knows how to market musicians and singers AND has done it before.

In April, 2007, I received the following e-mail:

You played a role in changing the course of my life 17 years ago. I was at home having my "29-year-old mid-life crisis" when I got tapes of lectures you'd given. I spent hours walking the country roads and railroad tracks around our house listening to those lessons ... concentric circles, the growth matrix, etc.

Cutting to the chase ... The material "clicked" something inside of me and I contacted a former sales training client about their marketing. I walked in, and using the principles in your lectures, generated an extra $30,000+ for the next year.

Thanks!   *Robert Stover*

Drawers full of similar messages from performers have been received. Musicians who have attended my Marketing Master class and applied its principles have dramatically improved their income and, most importantly, received more performing jobs.

WARNING: These are NOT my principles, however. You don't want new principles. If anyone tells you've they've come up with a new marketing principle, run. It's a con. New marketing principles have not withstood the test of time.

Instead, these principles of promotion I teach have worked for eons and for millions of people. I have invented nothing. I have simply molded time-proven marketing principles to fit musicians and others I have taught, from non-profit leaders, to millionaire business leaders needing to grow their businesses.

And I have done it again and again and again. You can too. I'm no more talented or smarter than you. I just never quit.

I am currently working on a marvelous project involving some low-tech inventions, and the inventor recently told me that "the technology sells itself." Nothing sells itself. I understand, however, where he got that idea. People often see salesmen as smooth talkers who know all the right words and can talk an Eskimo into buying a refrigerator. I have fallen prey to them and probably will again.

While this is indeed one type of salesman, these sales skills do not apply to the vast majority of sales jobs. Certainly they do not apply to you as a performer.   Instead, great salesmanship consists of the ability to know both your product and your audience, and how to carefully share the product's benefits with the audience. This includes educating them in what the product can do for them, and finding ways to continue contact. No clever words or lines are needed.   Rather, a performer must be able to intelligently discuss the opera field; he must understand and be conversant with accepted (and even outmoded) techniques so the performer can distinguish himself by his acumen.

Performers must also be able to understand financial arrangements and what they mean. They must understand the basics of contract law – when to sign, when not to, what kind of contracts matter, and when a handshake or e-mail is sufficient. This is all part of the business or marketing side of this gig.

Marketing yourself does not take a degree; but it does require some good practical experience and an acceptance that this is your responsibility – not that of a mysterious agent who solves all your problems without you having to think one iota about the messy details.

Why this is not taught in music schools is understandable. Music schools teach music, and it takes so long to teach the techniques that they can focus on little else.

Now it's time to step back and make sure we agree on what we are trying to do with "marketing" in the arts. It sounds like oil and water, Mutt and Jeff, or Beauty and Beast.

In many ways it is.

But start at the beginning. What is it you want from your voice? Likely it is not a way of entertaining yourself in the shower. You want to perform. You want to move an audience.

To get that chance you must venture out of the shower and demand an audience. The alternative is to wait and hope someone makes the demands for you. That would be nice, but it never happens.

Overnight sensations are meat for the gristmill, but have nothing in common with real life. Those overnight sensations were actually years in the making and get quite offended when anyone suggests it was all a matter of "luck." They were where they needed to be, ready for the opportunity through years of performing.

You need to be the one finding an audience so you can be discovered for the next job. Getting these jobs (performances) and getting paid for them is simply marketing.

Do not confuse marketing with sales. Marketing is your overall plan of creating performance opportunities. It *includes* sales, negotiating and public relations. It includes a written record of who you are with your resume, bio, websites and business cards.

Marketing also has to do with networking, keeping track of contacts and writing them, calling them or in some way notifying them of your desires – be that selling a CD, tickets or seeking sponsorships.

One final thought: All of the philosophy talk we do doesn't lead to success. Rather, effort constantly applied yields results. Great effort using weak principles succeeds far more than weak effort using great principles.

As my ninety year old grandmother lay dying, she was nearly in a coma. She slept most of the time, but one time when I visited her, she woke up and starting speaking in the language of her youth: Swedish.

In a few minutes she opened her eyes and welcomed me to her room. Slowly she became more and more coherent.

When she had aroused her faculties she said, "I have a poem you must learn, Mark." She then quoted from memory, with surprisingly sweeping gestures and oration, this poem by Edward Sill. Fortunately she recited it to me in English.

Whenever I'm a bit down or feeling sorry for myself, I recite this bit of verse to gain perspective.

Here it is:

Opportunity
by Edward R. Sill

"This I beheld or dreamed it in a dream.
There spread a cloud of dust across a plain,
And underneath the cloud, or in it,
A furious battle raged; swords shocked upon swords and shields.
A prince's banner wavered then staggered backward,
Hemmed by foes.

A craven coward hung along the battle's edge and thought,
"Had I a sword of keener steel like that blue blade the king's son bears,
But this blunt thing!" he snapped; and throwing it from his hand,
He loweringly crept away and left the field.

Then came the king's son; wounded, sore bested and weaponless,
And saw the broken sword, lying hilt buried in the dry and trodden sand.
He ran and snatched it up.
And with battle shout lifted afresh,
He hued his enemy down,
And saved a great cause that heroic day.

Read at the Funeral of Carla Bates

"Carla Bates would tell you "I grew up in the 'hood and was on hard drugs and prostitution to pay for it by 16, followed by the use of tobacco, alcohol and the rest. "In my 20's I was a junkie with a junkie husband who tried to hit me and I knocked him out. I could see my life was in ruins and decided, that day, that enough was enough. I quit everything that day."

I asked her many years later when she was in her 40's how she could quit hard drugs, tobacco and the rest when others spent years in rehab. This wonderful person who died too young, had great compassion but little tolerance for excuse makers and whiners. Her answer was profound:

"If you want to, you will.
If you don't, you won't.
Your choice."
-Carla Bates, Akron, Ohio 2005

Chapter 2

The First Marketing Principle

In this picture notice the ripples caused by dropping something into a still pool of water. From the central point of impact, ever larger circles are created. These are concentric circles. They illustrate a profound marketing concept: the Law of Concentric Circles. When most people begin marketing anything, they tend to think the potential buyers are people they have never met. Not so. The most effective marketing you will ever do will come from people who see you as credible.

If you take a new product to a new market you have zero credibility.

If you sell an existing product to a new market, you have the credibility that someone has tried the product before. That helps, but it is a long, difficult task ahead of you to become profitable.

If you take a new product to people who either know you or know about you, your credibility will allow them to brush aside their skepticism about the new product and give it a try. This is a good place to be.

Even better is if you take an existing product and invite people who know you, or know of you, to a concert that features you. That existing product could be songs they know or songs from a composer they respect. Chances are you will succeed.

This all stands to reason.

It follows a natural law.

Any time you want to sell a CD, find students for a voice studio, sell tickets to a concert, find donors for your cause or a sponsor for your talent, begin with your inner circle. In this book we will show you how to record the name of everyone you know, i.e., family, extended family, friends, neighbors, soul mates, church mates, civic friends and so forth. This is your inner circle. You may not think they like you. It does not matter. Even those people can become fond customers.

It is to your inner circle that you send your first marketing piece.

Then you use the methods we'll show you to suggest ever so gently that these people invite their friends. You make it beneficial for them to do this. You incent them. This is the next circle.

You might even offer a reward for them to sell blocks of tickets to their friends. Let them volunteer to be responsible for 10 tickets. Either they sell them or they pay for them and give them away. Of course you will be keeping track of all of these names and they will go into your house file for future events.

Each layer beyond this is reached via the previous layer. The further you extend from the center, the larger your world of prospective customers becomes. Your reputation grows. You utilize these new connections to obtain more press coverage and to gain contact with the right people in the right houses at the right time, thus expanding your influence.

All the while you are:

* getting paid

* finding more jobs, and

* establishing a perpetual job machine.

Simultaneously, you are doing what you love – singing for wonderful, supportive people who are paying you because you are giving them something of great value.

Such is the Law of Concentric Circles.

Later chapters will expand on these concepts, fill in the blanks, and prepare you to be a performer with a marketplace willing to pay you for sharing your great talent.

Welcome to the essence of good marketing.

Chapter 3

What Does This Have to Do with You, the Performer?

In review, ask "Who is in marketing," or "Who is in business?" Is there really a meaningful difference? Maybe in theory, but not in the real world. So the question is the same. Who is in business?

As a writer, I'd like nothing more than to spend my days penning some marvelous script, writing some music, and finding just the right lyrics to fit the notes, rhythm and mood. Then take up a chance to finish my latest book.

But, reality intrudes yet again. I have to buy food and pay the mortgage. No one ever comes along, rips the transcript from my hands and hands me a check. Instead, I have to find a buyer. Yes, this is a pain.

About five days after my wife Elizabeth and I returned from our honeymoon, we were sitting around the apartment on a Sunday afternoon reading, listening to music and generally enjoying the solitude together. Then a thought came into my head: "I think the first rent check is about due." So I asked Liz, "Ahh, how much money do we have in the bank account?"

She looked up at me and said, "I haven't a clue."

"Hmm," I said, "Neither do I. Maybe we ought to check."

We balanced the check book ... it was a mess. We'd combined our meager bank accounts before getting married. Once the adding machine did its thing we saw the balance and laughed. We weren't overdrawn, but were very close. We had nothing in savings and not much cash sitting around the house.

"What are we going to do?" her look said to me.

"I guess one of us ought to get a job."

"Let's both get one," she said.

We did. We made ends meet. Liz, my artist wife, found a job at a construction company as ... are you ready? ... a bookkeeper! I flipped hamburgers and made milk shakes while I finished off my English degree and my great American novel and short stories.

As life happened, no one beat an Agatha path to my door to read my better Mousetrap. I had to send my story out to find a buyer. And I did.

Since that time, I've learned the art of advertising and marketing and it has served me and my family well. I've written 18+ books and have self-published them all so I could market them myself. The mark-ups beat the heck out of royalties. I've also learned to start businesses. I've seen wonderful successes and mind-numbing failures as I've started companies in construction, advertising, publishing, tour operations, fund raising, adult education, vehicle transmissions and others. I've staged musicals, and created a venue for more than 100 sold-out concerts for my friends in the classical music world. I've even been a lobbyist for a free-market grass-roots lobby where I wrote and helped pass the only unanimously approved resolution in US history supporting freedom fighters. It's been a wild ride, but one filled with great adventures.

Reality bites; but just like me, you're in marketing and business too. The key is getting your mind right. No one owes you a living, a job, or much of anything else. If you want it, you have to ask for it and go get it.

The choice is yours: you can do what you want, when you want, how you want and somehow get by; or learn some business/marketing principles and actually get some financial value out of your talents.

Marketing is simply persuasion. It's getting what you want by convincing someone what they have of value should be traded for what you produce of value. It's fairly simple.

Just commit a little image suicide, stop thinking yourself above marketing, and start getting what you want.

Becoming a performer, not a singer

In all marketing, at some point you must put yourself on the line, or stand up and physically make your case. In dating, having a Cyrano or Miles Standish to speak for you is a luxury that can backfire. You must speak your piece for what you want.

In business, the business owner must be the greatest spokesman for his company. The lowest employee had better be his best advocate or he or she will remain the lowest employee. Meg Whitman rose to the top of E-Bay and became one of the wealthiest women in California. She got her start selling magazines door to door. She learned the art of "eye contact" by reading people's eyes as she sold magazines face to face. She hadn't lost her four-year-old ability of reading people to get what she wanted.

When their eyes told her she wasn't resonating, she switched approaches and found one that meant something to her customers. She found a benefit they couldn't live without. She then went on to a university education in business and landed a job as a Brand Manager. Sounds sophisticated and impressive, but a Brand Manager is simply a higher paid door-to-door salesman. She mastered that and sold her products for Proctor and Gamble, and then advanced to become a Vice President. I suspect some think she got to the top because someone felt sorry for her as a woman, or felt she was an oppressed minority and needed a free hand up. Whitman shudders at such a suggestion because she knows all the hard work that has gone into her career. She got what she wanted because she knew what she wanted and knew how to be her best spokesman. At press time she was the leading candidate for the governorship of California. Once again, she's her own best spokesman and must be.

One of the keys to becoming your own best spokesman is to understand that your knowledge of the technical side of your business must be joined by your ability to read your audience and present your skills in such a way that they'll get out of your discussion what you wish them to get.

One way to do this is to understand human beings. Surely even the most erudite, sophisticated or cerebral man finds himself useless without an understanding of human nature. The reclusive Stephen Hawking, as brilliant as he is, knows he must frame his opinions in a way people can understand and accept. This is done by finding similarities in different universes.

Anyone can point out how one person is different from another. It's the hallmark of racism. We see a person with a different skin tone and draw conclusions. But race is a terrible predictor of behavior. When I lecture on college campuses, I enjoy watching students come to grips with this concept.

Those in the more intellectual or artistic pursuits have the most difficult time comprehending that they could possibly be one who takes the easy way out by focusing on differences. But they do. It's almost reflexive in their chosen professions.

My comedy, "An English Toffee in American Molars," won a local university theatrical competition. Much to my delight, nearly all of the audience cried with laughter. One gentleman near me was literally on his hands and knees laughing. At the end, they called for the author. That was fun. But, the next day the university drama club assembled to evaluate the competition. One of the professors was asked what she thought of my play. She responded, "I heard it was well-received but I also heard it had some problems." I had snuck into the back of the hall and just had to shake my head as such a desire to find the differences.

Anyone, however, can fall into this trap. As Teddy Roosevelt once said, "It's not the critic who counts, not the man who points out how the strong man stumbled, or when the doer of deeds could have done better. The credit belongs to the man who is actually in the arena; whose face is marred by dust and sweat and blood; who strives valiantly; who errs and comes short again and again; who knows the great enthusiasms, the great devotions and spends himself in a worthy cause; who at the best, knows in the end the triumph of high achievement; and who at the worst if he fails, at least fails while daring greatly, so that his place shall never be with those cold and timid souls who know neither victory or defeat."

Being a critic is easy. Being a creator is tough.

Back to finding similarities in different universes. Let's test your ability to find similarities. Quickly list how a cat and a refrigerator are similar.

Go ahead. Write them down.

They are, indeed, very different universes. We have no problem listing how they are different. Fur vs. metal. Living vs. inanimate.

But listing how they're similar is tough until you change your view point. Then it's fun. Go ahead. Make your list.

When I do this exercise with students, artists have the toughest time. They are almost overcome by a stupor of thought because they aren't asked to think like this. Normally they watch a performer and point out flaws. As I said, that's the easy part.

How many similarities were on your list? Most people mention that both cats and refrigerators:

* come in an assortment of colors,
* hold fish and milk,
* are cold, and
* do not come to you when you call.

Once people change their mind sets, they start getting creative (hmmm, is there a lesson here?). They start noticing that both have four legs, a tail, they both purr, have hairballs, sit in a corner, and so forth.

We recently attended a performance of several singers. They were terrific. Blended voices, active music selection, great range ... and in fact were quite at home on the range. They were the Bar J Wranglers, a cowboy singing group. Every singer could learn some lessons from these guys. They were performers first, singers second. Robert Swedberg of the now-defunct Orlando Opera once told me he was tired of hiring singers and only wanted to hire performers. Apparently his audiences tired of singers, too.

People go to theatrical events to be entertained, not educated. If we learn something as well, that's the clotted cream atop the butterfat rich ice cream.

The art of persuasion has, at its core, the ability to perform. Performance is all about blending art and reality. Great music elevates the soul, but a musician singing aria after aria after aria is mind numbing. Performance is all about engaging the audience. This means speaking to them, telling them stories about the music, joking with them and making them laugh, touching their souls and making them weep. You've got to have a shtick, an entertainment routine.

It's no different if you're holding a stock holders meeting, making a Power Point presentation, going to a job interview ... or dating for that matter.

Developing a performance ability can be tough work. In career singing it takes talent to conceive of routines that add to the music rather than distract. More than that, it takes experience. You must perform for enough people until you come to know what moves them, makes them laugh, cry or chuckle. You must organize the music so it crescendos to a climax that drives the audience to leap to their feet and demand more.

The same thing applies to any other presentation.

Watch the Bar J Wranglers and you'll see a finely tuned performance. They touch all the buttons. In college courses, we tell students that plagiarism is stealing from another person – but research is taking from many! Bits here. Ideas there. But take only from the best and only those ideas that fit you and your stage goals.

One rather stuffy teacher once preached for classical singers to "never look their audiences in the eye because that diminished the music. Let the music speak for itself and don't get common." Nice advice if you want to bore people. Instead, consider a tip from Gladys Knight. She states that every time she enters the stage, as she walks to the center or her starting mark, she scans the audience for the most positive, receptive person and then zeros in on that person as she sings her first song. She draws energy from that audience member that flows through her and back to the rest of the audience. Gladys is a great performer. Take her tip.

I wrote this chapter after a trip to Graz, Austria, where I gave a couple of lectures on marketing. Every time I talk to singers I am struck by their commitment to their talent, and their determination to build singing skills because they love it so much. Too bad more people don't have that kind of dedication in their respective professions.

However, I am bothered by the number of singers who just cannot picture themselves promoting themselves. I do understand their reluctance for self-promotion. I can easily promote others, but I feel uncomfortable talking about myself and pushing what I have to offer. I would love it if everyone who needed help marketing themselves would just call me. But that is foolish. Only in our Horatio Alger stories of Rags to Riches does a person hang out a shingle and the customers come running. Yet we dream.

One situation I pose to singers is, "You try a little marketing, test it, keep track of the results and then try again. You finally discover something that works. Then later, what do you do when you find out what worked yesterday does not work today?"

Screaming, we throw up our hands and ask, "What is going on? It worked last time. Why not now?"

It's important that you understand this, so let's go deeper.

Just look in the mirror. How are you different today than one year ago? I'll bet you have changed. Different jewelry. Different hair style. More up-to-date clothes or retro clothes. Around your apartment or home you have new conveniences only dreamed of just a year or two ago.

You are the problem. You keep changing. But it's not just you. Everyone else does the same thing. The technique or slogan that attracted people to you yesterday does not work today. Perhaps they have heard it too much and it no longer attracts attention. This is marketing death. Perhaps others are using a similar approach, so instead of being Rocky Road, you have become vanilla. Your marketing is passed over. You might be passé. Old news. Been there, done that. Predictable.

You can and must keep experimenting with the market place. Do not ever be afraid to try an approach to promote yourself. If you fall flat on your face (done that a bunch myself), lick your wounds and ponder what went wrong. Then try something else. You are learning and getting better at marketing as you do it.

As a performer, you generally know who the current market is for classical music; but do not think of the market as a stratum of humanity – rich, old white people. Think instead of the market being a stratum of a human being. Each human has an enormous variety of stimuli that can affect them. Just about every stimulus affects us to some degree. At times we like a raucous beat, wild ideas and crazy notions. At any age. Perhaps as we grow older some of us resist some of those beats, but I theorize we are all affected by them. If classical music is truly classical, it is timeless and reaches all humanity. It carries universal emotions that can touch everyone.

If this is true, it's time to take the wonderful voice you have developed and constantly share some portion of classical music to touch the human soul. Perform everywhere, anywhere, any way, constantly, never ending. As you share, you will gain the feedback you need to 1) get better, 2) know more what the market needs, and 3) know what affects the market in the best way. As you share, you gain the joy of having touched people, which builds you in a positive way.

And charge people. Find ways to get money for what you do. Remember that price is always determined by perceived value. Know your value to people and help them know that value through effective marketing and promotion.

The market is ever changing just as you are. Learn that one of the prime principles of marketing is understanding your fellow human beings, how they live their lives and how you can help them. Then be flexible to appeal to them in their current state of living.

In summary, marketing (and business) requires us to know what we want, understand human beings, and persuade them that the value we give is worth the value they give. What you are selling doesn't matter. It's all the same.

Choose the shape that is different from all the rest!

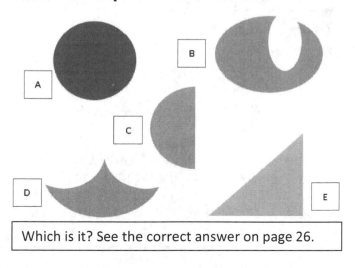

Which is it? See the correct answer on page 26.

26

"If we treat people as they are, we make them worse. If we treat people as they ought to be, we help them become what they are capable of becoming."

-Goethe

"If a million people say a foolish thing, it is still a foolish thing."

-Bertrand Russell

The correct answer for the "shapes"?

A – The only shape with no points.
B – The only shape that is asymmetrical.
C – The only shape with a straight and curved line.
D – The only shape with a Euclidian triangle in a non-Euclidian space.
E – The only shape with three straight lines.

Marketing is messy. Usually there are MANY right answers. That is because it involves dealing with the public and people are constantly changing their minds. You must be creative. Armed with the principles taught in this book you'll be prepared to create new techniques that best fit your immediate circumstance.

Chapter 4

Speed and Actions Matter

I was once crestfallen after reading a beautiful poem and hearing the author confess she had never written anything before. I had previously figured only those of us with writing training could produce such a tome. The fact is, anybody can write. About anybody can do about anything any of the rest of us can do.

Not long after this deflating experience, I was working as a carpenter/laborer on one my father's construction projects. After a few tries of using a new nail gun, the foreman said to me, "See, I knew you could do it. Anyone can build a house." He saw my confused look and said, "Hey, don't get me wrong. My brother is an accountant and thinks a hammer and screw driver have the same use. But, given enough time, he could build the house I'm building for him. Given enough time."

That was the answer. Time. Given enough time and enough effort, anyone can write a book. However, a skilled person can do it in a fraction of the time.

In your business and professional pursuits, understand the power of time. Anyone can find a way to sell a product, but if they take months or years, think of all the lost opportunities. So if someone contacts you for business, and you want their business, the clock is ticking rapidly.

My friend Benoy Tamang recently gave me an MIT study which found that if you get an Internet inquiry and you call them within 5 minutes, you have more than 20 times the chance of landing their business than if you wait 30 minutes. Wait a day and you wasted your money. Let me illustrate. One November, a guy told me of a chance to sell real estate in Switzerland. At the same time, several major real estate companies were presented the same opportunity. I'd never sold real estate before and knew nothing about Swiss law, but it seemed like a great opportunity.

By the end of December I'd videoed the properties, videoed myself explaining the deal, edited it, made a one-hour sales video detailing the offer and benefits, and sold more than 400 videos for $100 each.

By the end of January, I had a list of more than 100 prospective and qualified buyers willing to pay their way to Switzerland to meet my sales team for a tour.

By the end of February I had the team in place including the Swiss property lawyer.

In March we started meeting groups in Geneva for one-week buying tours.

By May we'd sold every unit.

By the end of June we'd closed on $20+ million in Swiss condo properties in the Valais Valley.

I made the decision and got to work immediately. The major real estate firms arrived in Switzerland in May, ready to complete their "due diligence." The look on their faces was priceless.

As Andy told Red at Shawshank, "Get busy living, or get busy dying." So much of business success is speed to the market. The guy or gal who can get a project completed this week is rare. Most take a week to clear their throat, or a month to get board approval to investigate. Tis worse to be irresolute than wrong.

Marketing has a couple of other ways to look at speed. Many wait until too late to do something. They fear rushing in. They don't know how to manage speed. Speed kills, they say.

As one can see, I have a different point of view. General George Patton (never one for being irresolute) stated, "A good plan, violently executed today, is better than a perfect plan next week." If the violence bothers you, then say it as "Entrepreneur of the Year" (and great friend and business associate) Byron Boothe said it, "About right now is better than exactly right later."

Fear of failure gets people into the fuss-budget mindset where they keep doing market research, fiddling with figures, and carefully mapping out strategy - never getting to the job at hand.

While these fuss budgets are fiddling while Rome burns, I'm out doing, making mistakes, learning from them and eventually getting it right. That "eventually" has some advantages. Eventually you learn the skills to do it right the first time and do it right quickly. If you're taking action, you learn, adjust, adapt and move on.

In 1984, I was at a reception in Washington, DC. These are dreadful affairs where everyone wants to be seen with someone special. I was semi-enjoying a mindless Tuesday evening when Neal Blair, my partner in political grime (we were lobbyists), came up to me with Phyllis Schlafly in tow. The Equal Rights Amendment had spent years being rejected by state legislatures and the time had run out for the amendment process. But die-hard supporters were trying to change the rules and grant it an extended time so they could get their way. Both parties participate in such shenanigans.

Mrs. Schlafly told Neal that she needed a commercial written that could convince the 17 wavering congressmen to spike the bill once and for all. Neal magnanimously told Schlafly that I would be happy to write a commercial for her. I nearly croaked on my Sprite. I managed to say I'd give it a try. She said, "Good. We must have it Thursday morning." Blair said, "No problem." I could have strangled him.

So I went home that night and wrote the script; a little one minute play about two GI Janes in a fox hole leading a platoon of Marines and saying that their congressman assured them that if the ERA passed it would not mean a mandatory equal draft. Even if you didn't agree, it was quite funny and hard to refute.

The next morning, Wednesday, I was at the sound studio. Before leaving I called the producer and read him the script (we didn't have faxes, cell phones, scanners or computers). By the time I arrived he had assembled five actors who grabbed my script and started rehearsing. By 5 PM we were finished. The producer spent the evening squeezing everything into the 1 minute spot. The next morning, Thursday, Schlafly had her 17 cassettes, each with an ad naming that specific congressman by name as the person who voted to force Mom to be a Marine.

By Thursday afternoon, Schlafly had walked into all 17 Congressmen's offices and played the commercial "that will air Monday both here and in your district if you vote to give an unfair extension of time to the ERA." She used a bit of strong arm and localized persuasion to counter a special-interest power grab.

On Friday morning, all 17 voted against the extension and it killed the ERA once and for all.

Speed matters. Getting the job done quickly is a must.

Many other successful marketers are out doing exactly the same thing, while all of the careful plodders are still trying to make it perfect. They really fear failure. Afraid yet another person will find a reason to reject them. Marketing is so much about learning from the rejections and turning them into opportunities.

To those fine people and everyone else struggling to get started, understand that anything worth doing well is worth doing poorly to start. Grow into it by doing something today. Make a fool of yourself - just because. Now that it is out of your system, and you didn't get eaten by a bystander viewing you, it's time to get on with the task of accomplishing your dreams.

Speed. Go to it. Do it now. Don't wait another minute.

Marketing is Motion, not Magic

Much is made of genius. It's a magical thought that someone does better than you because of their innate, born-with mental acumen. It gives us comfort to know there is nothing more we could do to achieve what they've achieved because ... they were just born that way.

In this current world of rationalizing so many things because of gene pool back strokes, let's talk common sense (which isn't so common).

Genius accounts for little. Few have it, and those with it often nominally contribute to the greater good.

In marketing, genius is greatly used to dismiss our own lack of success. But it's best to put that behind us and get to the real heart of what matters. My little maxim for all this is "marketing is not magic, but motion."

In nearly all advertisements or marketing campaigns I've conducted that have been wildly successful, the path behind them is strewn, littered and piled with massive mistakes. I've tried one idea followed by another. Smartly, I carefully tracked what worked and adjusted my aim. That led to the "genius" idea... eventually.

I've worked with dozens of "marketing geniuses," and have spent time around many others. Their tale is no different. The notion of motion matters most. I advise many people, and nearly all of them take the information and stew on it and then look for magic that never comes.

I'm reminded of the two turkeys who read the advertisement for flying lessons. Excited to fly, they attend a wonderful all-day flying session. They soar, flap to the sky and see life from a new vantage point. As they walk home at the end of the lesson, they declare how worthwhile the day had been and wonder, "When's the next lesson?" Yes, they *walked* home.

How often do we read or hear great advice and then WALK home?

The great entrepreneur Larry Miller (lacked formal education, worked in car parts stores and ended up with dozens of car dealerships, owned the Utah Jazz and a world-class speedway) was once asked the "secret" of business success. Miller's response was, and I paraphrase: "60 percent of success is just showing up. Another 20 or 30 percent is showing up with the right attitude."

Edison is remembered for his quote, "Genius is 90 percent perspiration and 10 percent inspiration."

To further illustrate: I received a call the other day from a very bright and well-seasoned fellow who is an administrator at a local university. He wanted to know why the Entrepreneur conference he was holding this year was drawing so many fewer people than the one I held last year.

He figured correctly that the university should have been able to use last year's successful conference as a foundation to build upon. Last year we were told that - being the first year - we should only plan on 80 attendees. We had more than 600. Afterwards we left the university all of our notes, ads and plans, the email and mailing lists we used, and evaluations and testimonials. Thus the second year's conference should have attracted more than the 200 or so reported attendees. The first year we had no credibility and couldn't even get a local mayor to come. This time, using our credibility combined with the university's contacts and effort, they were able to get the governor to attend! Sadly, he spoke to a partially filled room.

I admire the administrator because he sought to evaluate the program. Instead of making up excuses, he sought to find reasons for the less than stellar attendance. Most people blame the economy (it was worse last year), conflicts in the public's schedule, or something.

So why didn't the conference exceed last year's attendance numbers?

The answer is fairly simple.

I have a blog we used to call "Marketing Magic." After we'd found enough readers, I changed the name to a more accurate description, "Marketing Motion." We did it to drive home a principle: Marketing is NOT magic, but motion.

The reason the conference didn't attract as many is they didn't have the marketing motion. They did a few things, but we did many things.

We did some controversial things – we dared to go outside the academic box. We made some enemies with campus advertising department folks by using art for ads that didn't look pretty. Our ads had more words than pictures, and not enough white space for their taste. But the words were powerful, full of emotion, and they attracted people. Their ads were picture perfect and bland. Tombstone advertising.

Their conference name seemed academic and ours stated how the customer would benefit. We really ticked off the university's conference and workshop people because we made up tickets and put a high price on them. Crass.

Then we sent tickets to groups and gave them a whale of a discount. We sold them on an option basis to students in business classes for a low price and told them they could go out and sell them for whatever they could get and keep the difference. Funny how the profit motive works.

We had an email campaign, a direct mail campaign, a poster campaign, an affinity campaign (sell wholesale-priced tickets to groups of like-minded people who meet regularly), several referral campaigns, and got all of the business students involved with self-interest motives. Every day we tried something new.

It wasn't magic. It was motion. Lots of motion. That's what it takes.

Marketing is a pain in the neck. It is a lot of work. But if you want to succeed, that is the key.

Right now I'm involved in selling a vehicle transmission technology. In case you're engineering inclined, it is the ONLY positively displaced, infinitely variable transmission. That means it doesn't disconnect gears to change speeds and ratios, has no belts that use friction so it has race car performance but hybrid car economy. This technology should save the average consumer 30 percent or more on fuel. It can put a hybrid engine in a large pick-up and burn rubber while getting two times the gas mileage. Therefore, it is so innovative with such high customer benefit ratios that some have said, "the technology will sell itself." Wrong. It doesn't.

Using good, fundamental marketing principles – all involving motion and lots of it – we've managed in four months to get in front of the world's best transmission engineers. We're also in front of the biggest names in the auto industry (did you know $240 billion worth of transmissions are sold every year?). We've been in front of Americans, Germans, Japanese, Koreans and more. But every step along the way we've had to overcome their mental roadblocks. We manage to sell the CEO but he wants his engineers to approve ... but it takes time for them to figure out all of the great features we have, and people don't want to think outside their box. Slowly we're succeeding. But what a pain.

Why didn't they jump at it instantly? The benefits are so obvious. Because they're human beings and human emotions and needs are immutable. They must be persuaded, coddled, cajoled and romanced. It's how we humans all are.

Jason, a reader of my blog, took what was said in a previous post on negotiating and the same week put it to the test. He had a product, and he wanted to know if there was a market for it. Jason did the following very right things:

1. He immediately asked the customer what he needed. He learned that the customer's budget was very small, and couldn't afford even $100 to $300.

2. Jason then met with the customer and offered solutions to the customer's problem (in person is always best).

3. Jason established the value he could bring and got the customer excited about the possibilities. (You do that by knowing his needs and showing him how you can fulfill them.)

4. Once the value was established and the desire was high, the customer asked the price.

5. Jason astutely said, "I've asked another professional what he would charge and he said his fee would be $3,000 to $5,000." He stopped and let the high price sink in. The customer gasped a little and said, "Ouch. $5,000 is beyond my budget."

6. Jason heroically stepped in and said, "That's okay. I can do it for about half that." A 50% discount is always compelling.

7. The customer was quite pleased to get such a good deal.

8. Jason was quite pleased to have gotten the job for $2,500. Better than the $100 to $300 the person originally thought was their maximum.

The same principles work on any product or service.

The same principles work on any amount - $1 to millions. I'm working on a deal right now worth a great amount in excess of monetary imagination, and the offer has been tendered for far more than I first thought. Happily.

The prime lesson here: Never think marketing is magic. It's motion, and lots of it. You must do something every day, even if it is wrong, because you'll learn more from your mistakes than your successes – although success will seduce you into thinking you're the cat's meow.

Welcome to the game. Do something today. Now.

Just do it. Go do something. Go fly. Don't walk home.

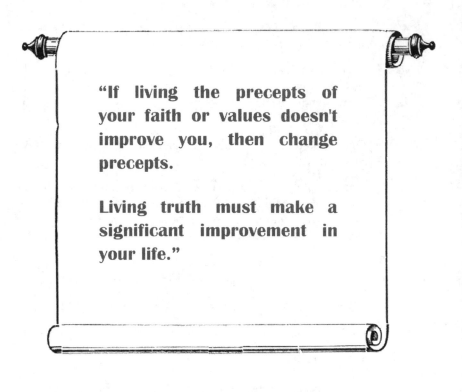

"If living the precepts of your faith or values doesn't improve you, then change precepts.

Living truth must make a significant improvement in your life."

Chapter 5

A Matter of Success

We've all heard a hundred folks bemoan their lot in life, and reduce all the reasons for their woes down to bad luck. Or they diminish the accomplishments of others by declaring that their fortunes were a matter of good luck. Either way, luck was the master.

Thomas Holdman decided his love for art ought to be expressed in creating stained glass windows. Soon after taking a university class in stained glass, he began creating windows for friends. However, a hobby was in the making unless he could actually make money from his art. So he got out of his studio, walked down the street, knocked on doors and struggled to tell strangers how wonderful it would be to have a stained glass window in their entry way.

Struggled is the operative word, for Tom had difficulty speaking. His stuttering caused him to freeze up in front of people. But, he had what too many of us don't have: the determination to ignore discouragement and obstacles.

He rapped on doors until his knuckles were sore. He spoke so much his speech improved. One window turned into dozens. Dozens became hundreds. A solo struggle became a team effort with many employees. A craft became an art, and his art became his business. In just a few years, Tom Holdman and company nailed a contract to put beautiful windows in churches and temples across the world. Other contracts followed.

His small basement studio is now an impressive commercial building half the size of a football field.

Where was his luck? Just where Seneca said it would be way back in 25 AD: where preparation meets opportunity. Ever was it so.

Notice who created the luck? Yep, the artist. He didn't wait to be discovered. He prepared himself artistically, yet knew no one would market his art but himself. So he did. Marketing wasn't beneath him. It was a part of him because his success was his responsibility.

Planning for What We Really Want

An old maxim reads, "Those who fail to plan can plan to fail." Too often the neophytes in the art world equate spontaneous thinking followed by immediate action with creativity. It does happen, but rarely. Great performers didn't become great by following this foolish reactionary methodology. At an early age they committed to their end game by putting themselves through voice lessons, methodical practices, rehearsals and auditions.

I've written a number of plays and musicals as well as books. In every case, the process began with a plan. First an idea, then a description of the characters in fiction works and principles in non-fiction works. An outline of the work soon followed. Within the outline I noted ideas I needed to cover for that section and the concrete examples to illustrate the principles.

Finally the time came to write. Certain times were set up for writing. A deadline for completion was established. I then followed the plan.

Directors and producers must do this. The near-genius spontaneous moments during the blocking of a play come about only because the director methodically stages the play *before* the actors show up.

Did the plan ever change? A better question is "Did the final product exactly follow the plan?" Never ... but close.

My father was an officer in the Air Force. He told me that it was standard training procedure to heavily plan for each mission, and then be prepared to change the plan once he hit the field. Adapt. Improvise. Overcome.

Michael Kami, one of the founders of Xerox, was one of the first to go against the pop trend of 3 and 5 year plans. He said they first established their general goals and general directions and considered them inviolate. Next they discussed the more specific goals for this year. Following that, the team met every Friday to evaluate the week, and then laid out the next week's goal and the tasks needed to accomplish that goal. Week by week, Xerox accomplished its goals. Soon the company accomplished their annual goals, and eventually achieved their long-term corporate goals.

That's a sound planning process.

Assuming you have end-game goals, my first question today is: "What did you do last week to accomplish your goals?"

My second question is: "What will you do this week to accomplish your goals?" Write them down. Hold yourself accountable.

Make sure you consider all three phases of business: marketing, operations and finance. Do something every week on each of these. It doesn't have to be much, but it does have to take a step toward your objective.

Self-Interest is Reality and Good

In a previous section I made a very seemingly political statement. I said you shouldn't be like the socialists that want to change human behavior. Some editors wonder why I would say such a provocative thing in a business and marketing book.

Primarily I say this to help you understand human behavior. We can't persuade people if we don't understand their desires, actions and what benefits them.

Simply put, marketing reaches over all borders and philosophies. Socialism and communism are based upon the public ownership of the means of production; state ownership of such things as banks, car companies, health care, etc. These methods don't work because they violate the basic laws of human behavior by legislating that people will NOT do something out of their own self-interest. But everyone works from the basis of their own self-interest. It is natural for EVERY species on Earth to protect themselves from danger. That's self-interest.

I lived in England at the height of its socialist push in the 1960s. I lived in France and watched what happened to its people in the 1970s. And I spent 10 years doing business in the Soviet Union and Russia. Socialism destroys minds and abrogates personal responsibility in favor of the state. That's stultifying.

Communism and socialism demand that you ignore what is best for you and put it aside for the benefit of the state. Trouble is, the state also acts out of its self-interest and if you don't like it then the state has ways to crush you. Freedom is the casualty of socialism. Freedom is in everyone's individual self-interest. You do not like someone telling you what to do. You believe that you know better than some faceless person in the capital deciding what's best for you.

Socialism loves the Marxian maxim, "From each according to his ability, to each according to his needs." Clever but cruel. Who decides what your *ability* is? In a free market you and the marketplace do. In socialism, someone else decides. Who decides what your *need* is? In a free market, you take what you earn and determine how you'll spend it. You may spend it on wants or needs. Your choice.

The movie "The Patriot," is loosely based upon the life of the Swamp Fox Francis Marion, who fought in the Revolutionary War. He served in his local legislature at a time when the people were deciding whether or not to break away from England. Much was made of the king's tyranny in deciding how colonists living 3,000 miles across the sea must live. Yet members of the legislature all had their own bills locally telling others how to live. The Patriot states boldly to his fellow legislators, "I'm not sure which is worse: one tyrant 3000 miles away, or 3000 tyrants one mile away."

Thomas Jefferson wrote, "I have sworn upon the altar of God eternal hostility against every form of tyranny imposed upon the mind of man."

When you decide what is best for other people; when you insist they need this more than their wants; when you decide what they ought to have, and that they need to be educated to appreciate what you're selling; then you've entered the world of socialism. Socialists push legislation that people don't want or doll it up so that it looks alluring but is ensnaring. They want what they want regardless of what you want.

More than 80 percent of Americans like their own health care plans. Mandatory health care run by the government is disliked by 60 percent as of July 1, 2010. But the proponents think they know better than we do, and are going to push it down everyone's throats. I've seen the same thing with those who favor or oppose abortion. Steve Forbes once pointed out that until the majority of Americans favor a ban on abortion, we have no business dictating to the majority – even if we find it morally repugnant. Freedom ought to rule even if it is inconvenient.

Good marketers believe in freedom because they're confident that their products are so beneficial that no one could possibly resist wanting them. They understand that no one owes them anything. No one MUST do something for them. Instead they learn the words: irresistible, compelling, alluring, unavoidable and enticing, because all are words of freedom ... words marketers live by.

Patterns

By now you should be well aware that marketing is the art of understanding human patterns and behaviors. In marketing, you seek to observe patterns of human actions to see if you have something humans want or need. WANTS are the most powerful. People sacrifice wants for needs all the time. People need education but want a new TV. TV wins. People need good nutrition but want booze and drugs. Booze and drugs win all too often. People need to be slim but want a donut.

Check out this pattern of doing business: Find that need or want. Find a product or service that fills it. See if you can make money on supplying that. Find the customers and find a price that they'll pay.

Don't find the product first and try to foist it off onto people. Clinton Felsted built his business doing exactly the opposite, which is the right pattern. He was doing programming for companies and asked if they needed anything else. They did. He built a program to meet that need and sold it to them. Low cost marketing results.

Sophistication often gets in the way of marketing. It loves to over complicate things in order to make things seemingly more meaningful. Keep marketing simple.

When I was in the Soviet Union teaching a ship load of highly acclaimed Soviet business leaders (they were leaders, but I use the term "business leaders" loosely as you'll see), I tried to help them understand the process of commercializing a product ... finding a product and selling it.

I asked them a simple question, "What one thing do you need to have a successful business?" They first said money and I said, "No, I've started businesses without money." They said "a great product" and I said, "No, many successful businesses have started with a weak product and managed to transform it to a good one – see Honda." They said many other things that exhibited their failure to really understand business. When I ask this question to university students, they instantly say, "a customer." Right.

When I finally pulled this answer out of the Soviets, they shook their heads in disagreement. One said, "In Socialism, we make what they need and they must buy it from us." He was right. In the fantasy land of Socialism, customers are at the bottom of the heap. But in a free market, as I told them they would soon have, customer is king.

To illustrate the point I brought up a 17-year-old boy from the dock at Gorki (now Nizhny Novgorod) who sold soldier hats, paintings and dolls. I asked them what his business model was. They managed to state that he did the following:

1. He noticed that tourists were coming and they all wanted souvenirs.

2. He researched which trinkets the tourists wanted and how much they were willing to spend.

3. He found suppliers and artisans who would make these items for a price he could afford.

4. He sold the trinkets and made a profit.

I then asked them what I'll ask you: how does this differ from your business model? In all likelihood you'll say it fits about what you do. But the Soviet leaders were horrified to be compared to a young speculator (a really nasty occupation in a Soviet Socialist land)! Then I horrified them more. I said the only differences between him and these leaders were two-fold: the boy made a profit and didn't live on subsidies, and the number of zeroes to the left of the decimal was higher in their bookkeeping.

After some gentle discussions, the light finally dawned.

Notice patterns. Follow successful ones.

Negotiating Value: Getting What You Want

A brief overview on negotiating is necessary in this point of the discussion. Later in the book we'll go into greater detail about how to become your own best negotiator.

First, are you a candidate for the Emily Dickinson Award? This is an award for a creative person, cloistered in her own creative castle, who no one has heard of and won't until after she's deceased and some marketing-savvy person finds and promotes her works. (I love many of Emily's poems – particularly "The Bustle in the House" – but find it a shame she couldn't enjoy her own success and find the solace and joy her poetry later gave to others).

To help avoid becoming such a candidate, you need to promote and negotiate your work. Negotiating is a vital life skill because you don't get what you deserve – you get what you negotiate. We'll save the full discussion negotiating for Chapter 34 .

Final Negotiating Thought

Because all prices are based upon PERCEIVED value, the first thing you must do is establish your value. The second thing is show more value. The last thing to discuss is price ... only after your value has been established.

Chapter 6

Summary of Marketing Thoughts

I am overwhelmed with ideas on how performers can do a better job of getting jobs that pay. Rather than have a chapter on each of these items, allow me to give you some quick thoughts as I end this section on "Creating a Marketing Mindset." As you develop your marketing mindset, you will create all kinds of marketing avenues to explore. The more you focus on marketing, the more natural it will become.

Thought #1: Where's the Problem?
Remember that repeatedly doing the same things, but expecting different results, is insanity. A singer once said she was promoting herself the way everyone else was promoting in the opera world, but she was not seeing any results. Her question was, "How can I find out what is wrong with the way I sing?"

Having read what you have in this book, how would you answer?

This question is like saying "My airline is doing all the things airlines have done– serving bad food, killing knees and shoulders of passengers sardined together, making complicated pricing, adding rules daily, talking rudely, choosing routes where people do not want to go en route to where they are headed," and then wondering if "the reason I'm not getting passengers is because there is something wrong with my engine."

Now, something in your engine or voice might need tuning. The voice, in the end, is what truly matters - although constant exceptions tend to kill that rule quickly.

In truth, it is not the engines on the planes, but it is all the other things United, Delta, Northwest, PanAm and other airlines have done wrong for years that have cost them their customers. And it is the positioning in the market place, proper cost structures and understanding how to take care of customers that have made Southwest, JetBlue and others exceptionally profitable.

Conventional wisdom says opera cannot grow or be profitable, thus it must bow, scrape and beg to acquire enough money. Yet, it is the way opera is marketed that prevents it from being profitable and expanding.

The performer with an opportunity to make money refuses to listen to conventional wisdom, keeps track of her customers, searches out new avenues to reach potential customers, speaks and sings so customers want more, and unabashedly and unapologetically promotes herself.

One prominent and respected teacher of singing – and she is good – castigated me for teaching what I teach. She insisted the marketing she teaches, the accepted wisdom of operadom, was the only acceptable method.

My answer was simple. Does it work? Do these performers get the work they deserve after all the money and time they have put into their craft? I told her, "I'll give you $1,000 if you will show me a brochure, a letter, an email or anything that actually caused people to come and pay money to hear a singer. But, you must show me the proof that it was THAT advertisement, or brochure that actually brought them in." She couldn't do it then, and has not done it yet.

Thought #2: Modesty vs. Fear

Do not confuse modesty and shyness. Modesty comes from an inner sense of purpose that rises above fashion or stylistic clichés. Modesty becomes a standard unto oneself born from seasoned confidence.

Shyness is just fear. In fear, little good is accomplished.

Fear sees failure as an ending.

Modesty understands it is on the road to something better, and recognizes failure as a means to progress.

Thought #3: Relish All Victories

Small victories propelled George Washington to the presidency of the world's first republican democracy. Sometimes he relished a loss merely because it could have been much greater, and recognized that his troops gained determination and purpose through defeat.

Yet even his many disastrous defeats never overshadowed his belief in his ultimate purpose and were each learning moments on the road to glory for his cause. He relished even the smallest victory because it took him one step closer to his ultimate destination.

The same goes for you. Do not let a psychic vampire tell you, "You won that competition because no one else was any good," or "Yes, you got the audition, but it was for a mediocre house." You may decide not to take the part, but for heaven's sake, bask in the victory of being offered the part. Now you have a choice!

Thought #4: Self-worth vs. Net-worth

Never confuse your self-worth with your net-worth. These pages are all about how to get your net-worth up on par with your vocal-worth. But neither your vocal-worth nor your net-worth is who you are. I think you are divine, and do not forget it. (If you knew me, you would know I am not being hyperbolic on this, but literal!). I never cease to marvel at how truly interesting and wonderful most people are, and in nearly every case they have far more in them than they respect or understand.

The world is filled with timid, anxious, depressed people lacking in self-confidence. In the same breath they decry someone with self-confidence as someone who is arrogant.

In truth, most seemingly arrogant people are trying mightily to hide their lack of confidence.

It's all very sad.

You are a person of great worth. Value yourself. We're all reaching for the stars while our feet are mired in the mud. That is to be expected. Earth existence is all about becoming, and we don't become unless we struggle to overcome. The key is to know that you truly are worth it and deserve every blessing in life. Do not accept less.

Work to make it happen, follow correct principles, and you'll be floored about how great things can become.

In closing, here is a quick summary of several key points we've covered:

1. When someone inquires, don't call them back the next day. Call them in 5 minutes and you'll increase your chance of a sale by at least 20 times.

2. Only God is not in marketing. The rest of us rely upon customer satisfaction to validate our fiscal existence.

3. Collect today one email address you don't already have. Add it to your "house list." Do the same tomorrow. Soon, you'll have a database of people who know you. If you can't figure out what to do next ... stay tuned. I bet you can't collect just one!

4. Once you gather the names and emails of everyone you come in contact with on a professional basis, use this list when you sell something. These people will bring in 5 times more

money than any other list of names - except one. When you have something new to sell, use a list of *previous* buyers, as they are 10 times more likely to buy again.

5. If you can't fix it, feature it.

6. From Carol Vaness, the famed Met opera singer: "Enjoy your craft. Love your craft." It's the best marketing advice ever.

7. If you believe it, they'll believe it.

8. No one cares what your product IS, they only care what it DOES for them. No one wants to buy a drill, he/she only wants something that will make a hole.

9. About right now is better than exactly right later. Marines and marketers adapt and improvise on the move.

10. Plan your work and work your plan. You'll thus be true to yourself and your dreams.

Chapter 7

Getting the Mind Right
While Waiting to be Discovered

Who said, "All I need is a break!"? In truth, just about anyone who has ever succeeded has said this phrase at some point.

Performers are no different than composers, conductors, inventors, engineers with spunk, athletes, writers, actors, politicians or anyone in a competitive profession. However, performers do not like the idea that they're in competition, preferring the more languid image of the "artist suffering for his art." But in reality, every performer competes against not only other performers struggling for the same job, but against every form of educational or entertainment venue that can distract paying customers from a performer's performance.

Every "overnight success" takes years to create. The successful performer invents herself by repeatedly doing the right things. It's not easy.

So how do you get a break? To begin with, choose what the poet Robert Frost deemed "the road not taken." Following the well-trodden route traveled by tens of thousands of performers every year who earn a pittance will certainly guarantee the mediocre non-careers most singers receive.

Making it to the next level *does* require a break. But breaks are not the equivalent of luck – if luck means the presence of something freakish or undeserving.

"Breaks" are when preparation meets opportunity.

In Malcom Gladwell's book, Outliers, he makes a compelling case that one of the prime things that separates marginally successful, successful and wildly successful people is how much time the person spends doing the task at hand.

The magic number is 10,000 hours that lead from good to great. Violinists at a Berlin Conservatory who had practiced 2-3,000 hours since they started at age 5 were destined to teach school orchestra; those who practiced about 5-7,000 hours played for city orchestras; those who put in 10,000+ hours were soloists in great demand. The Beatles played for 10,000 hours in striptease clubs in Hamburg often for 8-10 hour days. Mozart penned his first true masterpiece after 20 years of composing (they did the estimations and found that to be... 10,000 hours of composing).

Singers wishing to become performers must not only practice constantly, but must perform at least 3 to 5 times a week. One can include in that auditions and competitions for they are still performances. Singing careers are about learning to be a great performer and you can't get that any other way than performing until you are the master of the stage.

Preparing for success is more than preparing your voice. Vocal preparation is critical, but complete preparation means far more. You need to have your Foyer in near perfect shape. A Foyer consists of your resume, head shot, biography, website, repertoire, press releases and clippings, stationary and business card. It's called a Foyer because just like the foyer of a home, it's the first thing people will see of you. Your Foyer determines how people perceive you. It's your brand, the positioning you place yourself in the market. This has to be ready now.

Notwithstanding the declaration of Rossini (some say Verdi) that "voce, voce, voce" is the key, voice is not enough. I have heard dozens upon dozens of unemployable "grade A" voices. Their voices were sweet, but they lacked the whole package.

On the other hand, I recently listened to a world-famous soprano – one of the ultimate divas. I have heard better voices, but seen fewer performers more captivating. Voice is NOT enough. The voice must be tempered by, and enhanced by, performance presence. That does not happen in the studio, but in every gin-joint, flop house and regional stage between Tacoma and Tampa, Bangor and Burbank.

The path to the great career or even the next level goes straight through the less-traveled venues, for here the great artist sees the eyes of the audience and moves them to tears despite rotten conditions. It is here the trade is learned. Great comedians start in comedy clubs and return often to sharpen their timing and skills.

Seeking these "bridge jobs" such as concerts, recitals, conventions, specialty restaurant gigs, small-town opera guild performances, etc., enables you to hone your promotional and marketing skills to leverage these gigs into better and better jobs. They also provide added exposure to the right people and that all-important ingredient of significant experience.

No one can get you the A job. No one can guarantee you will ever hit the next level – let alone succeed. This is entertainment. Stardom requires bizarre circumstances. But I can guarantee you will NEVER see the break you need unless you are doing everything to prepare yourself so when it comes, you will be ready.

Simply put, the time-tested principles in this book are essential for bridging the gap between where you are now and where you want to be. Again, these principles are not new; Geoffrey Chaucer laid out many of them in 1380. He did not make them up either, but borrowed from others who had been using them long before him.

I just package and present them uniquely for performers.

I cannot convince Christina Scheppelman to hire you for the Washington National Opera, but I can surely show you how to earn the money necessary to keep you in the game and prepare you – so when you do audition for Christina, you will make a great impression even if you don't have the top Grade A voice. She might hire you with a B+ voice because you've developed the stage presence born from seasoned performance skills that will move an audience.

And if the main stage is not your cup of tea, fine. The rest of the world is waiting for you to stir their souls. It is up to you, but only if you have both the voice and the marketing skills essential to success.

Do not expect much help from the traditional opera establishment. They are still clinging to marketing techniques established in the 1800s. Effective techniques grow out of time-proven principles, but they must be tailored to current conditions. Hanging on to outdated techniques is akin to marketing Ferraris using buggy-whip promotions. The opera world keeps repeating the same marketing mistakes, each time expecting different results. This is insanity.

Miriam Kreinin Souccar recently reported on the front page of Crain's New York Business paper, "Executives at even the most renowned houses are desperately searching for ways to cope with graying audiences and declining ticket sales. Last month, the Metropolitan Opera announced halfway through its fiscal year that it would have to make budget cuts, for the third straight year, to compensate for an expected $4.3 million shortfall. And subscription sales are down at City Opera."

This is bad news for every classical singer because it has an immediate impact on your ability to earn income from your talent. If the big guys do not create more demand, they cannot hire you. If they fail to enlarge the audience base there is a trickle-down effect that results in a smaller and smaller market for non-theater work.

Jay Meetze, of the Opera Company of Brooklyn, recognizes the insanity. Namely, he has watched up close and personally how big theaters promote opera, and he is doing something about it. Using a technique we discuss in this book, he has been increasing demand by holding a series of HOME CONCERTS. He charges $20 a seat, and 50 people crowd into an Upper East Side apartment. In her news article, Souccar reported, "They came to enjoy a live performance of Tosca featuring singers who often grace the stages of the country's finest opera houses."

This small arts organization is gaining national attention for cultivating a new generation of opera lovers by offering cheap tickets and performing in unconventional venues. The first five performances sold out almost immediately, and 80 percent of the audience was new to the world of opera.

Now it is your turn. Let's get going. The opera and the classical music world need you to be successful, and to introduce new audiences to the joy of the greatest music in the world.

Can one person make a difference? Can it be you? Of course. It all depends on your clarity of vision and determination. Someone once told me that "no one had ever gotten a congressman elected on a write-in campaign. Both political parties and the White House were against our candidate. But we wanted to do it, and he won."

You can win your victories. Follow the marketing principles in this book.

Being Discovered

The bane of all artists is the story circulated about the singer or painter or composer who labored in obscurity and then one day, almost magically, was "discovered." He did not need a resume, did not need to ever touch money or sell or advertise. He merely performed and the money flowed. Artistic directors and impresarios lined up to beg him to perform at their theaters.

The more I write, the more fanciful and even sillier this scenario sounds. But in artistic circles it is believed so strongly that entire fictitious careers are based upon this delusion of being discovered.

You are NOT going to be suddenly discovered. In fact, most stories of an artist being discovered are filled with sadness and include substantial deprivation and difficulties just before finally making it big.

In the classical singing world, the price of preparation is probably greater than nearly all other artistic disciplines. Even a wonderful voice must be developed to withstand the rigors of constant performance. Being on stage requires honing performing techniques including breath control, movement and dance, acting, stage presence, language and diction, character study, and concepts of direction.

All these require great quantities of time and money from the singer.

Yet the number of good jobs on stage diminishes each year while the legions of new singers increase. One estimate showed that in the United States fewer than 3,500 roles become available each year in opera; yet more than 600 universities and conservatories graduate, on average, 17 new singers every year. Let's round that off for the ease of discussion to a total of 10,000 new singers hitting the market each year. Add to that the 10,000 for each of the past 10 years and we are talking about 100,000 singers vying for 3,500 roles.

To make matters worse, of those 3,500 paid roles, the majority are filled by singers who have performed well for the theater or house and are locked into a contract for future roles.

Of course, over time many of the 100,000 singers lose heart and their passion to sing Carmen or the Barber or whomever else has died onstage from the complications of life and discouragement. Others choose to teach or find alternative careers and keep singing as a hobby.

To think that a director should accidentally happen upon an undiscovered talent in this swirling, complicated and highly competitive singing world is absurd. Overnight discoveries come only after decades of preparation.

An Example

In the Hollywood film "The Castaway," Tom Hanks plays a FedEx executive who crashes in the ocean and is washed up, alone, on a deserted island. He does what we all do. In the beginning, finding himself alone and seemingly without hope, he has a pity party. Once he gets over that, he begins doing the logical things to be rescued – he builds a fire hoping a search plane will notice. He uses rocks to create the word "HELP" on the beach. He does his best to get recognized.

Nothing works because there is no one nearby to notice.

After years of surviving alone, he observes that when the winds blow in a certain direction, the waves lessen over the reef so that if he were to build a raft and try to sail away, he could actually get over the reef.

In the midst of his survival, various things wash up on shore. He has to determine how he can use them. Among them is half of a construction toilet wall made of hard plastic. He builds a raft and places this wall as his sail.

When the winds and tide are right, he gives a mighty effort and sails over the reef into the ocean. Once there he figures he has won. But the ocean is so enormous, and he is just a speck. When he is out of food and water, the exhausted sailor falls asleep – but wakes to learn he is an "overnight discovery" found by a passing freighter.

By happenstance, the castaway had drifted into the shipping lanes. If one ship hadn't noticed him, another would have come along soon because that is where the ships like to travel.

Does this sound like a singer's career? I will not belabor the analogy because most analogies are like a car – when driven too far they fall apart. But consider it.

One point must be made abundantly clear.

The castaway was not discovered until he first made a strategic effort to put himself in the shipping lanes. As a performer, until you know how to place yourself in the "shipping lanes" and be noticed by the right people, you're like the atheist in the funeral parlor – all dressed up with no place to go.

Learning how to market yourself is all about learning how to put yourself in the right "shipping lanes" of the opera world.

Chapter 8

Forced Paradigm Shifts

I deal in the world of money, business creation, spreadsheets, profit and loss reports, and the like. But at heart I'm a romantic. I tend to see things as they are and imagine how they could be. Having immersed myself in the liberal arts with university degrees in English, humanities, history, theater arts, communications and journalism, I come by my romantic streak reasonably. In addition, my parents were musicians who contributed to my understanding of some fundamental truths about life.

These notions dominate my thought process, leaving me with many great wishes that I've spent my life fulfilling - sometimes to my detriment. Several of these wishes are way too ethereal and impossible to become reality, but still I fight for them.

As I've taught thousands of performers and other artists about marketing their talents, I've discovered most share similar fond wishes at heart.

Performers nearly universally have at least 12 wishes:

"I wish ... I could say 'here I am,' and people would line up to give me money.

"I wish ... people would instantly recognize talent.

"I wish ... I could send a simple and inexpensive message to 100 people in a mass email (yes, that's spamming), and 100 people would buy my CDs.

"I wish ... 10,000 other singers would give up and stop the info clutter and persistent marketing noise.

"I wish ... the media would stop charging for my notices of an important event.

"I wish ... the media would print what I tell them to print.

"I wish ... success was based upon sincerity, effort and talent.

"I wish ... I would be discovered when I'm ready.

"I wish ... a manager would see my talent, demand to represent me without any upfront fees, and then work hard to promote me.

"I wish ... the opera world would learn to market great music and productions so opera would be in 'American Idol' demand.

"I wish ... Americans would become educated about opera so they could appreciate my talent.

"I wish ... I did not need money to live on and/or my talent would pay all my bills."

We have probably all experienced at least half of these thoughts to some degree. But in our quiet moments we confess that the Utopia of which we dream will never be. However, when you finish reading this book, return to this spot and review this wish list. You should be able to understand every wish and how to make each come true using practical means and principles that work.

Paradigm Shifts

Even the most amazingly talented performers face a challenge in today's opera scene. Never has a more highly skilled and talented group been so silent on the world's stage. Something must change, but surely we can't count on the world changing for you.

Years ago, the Soviets tried to change the world by declaring that singers were honored and must have jobs. If a child had an obvious singing talent, he or she was ushered into a program path to become a professional singer. In the Soviet Union, jobs didn't exist naturally. They didn't grow out of a need or want but instead were created by the Party. Mandated singers were paid the same as a doctor - about 200 dollars a month. The system created an enormous number of singers, many very good and many not so good. Regardless of skill, they were paid the same.

Because the supply of singers vastly exceeded the demand, the Party attempted to increase the demand by lowering the price of admission. By subsidizing performances, the Party was able to drop ticket prices to a few kopkets – mere pennies in equivalent U.S. dollars. As this false economy stumbled along, U.S. dollars became more desirable to the Party. Tickets to the illustrious Bolshoi theater were soon only available in U.S. dollars and the vast majority of Soviet citizens were excluded.

In the end, the false economy faced reality and the Soviet Union folded. As Prime Minister Margaret Thatcher once said, "The problem with Socialism is pretty soon you run out of other people's money." What was left in the shambles of economic collapse were tens of thousands of very good singers with no audience willing to pay them.

Some of this sounds like the U.S. opera world today. Something has to change. My task is to help singers and musicians change their paradigm (way of thinking) and deal successfully with the world as it is, not as we think it should be.

The most daunting task of changing a singer's or musician's paradigm is in altering how they view the market. Most performers consider self-promotion unseemly. It's time for a paradigm shift.

Our society loves to create classes of victims. Performers too often allow themselves to be categorized as victims. This must change. Victims are "acted upon". To be successful, a performer must determine to "act", rather than be "acted upon." This same society tries to tell us "we are who we are and that is the end of that." Nonsense. You are where you are, but *who you are going to be is up to you*. The victim mentality says, "I can't change who I am." The responsible person says, "I want something, and I'm willing to change myself to get it." This is a forced paradigm shift – a positive change of thinking. Make no mistake. You constantly make paradigm shifts, and you do it instantly.

Consider the story about the famous actor Clark Cable. As a young man, he was Hollywood's most eligible bachelor. On one particular movie set he saw Carol Lombard, a rising star and one of the original blond bombshells. As he watched her, he observed how she worked with people and noticed her grace, charm, kindness and talent.

Gable fell deeply in love with her; so much so that when he met her he would stutter and stammer and turn away. She thought he was funny-looking, rude and above all, stuck-up. One night as Carol left the studio, she was confronted by several muggers. She attempted to run and even thought of standing and fighting. Just then Clark Gable appeared. He leaped over the stage door guard railing, grabbed one mugger by the lapels and flung him away. He struck the other two repeatedly until they fled.

Now ask yourself, "Did Carol Lombard experience a 'paradigm shift?'" Yes. And how much counseling, deep study and days of meditation led to that shift? She changed her mind about Gable in seconds. As Bogart would soon say in another film, "This could be the start of a beautiful friendship." And it was. The Gable-Lombard wedding was a classic.

Not long after they had settled in, Cable made a confession. He asked his wife to recall that heroic midnight rescue. With admiration she did. He confirmed that without that event it was unlikely the two would have made a connection. "Yes," she agreed. "I thought you were a hopeless, helpless sort." "Well, frankly, my dear . . ." (whoops, wrong movie).

What he said next caused another paradigm shift. He said, "I must confess. After the fight it cost me a pretty penny to pay off those stunt men I hired. Can you forgive my deceit?"

What would your paradigm shift have been? Lombard looked at Gable and laughed. He grew more wonderful in her eyes because he went to such efforts to win her affection. Such a clever idea! We would be wise to follow Lombard's lead by carefully evaluating new information (provided in these chapters) and making the necessary changes.

Marketing for Singers and Musicians

In every area of the fine arts and music, artists labor over the most minute details to perfect their craft. Yet they purposefully omit learning the one thing that will help all this work pay off in something other than applause: how to earn money. Performers can and must learn to use the principles of common marketing. This might take a good dose of "image suicide," but that can be healthy. Too often artists consider anything in marketing beneath them, or at the very least sullying their hands with the dirt of lucre. Cries of "prostituting" or "whoring" talent are frequent.

Get over it and get on with life. If you want someone to pay you for your talent, it is essential that they WANT to pay you. They are the customer. They are NOT obligated to support you. You must give them a reason. As difficult as it is to hear, this is salesmanship.

I often ask groups "Who in this room is already in marketing?" Imagine if you were in that room. Would you raise your hand? Few do. I then ask, "How many of you rely on someone else to pay you something, so you can afford the food you eat and the house you live in?" Every hand goes up. Unless you are totally self-sufficient, you get your money from others. Here is the truth - only God is not in marketing. He is the only one who does not rely on customer satisfaction to validate his professional existence. One could argue government workers fit that as well; but, eventually, lousy and unresponsive bureaucracies are canceled and changed as legislators are pummeled by voters (voters are another customer).

We were all once terrific marketers. Recall being four years old, or watch a four-year-old at work. He is smaller, shorter, more ignorant and weaker than virtually any adult. He is often ignored and made to feel unimportant. But no one is better at getting what he wants than a precocious four-year-old. He watches, observes and never stops asking for what he wants. Once a parent succumbs, the four-year-old notes what worked and tries it again.

I watch parents with a disruptive child in church quickly take her to the outside foyer where she is allowed to run around and play. She has been rewarded; so each time the kid feels restless in church, she knows how to be carried to a suitable playroom. My father had a different approach. When we cried, out we went where we received a stern talking to followed by another entrance into church. Every time we cried, we went out, were disciplined, and ended up back in our seats. Drat. It did not work. Slowly I learned to listen and enjoy.

As we age, we become more sophisticated and build up an image of who we are and what others think of us. We lose our marketing instincts needed for survival. They return briefly to men and women when they look for a spouse. Once again we get to know the customer, learn his or her every desire and seek to fulfill it. We strive to make them thrilled, get their attention, arouse the interest and desire, and close in on the action to complete the sale. Most men, once married, promptly forget all sense of this kind of marketing - and both wonder how it was they grew apart. Take you dancing? Why? I already have the prize. Dance was not about foot movement, but marketing. If the sale is complete - why dance? Silly boy … marketing in relationships is never finished.

Universities do not help. They can't. Universities are set up to train in traditional ways. They cannot give you the latest marketing trends, or the marketing mindset. They can tell you how Claude Hopkins did it, but not how to apply it. Instead, they enhance the image of personal sophistication and the eschewal of anything so crass as making money from singing.

Hence the need for a little "image suicide." Marketing cannot be beneath us if we desire the underlying thing marketing gives us: selling our wares to customers.

For a performer, this image change, or paradigm shift, is critical. Many forget quickly why they want to sing, which is because they love singing. Instead they fall in love with being loved. They want applause, stardom and adoration. Singing takes a second seat.

For a true performer, performing is life and as essential as breathing. That is why singers will sing for their supper - just so long as they can sing. For them the joy of singing is everything.

For those folks only - the pure singers - I urge you to learn the principles of marketing. It will allow you more opportunities to sing and let you eat and have shelter and clothing in the meantime.

Consider this story of a real person. While I was in San Francisco a few years ago, I stepped out of the St. Francis Hotel and looked across Union Square. A decent-sized crowd had gathered. When I arrived, some of the crowd left and others filled in. I wormed my way to the front and found a gentleman dressed in a tuxedo standing by a large set of speakers that were playing the accompaniment to a majestic aria. He was singing his heart out in as good a tenor voice as I have heard in some time. The crowd was visibly moved.

When he finished, they moved toward his black velvet cape artfully placed before him and dropped bills - not change, but bills - onto the cape. He soon began another aria. Spellbound, the crowd hung on his every note, every syllable and every gesture. His drama was intense and real and emotionally genuine (meaning he faked it well - sincerity is the key - fake that well and everything is easy). Again the applause and cash followed. Slowly a few left and others took their places. This went on for a half hour before he took a break. As he rested, he sold CDs by the dozens. I caught him in a quick quiet moment and asked him why he was doing what he was doing. Why, I wanted to know, with such a lustrous voice was he not singing on the "legitimate" stage. As he had heard that question before, he smiled and responded, "I do sing in regular operas. But I need my practice time, and out here I don't get visitors dropping by or phones ringing. More important, I get to see the eyes of the people, see what they like, what moves them, what keeps them here, and which arias connect with them"

Now here was a fellow who understood the basic principles of marketing, which I'll outline in a bit. I asked, "How's the money?" He smiled broadly and whispered, "I make more here in three hours than I make at other singing jobs in a week." And I continued, "I doubt the IRS has much to say." He held up his finger to his lips.

This performer confided that he often makes more than $100 an hour doing this. "But I would do it for a whole lot less - maybe for nothing. Just knowing how my music affects people tells me so much. And I get to sing. It's who I am to the center of my being."

The first step to advancing your career, then, is to understand you are already in marketing. The only question is: will you market well or poorly? It is within you to market superbly once you believe it is important (and that only *you* are responsible for your career), and once you've armed yourself with a few basic tools.

Don't get caught up in the notion that it takes a person with encyclopedic knowledge of marketing to do well. Marketing is a human instinct. It's basic.

Marketing is knowing what you want and finding ways of getting what you want. I would prefer to say "finding ethical ways of getting what you want" but, in fact, people use great marketing principles effectively to reach the most nefarious of goals.

Communism loved to say marketing is immoral; many in the business say it's moral. In reality, it's neither, making it amoral. Marketing relies upon your morality, instincts and skills to achieve your goals.

It is up to you and no one else.

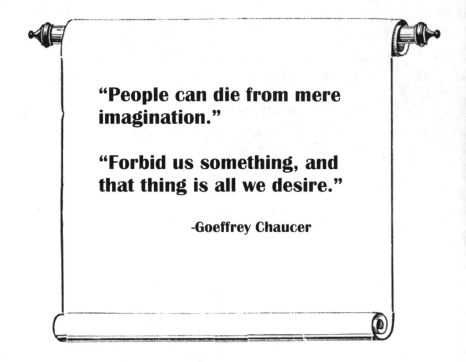

"People can die from mere imagination."

"Forbid us something, and that thing is all we desire."

-Goeffrey Chaucer

Chapter 9

Marketing with Chaucer

GEOFFREY CHAUCER.
Born 1328. Died 1400.

Remember that the tried and true marketing principles in this book have been around for a long time. As marketers we run the gambit from wanting the latest and greatest, to preferring something we are sure will work – low risk. The best way to get great results with low risk is to know and use proven principles.

I keep hearing about marketing gurus giving people the hottest new idea. The problem with these ideas is they may or may not transfer effectively from selling cosmetics to helping a performer find more work – unless you can look below the glitz and find the core principles, and then make an application to what you are doing.

To ensure success, search for principles that have worked across societal boundaries, across economic considerations, centuries and cultures.

I did this recently with Geoffrey Chaucer's great work, "The Canterbury Tales." I carefully read through the "Prologue to the Pardoner's Tale" – written in about 1380 (625 years ago) – and extracted the marketing principles he used to sell people pardons.

These principles work for Crackers or Kings alike ... because they are based upon immutable human behavior.

Here is a good translation from the Middle English text. Underline each phrase that is a marketing, advertising or selling principle. See how many you can come up with, and see if they jive with mine. I found twenty. You will probably find more:

The Prologue to the Pardoner's Tale

Radix malorum est Cupiditas: Ad Thimotheum, sexto.
"Masters," quoth he, "in churches, when I preach,
I am at pains that all shall hear my speech,
And ring it out as roundly as a bell,
For I know all by heart the thing I tell.
My theme is always one, and ever was:
'Radix malorum est cupiditas.'
"First I announce the place whence I have come,
And then I show my pardons, all and some.
Our liege-lord's seal on my patent perfect,
I show that first, my safety to protect,
And then no man's so bold, no priest nor clerk,
As to disturb me in Christ's holy work;
And after that my tales I marshal all.
Indulgences of pope and cardinal,
Of patriarch and bishop, these I do
Show, and in Latin speak some words, a few,
To spice therewith a bit my sermoning
And stir men to devotion, marvelling.
Then show I forth my hollow crystal-stones,
Which are crammed full of rags, aye, and of bones;
Relics are these, as they think, every one.
Then I've in latten box a shoulder bone
Which came out of a holy Hebrew's sheep.
'Good men,' say I, 'my words in memory keep;
If this bone shall be washed in any well,
Then if a cow, calf, sheep, or ox should swell
That's eaten snake, or been by serpent stung,
Take water of that well and wash its tongue,

And 'twill be well anon; and furthermore,
Of pox and scab and every other sore
Shall every sheep be healed that of this well
Drinks but one draught; take heed of what I tell.
And if the man that owns the beasts, I trow,
Shall every week, and that before cock-crow,
And before breakfast, drink thereof a draught,
As that Jew taught of yore in his priestcraft,
His beasts and all his store shall multiply.
And, good sirs, it's a cure for jealousy;
For though a man be fallen in jealous rage,
Let one make of this water his pottage
And nevermore shall he his wife mistrust,
Though he may know the truth of all her lust,
Even though she'd taken two priests, aye, or three.
"'Here is a mitten, too, that you may see.
Who puts his hand therein, I say again,
He shall have increased harvest of his grain,
After he's sown, be it of wheat or oats,
Just so he offers pence or offers groats.
"'Good men and women, one thing I warn you.
If any man be here in church right now
That's done a sin so horrible that he
Dare not, for shame, of that sin shriven be,
Or any woman, be she young or old,
That's made her husband into a cuckold,
Such folk shall have no power and no grace
To offer to my relics in this place.
But whoso finds himself without such blame,
He will come up and offer, in God's name,
And I'll absolve him by authority
That has, by bull, been granted unto me.'
"By this fraud have I won me, year by year,
A hundred marks, since I've been pardoner.
I stand up like a scholar in pulpit,
And when the ignorant people all do sit,
I preach, as you have heard me say before,
And tell a hundred false japes, less or more.
I am at pains, then, to stretch forth my neck,
And east and west upon the folk I beck,
As does a dove that's sitting on a barn.

With hands and swift tongue, then, do I so yarn
That it's a joy to see my busyness.
Of avarice and of all such wickedness
Is all my preaching, thus to make them free
With offered pence, the which pence come to me.
For my intent is only pence to win,
And not at all for punishment of sin.
When they are dead, for all I think thereon
Their souls may well black-berrying have gone!
For, certainly, there's many a sermon grows
Ofttimes from evil purpose, as one knows;
Some for folks' pleasure and for flattery,
To be advanced by all hypocrisy,
And some for vainglory, and some for hate.
For, when I dare not otherwise debate,
Then do I sharpen well my tongue and sting
The man in sermons, and upon him fling
My lying defamations, if but he
Has wronged my brethren or- much worse- wronged me.
For though I mention not his proper name,
Men know whom I refer to, all the same,
By signs I make and other circumstances.
Thus I pay those who do us displeasances.
Thus spit I out my venom under hue
Of holiness, to seem both good and true.
"But briefly my intention I'll express;
I preach no sermon, save for covetousness.
For at my theme is yet, and ever was,
'Radix malorum est cupiditas.'
Thus can I preach against that self-same vice
Which I indulge, and that is avarice.
But though myself be guilty of that sin,
Yet can I cause these other folk to win
From avarice and really to repent.
But that is not my principal intent.
I preach no sermon, save for covetousness;
This should suffice of that, though, as I guess.
"Then do I cite examples, many a one,
Out of old stories and of time long gone,
For vulgar people all love stories old;
Such things they can re-tell well and can hold.

What? Think you that because I'm good at preaching
And win me gold and silver by my teaching
I'll live of my free will in poverty?
No, no, that's never been my policy!
For I will preach and beg in sundry lands;
I will not work and labour with my hands,
Nor baskets weave and try to live thereby,
Because I will not beg in vain, say I.
I will none of the apostles counterfeit;
I will have money, wool, and cheese, and wheat,
Though it be given by the poorest page,
Or by the poorest widow in village,
And though her children perish of famine.
Nay! I will drink good liquor of the vine
And have a pretty wench in every town.
But hearken, masters, to conclusion shown:
Your wish is that I tell you all a tale.
Now that I've drunk a draught of musty ale,
By God, I hope that I can tell something
That shall, in reason, be to your liking.
For though I am myself a vicious man,
Yet I would tell a moral tale, and can,
The which I'm wont to preach more gold to win.
Now hold your peace! My tale I will begin."
HERE ENDS THE PROLOGUE

How many marketing principles did you find that this Pardoner advocated in his prologue? Here are the marketing principles I found in this Prologue of the Pardoner:

1- Select the best and largest audience possible.

2- Use attention grabbing, compelling headlines.

3- Know your message and product.

4- Love your product and let your joy be contagious.

5- Make a credibility reference with credentials and experienced references.

6- Use celebrity endorsements.

7- Use testimonials.

8- When a point is weak, turn up the volume. (In today's language, "Dazzle 'em with the pinstripes.")

9- Add some entertainment value to your advertisement.

10- Have an emotional appeal, an authority appeal, and a logical twist as well.

11- Use visual aids.

12- Specificity of benefits, benefits, benefits!

13- Do not say how the product works – JUST THE EFFECT!

14- No one cares what the product is, they only care what the product does – WHAT PROBLEM IT WILL SOLVE!

15- Price is determined by perceived value from benefits.

16- Use the "THEATER OF THE MIND" – it's the most powerful theater.

17- See the problem; figure out the solution. No one else will do this for you.

18- Use the two most powerful words in English – a person's name and FREE. The third is "BECAUSE" followed by powerful reasons.

19- PEOPLE ARE INWARDLY BEGGING TO BE LED.

20- Focus on the message at hand when marketing – DO NOT BRING IN SUPERFLUOUS INFORMATION OR THOUGHTS.

If you find more principles than these listed, use them.

The next trick is to keep this list around, add to it and use it to evaluate your marketing efforts. See if you are using these ideas in your efforts to advance your career, your fliers, your website and overall professional income goals.

Chapter 10

Discovering What You Really Do

If you wanted to sell a car to your friend Fred, and you wanted to keep Fred as a friend, what would you tell Fred about the car?

Perhaps the first thing would be to tell Fred what the car would do for him. But back up a second. We are jumping the gun. Before you decide what to tell Fred, your mind quickly flips through what you know about Fred to figure out what features of the car best fit his personality – his wants and desires.

You know Fred loves soft, spongy seats. His old car had those and he would brag about them. Your car has similar seats.

You know he is persnickety. So you clean the car until it shines – no speck of dust anywhere.

You also know Fred loves good music and, in fact, loves Bryn Terfel; so, you put in his latest CD. You know his last car was silver and yours is red, but you know he had admired red cars before.

You also know Fred hates foreign cars, so you mention how your Ford was built in Kentucky.

And you realize he needs to know the front window sometimes sticks, and the back left tire needs to be replaced. You bring these up BEFORE he sees the car. Chances are, because he trusts you and you have shown him how great the car looks on him and runs for him, he will buy the car.

So I ask you, "Who is in marketing?"

Naturally you say, "I'm in music, not marketing."

Not so fast, Chopin. The way you prepped Fred and the car proves you know something about marketing.

You now know that:

1. Customers do not want what your product IS; they want what your product DOES for them.

2. Appeals to the intellect do not make sales – appeals to the emotions are vital.

3. You need to give them what they want if you expect to make a sale.

4. Honesty up front is terribly disarming.

5. People buy from people, and credibility is the key to establishing buyer trust.

6. It is important to know your customer first – before you build the sales pitch.

See, you really are a marketer at heart. You knew all this. It might be tough to admit you are a marketer, but in fact, as noted, we all are in marketing. Unfortunately, most vocal programs seem to try to rise above customers, which tells you why classical music is in trouble. Classical music has become notorious in America for looking down on customers; expecting customers to educate themselves before they dare enter the shrines of music.

This is fine if you do not care where your next meal is coming from, but for those of us who have to work for a living and who have to fill a house before the show can continue, finding and pleasing a customer is vital.

In my many visits to the USSR (now Russia), I noted how loved opera was. A night out at the Bolshoi, Marinski (Kirov), Stanislavski or even the Kremlin Palace were treats – not for the wealthy (few were wealthy in the USSR except the apparatchik and nomenclature), but for nearly everyone. In Russia it was common to see babushkas, children, teenagers and parents at the opera. It was not uncommon to see people in blue jeans (an expensive commodity to them) or suits. Scruffy guys sat beside refined ladies. Together they laughed, cried and soared with the marvelous musical presentations.

Why? Here is the secret. Even the Soviets understood something about marketing that the American opera gurus do not know. They did not expect their customers to come to them worthy of the opera company. Instead, they figured out a way to make opera accessible to its potential customers. Ten-year-olds could go to Wagner or Puccini without ever having taken a class in opera, having read a libretto, or brushed up on their German or Italian. Teens could break away from the corner gang hang out and love the drama of a bold opera.

The Soviets brought opera to the customer and gave them what they wanted – a terrific musical experience they could understand.

How?

I shouldn't tell you. You will only think ill of me. But, I will even though I know the entire opera establishment in America is convinced that only through intense education are the unwashed masses of America ever going to appreciate opera. In the meantime, classical performers are scrounging for work while the pearls and diamonds of theater and music are being hoarded mostly by the pearl and diamond crowd.

If you do not believe this, look at *Opera News* which brags it is the magazine "reaching opera's affluent audience for over 65 years." Never mind the gross grammatical error in that sentence. The real problem is – it's true. *Opera News* focuses on the opera audience – and right now it is not the masses but the elite, the "affluent audience." And they want to keep it that way.

It does not matter to them that America is turning out some of the greatest voices, only to have those great voices face fewer platforms for performing.

Oh, I forgot to tell you the Soviet's solution. Have you guessed? They stumbled onto "outside-in thinking."

As you found out in other chapters, outside-in thinking is letting the customer tell you what they want. You then find a way to supply the customer what he wants. This is opposite to inside-out thinking that tells the customer what we think he needs.

I constantly hear from clients, "I have a product. Make people buy it."

I always ask, "What do people want? Supply it."

Here is the Soviet solution to opera: About 60 years ago, the Soviets commissioned a number of artists who could write up a storm to translate Verdi, Puccini, Wagner, etc., into Russian. They were exceptionally mindful of making the lyrics fit the notes and less worried if the text fit the original text exactly. They took great liberties with the words and even the meaning of the aria so long as it ultimately fit the plot and character.

So when you saw La Traviata, La Boehme, or Carmen, it would only be sung in Russian. Not a word of French, Spanish, German or Italian except in the name of the opera and the name of the characters and locations.

The result: the customer understood the product and experienced something nearly akin to what the original composer had wished to convey: the emotion, the memorable characters, the tragedy all combined with the soaring and majestic score.

Opera purists hate this, but marketers know you either give the customers what they want or they go elsewhere.

In Russia today things have changed a bit. In the old days their real reason for translating everything into Russia was not market driven. It was ideologically driven. They wanted Soviet theater. They wanted the proletariat to believe Verdi wrote the opera for Soviets. In fact, they wanted and tried to obliterate all other languages. Plus, they wanted the proletariat to think the government was doing something for them so they would have good things to discuss while waiting hours in line for bread. But choice has come into the Russian theater.

Today you can see opera productions in Russian from St. Petersburg to Ekaterinaburg, Omsk, Irkutsk, Khbarovsk and Vladivostok. One can also attend Puccini in Italian and Wagner in German. Enough customers wanted operas in the original tongue that they got them.

It kills me to admit that Russia, in this regard, allows for more choices than America.

If such a choice were available in America (and no, super titles do not count – they are patronizing and insulting), opera would find a rebirth that would overwhelm even the glut of out-of-work opera performers we now have. Remember – most people view opera as an unobtainable higher echelon of music. Kind of like incomprehensible musical theater done really well.

The principle is the same principle you must remember in your advertising: customers do not want the product, they want what the product DOES.

Show the customers what the product or service you offer does for them. Entice them with your headline. Then with every ounce of copy, every graphic image, cuddle that customer – wrap them in the warmth of your benefits. Make them feel they are your one and only and that life itself will end without you.

Until you have that overwhelming desire to ethically seduce them, your ads will remain sterile, product-driven, and you will be talking to yourself.

This is so hard for musical people, especially those who have a liberal arts education. They have been brainwashed into believing that money is evil, that customers owe them a living and that altering your dreams of SRO at the Met for a gig in Flatbush is tantamount to prostituting one's talents. They believe they should be subsidized, which automatically confuses a person into believing the world owes him. Nonsense. If the opera of America appealed to customers, they wouldn't need subsidies any more than CATS, Les Miserables, Phantom, Evita or Elvis needed subsidies.

Produce what they want and they will come. Of course that opens me to ridicule trying to compare Webber to Wagner – but I could not care less. Wagner and Webber both made their investors money and appealed to huge audiences. It is just that Wagner was smart enough to write his operas in the language of his patrons – as Webber does today.

Remember that fellow in San Francisco who appeared daily in a vacant spot in Union Square, armed only with his tuxedo, boom box and negative-tracks of famous tenor arias. He belted out the great arias with enthusiasm and a great voice. People stopped to listen and put money in his jar. But he told me a secret. When he sang in something other than English, people stopped for a bit and then moved on. When he sang appropriate English words, they were entranced by the music AND the message. They commented on what a beautiful song it was, and did not even know they were listening to opera. They gave more, too.

So that is the lesson. If you are selling a drill, do not tell me how fast, smooth and wonderfully it runs – show me the holes it makes because I do not want the drill, I want the holes.

Learn it. Use it. Wrap your customers in dreams and they will dream your troubles away.

If you insist on doing what you are currently doing tomorrow, then you will still be where you are today.

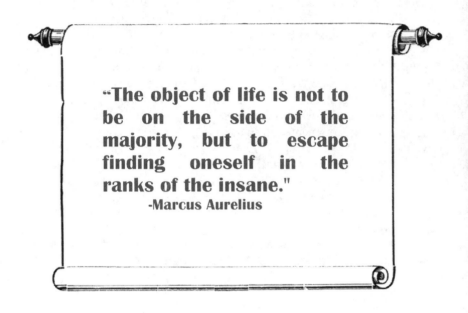

"The object of life is not to be on the side of the majority, but to escape finding oneself in the ranks of the insane."
-Marcus Aurelius

Chapter 11

Key Marketing Principles

Before getting into other matters, let's look at the big-picture view of 12 key marketing principles. Some may be obvious. Others need a bit more explanation.

1. There is no business without a satisfied customer. Find his or her need and fill it.

Opera, while much maligned (and justifiably so, I might add, for the way American opera has BECOME a non-user-friendly, lugubrious mode of entertainment), strikes deep into the human consciousness and stirs our emotions. People love opera and need it when it is properly presented. I'll tell you about Russian opera where they do opera right.

2. You must have a USP — a Unique Selling Proposition.

The San Francisco opera singer I observed (in chapter 84) was unlike any other street performer or opera singer. He captured a position by uniquely defining himself, AND he did not let the conventions and sophistications of his trade get in the way of his singing. HE defined himself and created something unique. Every product MUST have something that sets it apart from other competitors.

When listening to auditions at the Classical Singer Convention, I was struck by the lemming approach. Everyone sounded quite good, but they all sounded like vanilla ice cream. Where were the Rocky Roads or Tutti Fruitis? Why the reliance on obscure or esoteric selections rather than entertaining classics? They are classics because people love them. Wouldn't it make sense that those who run operas might love "Un Bel Di" too? But only one or two people dared to be interesting and entertaining with their repertoire, attempting instead to impress by esoteric selections. Those who defined themselves as entertainers and stood out from the crowd attracted our impressive judges.

3. Credibility sells. You must develop a professional persona.

The customer must have confidence that you can be trusted. You might have a boat load of talent, but until they believe you can deliver the goods, they will shrink back.

Cindy Sadler does a great job of detailing how a performer must build his image on paper and websites in order to be taken seriously. Paying attention to the details of resumes and websites shows credibility. The style you have on your website must fit the style of your head shots, resumes, and other public relations materials.

Some emphasize the need for self-confidence. This should not be a goal but rather a by-product of becoming professional - otherwise self-confidence turns to arrogance. During a Classical Singer Convention, Carol Vaness projected a sense of being at ease with herself and her career. Nothing about her was arrogant or pretentious. She fielded any and all questions from the audience for two hours while sitting on a simple classroom chair (we offered a nice lounge chair, but she preferred the hard-backed chair). Never did she act as if this was beneath her. In her words, "It's what I do — singing is my job." She was simply professional. This came from understanding her image, and making sure to project that image effectively.

More on this in Chapter 14 with the Credibility Matrix.

4. Develop a marketing mindset.

Once you have a marketing mindset, you'll start finding work in the most unusual places while still maintaining your artistic integrity. This mindset will broaden your understanding of your craft as well. When marketing is no longer a mystery, when it is part of your value system, you will begin finding unique strategies for marketing yourself.

This might require a paradigm shift, but you are capable of doing that right now. Just decide and do it. Accept the notion that singing is either your hobby or your business. The term "business of singing" should be a redundancy - not an oxymoron.

5. Contacts make the world go round.

Some call this networking. I call it business. Keep note cards with you and write down whatever you can about nearly everyone you meet. Either computerize or Rolodex them so they are easily organized by category as well as an alpha sort.

This data becomes your "House List," which is discussed more in the sections of this book about the Law of Concentric Circles.

6. Understand that human emotions and needs are immutable.

They do NOT change from day to day, year to year, or culture to culture. Humans are 90 percent similar and 10 percent nearly the same.

In the prologue to the Pardoner's Tale in "Canterbury Tales," Geoffrey Chaucer wrote strong principles of marketing which successful business people follow to this day. Once you have learned these principles, you can market anything. I personally have marketed artists, singers, composers, Swiss real estate, pearls, British Royal Mint sovereigns, teddy bears, educational seminars and conventions, magazines, newsletters, cruises, tours and on and on. By applying Chaucer's time-tested principles, my gross sales have totaled more than $200 million.

The process is the same regardless of the product or service. Speak to people; understand what they want; deliver the message so it is in their self-interest to act. Use the AIDA code (Attention * Interest * Desire * Action) explained in the advertising section.

7. Nobody cares what your product IS; they only care what your product does for them.

I will not expand on this one now - except to say if you are selling drill bits, nobody cares what the drill bit looks like, only if it will create the hole they want.

With performers, no one cares about the technique you are using or how much you prepared yourself, only how much they are entertained.

8. Be wary of experts out of water.

Occasionally I like to dabble in online forums. I mildly like the idea of forums as now constituted, preferring the original Greek and Roman public forums far better. They were open areas of public discourse where ideas could be traded, honed and either added or discarded. Today's forums are too often guilty of producing more heat than light, mainly due to the secretive nature. People hide behind pseudonyms to protect their identity from real or imagined bogeymen, and this cover gives them the courage to say things they would never say face-to-face.

Lack of courage has rarely produced anything of much value.

Examine a posting directed against me recently. The poster asserted my marketing comments were off the mark because I suggested pay-to-sing programs were a way to get more customers. She found it distasteful that I would advise pay-to-sing programs because she thought they were evil. She said I was helping to arm-twist poor ignorant singers into thinking these summer programs were worthwhile.

Was she right about so-called pay-to-sing programs? No. Pay-to-sing programs are neither good nor evil on their face, any more than are university pay-to-learn programs.

Her attitude may have come from having a rather low opinion of mankind. The truth is, consumers cannot be forced or coerced to part with money. Advertising NEVER made a person buy something. To believe this is to believe that "everyone else" (not me) is the lemming.

"Everyone else" is a funny thought. It is always the great unwashed masses (everyone else) out there needing our protection or condemnation. It is a rather cynical view of mankind. They are too stupid to make up their minds and are easily manipulated by oppressive advertising.

Wrong. Advertisers wish it were so, but their top copywriters get paid big bucks for continually creating something new to woo people. Were it easy, they could create the Orwellian ad that would force mind-numb robotniks to stand in line and give up the cash that somehow these fools earned.

In real life, people are smart. The smartest person is not that much smarter than the average person. Everyone makes choices. They succeed and fail and tend to learn quickly. Advertisers study people. So do you. You have since you were first conscious. YOU study people in trying to understand their wants and desires. Then YOU use that knowledge to persuade them to give you what you want.

Opera singers are no different. They want to sing great music. The trouble is that the opera industry in America is a dying industry because of the way it is marketed. It survives through beg-a-thons and government coercion to subsidize them rather than selling their product to the public and living on the revenue generated from sales. So fewer and fewer singing opportunities now exist, while the university-trained singers continue to increase. Diminishing demand and increasing supply results in an ever more stringent standard for performers. Musicians must have more on their resumes to impress artistic directors and greater experience to give them valuable stage presence.

Performers often wonder why no one will give them a chance. With a shrinking audience, would you risk alienating that precious audience with an unproven performer? Not a chance. So, performers need to find places to sing to simulate that all-important stage experience. If you cannot get it locally, try to get it somewhere else.

Add these factors, and a creative person might conclude that creating a summer program for performers in their 20s and 30s could be viable. If legitimate, these programs are expensive and labor intensive. Hiring good teachers costs more than minimum wage. All the housing, accounting for dollar fluctuations, food, transportation, etc., add up quickly.

"Will people come?" is a valid question and concern. According to the forum poster it is simply a matter of seduction. But it is not. It is a matter of tapping into an existing need and want. That takes advertising. Of course, what the poster fails to understand is that word travels quickly in proportion to the cost of a product. Summer programs, or pay-to-sing, have been around a long time. People who attend come home and talk. Word of mouth is a summer program's best friend or a worst nightmare. If the program produces the desired results, others will come from a referral. If it is poor quality, fewer people will come and more money will be spent to advertise their way out of the hole. That cannot go on long. Eventually the market place will deem the program a fraud and they will spend themselves into oblivion. In a free market, competition will drive out poorer quality - or experience will teach the organizers of a faltering summer program to hone their product and offer higher quality.

What has that to do with you? Simple. You are in marketing. Not in theory, but in daily practice. Your quality must constantly be improved in this exceptionally competitive singing market place. Advertising will not solve the problem if the voice is not the best. The poster fails to understand that advertising can only give the product the chance to be sampled. If the product does not meet the consumer's expectation, a sale is not made. You cannot trick people into buying your voice. Advertising can only open the door. PR will only do the same. Marketing concepts follow the same course.

9. Marketing & image or Branding should be simultaneous transactions.
Why do we market? Basically it comes down to two reasons:

1. To promote our image,

or

2. To sell products.

In many circumstances we hope to do both, although it rarely happens. Stay with one reason or the other. If both happen, great, but do not make marketing decisions while straddling two horses in a raging current. You are likely to fall and drown.

We must not spend too much time or money on image promotion, or "branding." Branding is trying to get other people to see a certain image, hear certain words or sounds, or smell certain odors and think of a specific product or company.

When we see an apple with a bite taken out of it, we think Apple Computers. When we see a horse rearing up against a yellow background, we think Ferrari. When we hear "Big Blue," we recognize IBM. When listening to a certain Tchaikovsky melody, we think Walt Disney's "Sleeping Beauty." Or who can hear the "Jeopardy!" theme and not think Alex Trebek. Advertisers also use smell – odors, perfumes, chicken frying, fresh cut grass, etc. – to evoke images that will brand their products.

On a less specific scale, when we create a resume, biography, website or a new photograph, we're concerned that the look of these materials accurately reflects our tastes. By doing this, we hope the viewer will link our good taste with our great voices.

But, does it work? Do these things brand us? Perhaps. At least in our dreams they do. The next chapter will go into more details on Branding.

10. When it comes to "wants vs. needs" -- wants win. No contest.

Not all business is marketing ... just the stuff that matters. Someone does need to make the product. But they've got to make something someone wants. "Wants" are all about marketing.

Often times inventors seek to create something they like that solves a problem that intrigues them. In the end, it doesn't sell because either no one else really cares, or his solution is worse than the problem. Inventors (including genre composers, writers, creative performers, etc.) need people who "need" their product.

Maybe. But here's the rub, Hamlet. It is far better to create something people *want* rather than something they *need*. Go to a poor section of town. What do they need? Most of all they need education. Everyone is six inches away from being successful, but that six inches is between their ears. They need to fill this space with something that's useful and accurate. The first American millionaire who came from African lineage, Madame Walker, once said, "It's not what you know that can hurt you, but what you know that just ain't so." Poor people know a lot. They just don't know what they need to succeed.

Can you make money from what they need? Sure. But it's more difficult. It's better to find out what people want. Many poor folks need education and skip that. They *want* televisions, DVDs, CDs, and cars they can't afford. **Obviously, they'll sacrifice what they need for what they want.**

How does this apply to performers? Quit trying to tell people you have what they *need*. Understand what people really *want*. Some call that selling out. That is foolish.

Shakespeare thoroughly understood what people wanted – action, romance, love, passion, intrigue, something new, something different, a way of looking at things they've never thought of, reaffirmation of values, power, and glory.

Even simpler, people are motivated by five simple wants: sex, power, love, money and glory. Human emotions are immutable - they haven't changed over the centuries. The entire human race deals with the big five constantly. Ask a crime detective what the motive for the crime was ... "one of the big five." Ask a marketer why someone bought something. Same answer. Ask a priest why someone sinned. As Sam once played again, "It's still the same old story, a fight for love and glory."

Don't be like the socialists who try to retool human behavior. "If only people acted another way." They don't, won't, can't and shouldn't. Goodness fills sex, power, love, money and glory. So does perverseness. Let your product lead the human race to the good side of these things.

Sell them what they want and they'll make you wealthy. As you do that, you'll be performing the job of marketing, the essential side of business. This can be summed up in the contrast of Outside-In Thinking (OIT) vs. Inside Out Thinking (IOT). OIT looks to the customers outside the company and sees what they need or want and brings that inside the company in order to create a product people want. On the other hand, IOT invents a product and tries to push it on the marketing place.

Inventors are notorious for Inside Out Thinking. They create something and believe everyone needs it. Few sales result.

Find out instead what people really want and need and then create something that fits their desires. When I counsel with classical performers, I ask them to write down the five arias they love to sing. Then I ask them to jot down the five arias people love to hear. If there aren't at least three of the audience's favorites on their own list, they might have an Inside-Out Thinking problem when it comes to creating a concert that will sell out.

While in the Soviet Union and later Russia, I created nightly entertainment for various cruises. I only chose the best classically trained singers, violinists and pianists. Their initial selections bored the customers, so I took over the concerts and assigned the artists their selections. Thereafter people lined up to come to the hour-long concerts held each night. . Both young and old loved them. We enjoyed great music in a great venue presented by wonderful artists ... but it all began with selecting great music that the customers would love.

11. Use risk reversal for immediate and long-term sales.

Risk-reversal should be a common-sense marketing concept, but as Mark Twain once said, "Common sense is none too common."

Risk-reversal (RR) is simply taking on the risk yourself and taking it away from your customer. RR comes in many forms, including guarantees, free samples, "try one", delayed payments, and the list goes on as far as your imagination works.

This principle works in every business setting, including the arts.

Let's get specific and look at guarantees. Some business people create conditional guarantees. Buy this and if it doesn't work, provided you did your part, we'll give you your money back. Many place conditions on the guarantee such as time restrictions, performance on the customer's part, and times of operations. They do so because of their belief that the customer will take advantage of them. He'll use the product, get the benefit and then try to get his money back. Thus by implementing a limited guarantee, the risk remains with the customer.

None of this is right or wrong. It's simply an opportunity for you. It's part of my Zig-Zag or Paradigm theory discussed later. If others offer conditions, you offer none. If they have time restrictions, make yours "unlimited time." If others say "you must perform," then you say "you don't even have to perform." This will catch peoples' attention and they will be more likely to try your products.

Of course, if your product is junk you might have a problem. I say "might" because I once worked (for a short time) with a company that produced extreme vanity products. Their diet products included ephedrine and other dangerous substances. The FDA had not banned them yet, but the owners knew of the negative effects. They also knew that nearly every product they had either didn't work or only worked temporarily. They preyed upon people's gullibility and weaknesses. This was most evident in their guarantees. Wisely, they had ZERO conditions for getting your money back (except for returning the product). Such a guarantee allowed skeptical customers to try the product without fear of being ripped off – which, ironically, they were as these products cost 2 dollars to make and sold for 135 dollars.

Having a zero-condition guarantee worked for this company because they understood a key principle about guarantees: no matter how bad the product, no more than 25 percent of the customers will actually return it. Of course, the higher the cost of the goods or service, the closer to 25 percent you'll be.

This company sold hundreds of thousands of bottles of diet pills, thigh shrinkers, fat lip salve, muscles builders while you sleep, and so forth. I'd go to their mail room every day and see large bins filled with returned product. They restocked their shelves with the unopened returns. The opened ones would be trashed. They had their standards.

Never did they have more than a 20 percent return rate; and after restocking the unopened items, they had no more than a 10 percent rate. Their margins and business plan used the 25 percent figure, so each month they exceeded their profit projections.

Learn from them about guarantees. Guarantees work. Unconditional guarantees work even better. Now that you know about the predictability of returns, make sure your margins can handle the returns. Above all, make sure that you have a quality product with good margins and you'll have a field day in the profit picture.

Special Note to Performers:

Have you ever offered a customer an unconditional money back guarantee – "Try my singing. If you don't like me, no charge." That will turn some heads your way because it screams "I'm confident and I'm that good." Someone you don't currently have as a customer will become a customer.

If you consider this "unseemly," it's time for a forced paradigm shift because you are saying you have nothing that is of sufficient value to exchange for something of value that you need from someone else. Get over it. You're in business and that's good; good for you and good for people who get to experience your music.

12. Free – turning the bad to good.

FREE is great for selling things, but bad for paying your bills.

When I advise performers, I stress that they should never again sing for free. And they don't have to in order to make a living from their talent. Don't give away your services. Ever.

Now, let me contradict that or at least set up the paradox.

In every business transaction one person has value that is traded to the other person for their value. When both parties get the value they want, a deal is made.

If a performer is asked to perform at a concert and the deal is "we'll be staging the event and have many expenses so we can't afford to pay you. We hope you'll donate your performance," don't let the conversation end there.

Most performers figure if they don't accept the free job, the organizer will just get someone else, so they cower and accept. Your position of advantage is lost, but it doesn't need to be.

Instead, when someone asks you to do something for free, listen and understand what they're asking and understand what their assets are. Then consider:

1. They asked you, so that is a great compliment. They want you. Work that.

2. Their event has great value because people are trading their value to come to the event. They value the event and sacrifice their free time to come and in many cases are paying for their tickets.

3. Now is your greatest time of leverage and you must use it.

First, say, "I'd love to help you and am pleased you think so much of my talent that you would ask me above so many other performers." You are establishing your value.

Next, say, "Normally the market rate is at least $2,000 for such a performance, but I understand your financial difficulties and would be happy to help you." You establish your value, again, and set a dollar roof that they must now consider. You've also let them know that by asking for "free," they are stating that they are not competent in their financial dealings. Be gentle, but make the reality point just a bit.

Now, come in for the opportunity and say, "Your audience must include some special people." Let them tout their abilities to attract people. Let them brag about what good people they know. Establish the value of the audience and you further increase your value, for you are being asked to stand before them.

Then say, "I'd like to thank them personally for coming." Then propose one or two of the following:

1. In all literature that goes out before or after the event, a gracious note be included from you thanking people for coming and endorsing the event or cause. Your name and picture need to be reinforced in the consumer's mind.

2. Ask for the email addresses (that's the cheapest, but mailing labels or something similar would be acceptable) of all the invited guests so you can send them a personal note after the event. The organizers have a list of people that they've invited. You're simply requesting that since you're sharing, they'll share also. Most organizations will cooperate. Some will give you the list. Others will agree to print what you need at their expense and include it in their mailings. However it turns out, begin by asking for the entire list. You may get it.

3. Tell the organizer you'd like to offer all of their audience members a special price on your product (your book, your CD or DVD, etc.), and offer that for each sale made you'll donate to the cause or give to the company. Turn their self-interest to your advantage. They'll be far more likely to give if they're going to get something in return.

4. Ask them to provide something else that you need.

Make sure you type up the understood arrangement in an email and send it to the organizer. Make it a Letter of Understanding and state "if my understanding is consistent with yours, please reply to this email that you agree."

Be sure to include in the letter a request that the organizers (on their letterhead) give you a stirring endorsement and positive evaluation of your abilities and contribution.

And yes, you will likely need to write that letter of recommendation. You may send it as a sample. Some will use that to help them get around to writing their own; but in many, many cases they'll take the words you write and use them for their letter.

I recently had our sales agents and engineers meet with some of the world's largest corporations who are considering buying our transmission. I had the agents ask each corporation to give us a Letter of Intent to do business. We wrote the letter and the agents gave it to them as a "sample of what we'd like." Sure enough, some used the letter almost word for word and others recrafted the letter in their own words. Either way we received great letters from huge companies positively commenting on our product and stating their desire to attain the product. These letters had a wonderful effect on our investors, our staff and future customers.

What about those who brush you aside and won't give you anything? People like this are very few. To them I say, "Let me get this straight. You want me to give of my time and talent as a value to you, but you're not willing to help me out in any significant way in return?" Most of the hard noses will reconsider. For those who don't, these are the words you must absolutely say ... "No, thank you." Walk away and don't look back. Literally. These kinds of people aren't worth dealing with. It will be a bad experience for you.

In the end, you must not sing for free. You must always receive significant value. It doesn't have to be money. While money was not exchanged in the examples above, you did get a list of names and rifle-shot exposure that would have cost you far more than the fee would have been. If you've followed the other advise in this book, you'll parlay those names into far more income because you now have a great many new people/customers to add to your house list. So as a result from performing in this "free" concert, you now have people (who know you) to invite to future events, sales from your product, and quotes or endorsements to add to your website and other promotional materials.

All because you refused to do things for free and understood never performing for "free" doesn't mean going without.

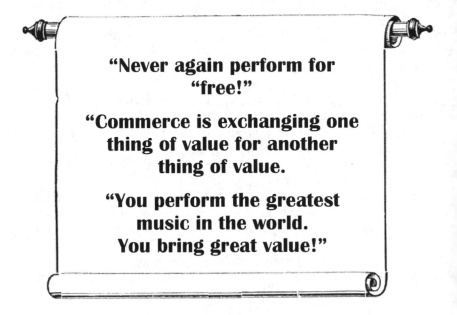

"Never again perform for "free!"

"Commerce is exchanging one thing of value for another thing of value.

"You perform the greatest music in the world. You bring great value!"

Chapter 12

Branding

In a recent marketing discussion with performers in Orlando, one singer named John made a good point. We were demonstrating the principle that when people perceive value, they are more likely to pay a higher price. John mentioned that Mount Blanc pens are about as good for writing as other pens, but are 100 times more expensive! Why? Because people believe these pens give them added prestige, which in turn does other nice things for them.

Too often we decide value and impose it on people. In this case, the pragmatic side of us says, "We need pens for writing," and concludes it can be accomplished with a really good BIC pen. Why pay more? We do not put aside our value and look at what the customer really needs. When we do, we find that some people do not want the pen for writing. They want people to "think more highly of me in a business setting, and this pen shows I know the finest and have class." People will pay big dollars for that perception!

Does a $5,000 Rolex tell time better than my $15 Timex? Is a Rolls Royce really that much more comfortable than my daughter's Chrysler Town and Country van? In a commercial, actor Kelsey Grammar does a voice over for a Korean car that compares itself to a luxury car and concludes by indicating that along with the $15,000 or more you save, you get everything in the Korean car except either cup holders or a luxury car that parallel parks. With the money saved, you can pay someone to park for you. Clever, but it carefully avoids one of the main reasons people will pay more for class. People believe if they are seen with classy things or people, they will be perceived as a classy person.

This is not all vanity. It is positioning to be sure. They are positioning themselves as having discriminating taste so those who hire or sign contracts will remember them in a positive light. Rather than argue against the concept, classical singers ought to use it. We use this opportunity to understand what customers really want from our music, and then fulfill it. Then you will be happy and they will be thrilled.

Mount Blanc has developed its brand so when someone hears the name, they think high quality, prestige and so forth.

Here is the main point: You are the Mount Blanc of performers. No other performers put in the time on their craft as you do. No others have the training regime you must follow to keep your craft at a consistently high quality. You wear high quality clothes in nearly every setting you perform, with some notable exceptions (in some operas where you might play Aldonza or a scruffy scullery maid). You get the point.

If you are a singer, you sing music only a genius could have written. Much of the music has a healing quality, an uplifting aspect and can be inspiring.

All of this needs to be part of your branding. We know part of human emotions deals with wanting the best. You provide that.

When consumers or those with whom you negotiate think of you, they must be led to understand that you are Mount Blanc, not BIC. You are a Mercedes, or Rolls Royce, not a Yugo. You are Harrods or Nordstrom's, not K-Mart or Wal-Mart. You represent the best the music world offers and supply the commensurate benefits.

Everything you do on your Foyer must be Mount Blanc. Great homes have great Foyers. When you first enter the great home and see the high ceilings, chandeliers, curving stairways and rich curtains, you know you have arrived in a great home. Your Foyer should be the same. Your Foyer consists of your resume, biography, website, business cards, cover letters, how you walk, how you talk, how you dress and coif yourself. It must reek of first class. Forget standard formulas for creating a bio, resume, etc. Look at your materials and see if they drip with class – do they exude confidence and quality? Nothing second best. Your business cards, website, resume, cover letters, and bio must have the same look.

Don't make the mistake of transferring this branding of first class with your advertisements. Artistic people are very susceptible to this mistake and then end up with artistic ads that don't sell. Your Foyer and your advertisements are two different animals. Advertising, for you, is NOT about branding, but about tracking Immediate Responses. Advertising class can be a real oxymoron like Young Gentleman, or Legal Briefs, or Country Music. Yes, make your advertising as nice as you can, but sales come first, not graphics.

Back to your Foyer.

Your head shot must include the following guidelines:

1. <u>Make it a current professional photo</u> so when they see you they think it is you and not your child.
2. <u>You should look approachable yet vulnerable.</u> I cannot explain it any more than that.
3. <u>Focus on your eyes.</u> Be sure your jewelry, hair, make-up and clothing attract attention to your face, not to themselves. For men, it is easier. A tuxedo will always do. For women, make the dress compliment you, not overpower you. Be modest and cover the cleavage. If you want them to look you in the eyes, make sure that is where their eyes will go!
4. <u>Consider color.</u> I predict the mode of black and white will be gone in a few years. Black and White is chic now and then, but its popularity originally came because color was so expensive. Now the costs for either are getting close to the same. I will take color any day. Save the blanc/noir look for the art schools.
5. <u>Get a professional photograph.</u> Most good photographers like Nick Granito, Devon Cass and many others who advertise in *Classical Singer* magazine know what to do to give you that professional look. Tell your friend with a camera, "No thanks," and get a professional. It is important.
6. <u>Use the right paper.</u> When you print out your Foyer, is the paper ordinary white? Why? You are not ordinary and neither is your product. Why is your resume white? Do not use ordinary white if you want to convey the extraordinary. Pick a color and texture that allows your black text to be easily and clearly read, but still be different in a classy way.
7. <u>High class does not mean stuffy or snooty.</u> Avoid arrogance. Be gracious and understanding. Let the inner class come through, unforced because you truly understand that when you sing, you uplift, inspire, challenge and heal. No need for pretense. Pretense is for those without talent pretending to have something they lack. You have the talent.

The $64,000 Question of Branding

Brand yourself in everything you do. One of the greatest ways you brand yourself is through your self-perception. If you believe it, they will believe it. The reverse is also true.

Think of the last time someone asked you, "What do you do?" How did you respond? If you are like most singers you said, "I'm an opera singer." When you said that, what was the reaction? Was it to your liking?

I have had singers tell me they have had people roll their eyes, or say "That is great, but I do not like opera," or some other less than positive remark. In your mind opera music is great, but do not forget that not all opera music is great; some of it is lousy. You have just put yourself in a category that includes the entire range of quality.

In addition you likely sing oratorio, lieder, art song and so forth. So why draw a circle around you that's not inclusive of your quality or variety of music?

My question is, "What will you say the next time they ask 'what do you do?'" If you say the same thing and get the same reaction, should you be surprised? As the cliché goes, insanity is doing the same thing over and over, expecting a different result.

My suggestion on branding yourself is to have the following conversation:

"And what do you do?"

"I perform the greatest music in the world."

I'll wager the reaction will be a surprised look where the brows are raised, the eyes widen and a smile ensues. Then the person will say, "Oh. Wow," followed by questions about that music. Nobody wants to look foolish or ignorant, so if they know little about classical music, they will simply think of the greatest music they have heard and assume that is what you are talking about.

Those who know classical music will assume you sing the best music they have heard.

Either way, that puts you instantly in great company.

You have totally branded yourself as the Mont Blanc of singers.

I once watched a couple of German opera directors sniff at a singer's resume and not-so-good photo. Instantly they had written him off. Then he took the stage, and emotionally "took the stage." It was his. The directors were his. He sang his heart out and they loved him. Others with stunning paper foyers were less impressive on stage.

However, some of us are marginal singers, and that is not a slam. Marginal singers are very good, but they simply do not have the extra edge to immediately garner attention. They are good enough to get a good singing job, but they just seem vanilla when directors are looking for Rocky Road. The marginal singers need every star to line up perfectly, and a well-done resume may be the one thing that pushes the directors over the edge to remember them.

For marginally good performers, branding is probably critical. For stunning performers on one end of the spectrum and not-so-good performers on the other end, branding does not matter much. (Marginal performers, however, can become stunningly great performers).

Branding or promoting our image is never a bad thing as long we keep it in perspective and do not fool ourselves into thinking those extra graphic lines we put on the resume near our name, or the font we select, or the mauve instead of burnt orange color makes much of a difference. Some people get so snooty about taste, when taste is just that. Subjective criteria change daily.

For example, my wife Elizabeth is a gifted artist. She creates advertisements for performers and those who sell to performers. Some clients thrill her with their good taste (which means it lines up with hers). Some clients crush her because they do not like something she has created. I tell her it is simply a matter of taste concerning something that really is not going to make a single difference to the performance of the advertisement. The client is simply over-caring about his or her image, thinking this shade of green makes a difference. One problem with strongly creative types that frequent the opera world is they are so dramatic in expressing their taste. It is all ego, because it does not have much to do with anything. One performer emphatically slammed Liz's ad for using "fonts that are clownish." Clownish? It is a font. No red nose. No puffy hair. No big feet. Wilder than Arial for sure, but clownish?

A response like this comes from the delusion that the most important thing is the font, not the message. Fonts exist to either call attention or to make a message easier to read. But the message itself is the most important part. Image enhancement, branding, and subtle advertisements waste your time and money.

Yet, when performers want an ad or create an ad, what do they focus on? The "look."

Yes, you ought to give it some attention, but if you have 10 units of time to devote to marketing, spend one of them on the image and 9 units on the message. Suck it up and do not worry about every graphic detail. Graphics are STRICTLY to set mood and, more importantly, call attention. Graphics, art work, fonts, photos or the like DO NOT SELL! Your BRANDING is not going to sell you. It is all a huge canard bit on by egocentric people who lack the skill to craft messages that sell.

When creating your message, beware of using Delayed Response Advertising (DRA). Ninety-five percent or more of all advertising you see is DRA. These messages merely say, "remember me." For example, "The next time you are in the market for a car, remember that Volvo is safe, fashionable and cool with the brie and cheese crowd."

Notice what it is NOT asking you to do. It is NOT asking you to buy their product now. Just someday. They may not even be asking for a sale. Just remember them.

You have neither the time nor the money to bother with this sort of advertising nor the branding that goes into this discussion. DRA is NOT for you. This means that 95 percent or more of the promotions, advertisements and flyers you see are wrong for you. You need to keep this in mind as you make your marketing strategy. The sirens calling you to fall into the DRA trap are all around you.

Message creation is more about skill than talent. Remember that marketing is not something that requires a master's degree to understand. Anyone can learn the art of crafting a message that sells. The best serious adult marketers never took a university class in marketing. They understand, however, that marketing is "GETTING WHAT YOU WANT."

Branding will rarely get you what you really want–a singing job. In order to obtain the singing jobs, in the moments when you are not working to improve "voce" with your best vocal instructor, coach or performance professional, pay attention to your message.

Your message is simple. What problem in the life of your customer are you going to solve? What are the benefits you bring to your customer? Work on that. Write every benefit you can give a customer. Spend most of your marketing time thinking about this.

We will discuss in the advertising and promotion sections how to apply this message.

Chapter 13

Is Marketing a Matter of Feeling?

As a civilization of the Western World, we have developed a severe sickness – over sensitivity. It has led us to believe that how we "feel" is how we are. If we feel something is wrong, it must be.

If we feel someone has been mean to us, they must have.

If we feel attracted to someone, it must just be how we are.

We have become a nation of emotional twits, twirling in the breeze of feelings.

Never mind reasoning something out.

Never mind applying principles of inquiry that require us to withhold judgment until the facts are in. If we feel something, it must be true.

As a card-carrying member of the liberal arts education establishment, I know too well the thinking patterns of artists, writers and performers.

Feeling is important in the liberal arts to the point of perverting the entire concept of intelligent discourse. Consequently, instructors teach us to feel throughout the education process in universities. When I teach writing classes, students' first papers are mostly just emotion, blubbering here and there and everywhere.

The anti-Christ to the liberal arts mentality is pragmatism. Should anyone wish to promote her talents, out come the machetes to hack her back in her place. Performers, writers and artists who dare to challenge the orthodoxy of the art establishment are labeled. "She is prostituting her talent," they say, by marketing herself and daring to find unique ways of getting paid for singing her music. The other words are "whoring" and "selling out."

Who is selling out?

In my Marketing Master Workshop, I show performers a foolproof way to get paid but never lose artistic integrity. I show them how to ask the right questions so they are sure to keep their art pure.

Students first understand their values and what is vitally important to their souls. It can be honesty, charity, integrity, or any of the things we consider morality. But, it might not. Whatever is at the core of your soul.

From these values, students create the strategies for success. Strategies can be things like reading this book to establish your marketing skills. It can be a determination to get yourself in a position to

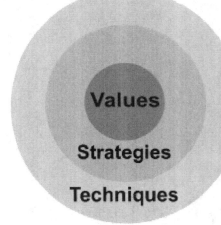

hire a manager, or to work your way through the traditional maze leading to the top opera houses. Or it can be a strategy of working in non-theater work to gain experience, so when your chance comes you'll be ready. These are strategies.

With these strategies firmly within your subconscious, you then create techniques to fulfill these strategies.

If you have positive, honest values and a strategy to deal with people directly, you'll likely create a technique like walking on stage at an audition with a firm grasp on your confidence, looking the audition judges in the eye and singing just as directly. You'll likely speak to your teachers directly and tell them when things are going well and when they're not. You'll not put up with others putting you down - be that person a teacher, fellow singer or an artistic director.

If you have a value system that says it's okay to bend the truth and form your own existential code, then you're likely to create strategies where you can deceive others. You'll feel others are as deceptive as you are and suspect each person's motives, degrading your own sense of confidence. Everything will become a game with perceived winners and losers and negative views of life. Your techniques will be backbiting and putting others down to build up your self-confidence.

Do not interrupt this flow. By all means change your values, but do not adopt other singer's strategies or techniques. They may work in the short term for you, but not in the long run.

By working from your values to your strategies, you have integrity in the truest sense. If you adopt someone else's strategies or techniques because they worked for that person, you sell out your core values. That is a recipe for emotional and spiritual conflict. It is a painted sepulcher; beautiful on the outside and rotten within.

If you follow this formula of only creating your techniques from your strategies, and only creating strategies that are consistent with your values, you will have great inner confidence. You will say, "Life was not what I expected, but it was exactly what I planned."

I love great art. It is essential to my soul. I also decry bad singing, bad pretentious performing, terrible technique and, worst of all, boring presence. Life is too short to be bored. But I love performers who have the guts to look at all the lobsters waiting to tear them down and all the psychic vampires anxious to make them as miserable as they are. These performers tell them to stuff it and go about the business of making money from their talent.

If you feel making money is somehow impure, unsophisticated, cheesy and Byzantine, you are reading the wrong book. Money is what you use to pay your mortgage and food bills. You earn it by exchanging your value for their value. This book is all about helping performers market – sell – their great talents to an adoring audience.

I rant for a reason. Performers who cannot stand up to psychic vampires are notorious for trembling at an audition. Within eight seconds most opera directors know if you are worth hiring. Confidence born of inner strength cannot be faked. It boils and spills over into performance. It gives power to a song, power to emotions and moves audiences – even tough opera directors – and make no mistake, an audition is just one more performance before an audience wanting to be moved.

Such inner confidence among performers is so rare that it is easy to spot. I want you to have that.

What does all of this have to do with marketing? Performers have choices.

Choice 1: Do the usual.

Tens of thousands of performers graduate each year, potentially clogging the audition arteries. But not really. Most are not serious and drop away after the first rejection. The Haagen-Dazs is grabbed and justifications are clung to like Linus's blanket. Those who object to the first rejection have a liberal arts training and believe that if they are just good enough, with great enough technique, the world will welcome them enthusiastically. One of the great lies is, "Build a better mousetrap and the world will beat a path to your door." That is a maxim from ancient times. Today we say, "If you build it, they will come." And it is true – in fantasies.

So the performer works hard, spends thousands to improve, goes to auditions and gets only a few church jobs here and there. He or she is never discovered. Of course, being discovered is another liberal arts dream. We have read about it often in our college texts and classic stories. But Rule # 1 is, "No one is ever discovered." If they are, see Rule # 1 again. Chances are this overnight sensation was 20 years in the making.

Doing "the usual" is how most performers live; eking out a living doing something else, living with someone who pays the bills for his expensive hobby, or paying back student loans with non-singing revenues.

Choice 2: Do the unusual.

Remember that doing the unusual is part of a clear marketing concept called Zig Zagging. When others Zig, you Zag. This reiterates our initial discussion. When the Western World is busy "feeling," there is an opportunity for someone who is thinking!

Marketing is all about thinking. It is all about analysis. It is not about feeling, except how to get the other guy to start feeling what you want them to feel.

Notice how many people are successful with "Choice 1." Few. Hardly any. Typically 10,000 singers graduate from universities every year. They compete for fewer than 2,000 paying opera jobs in the USA. They are competing with seasoned singers – hundreds of thousands. And next year it gets worse by another 10,000. Yet, these people whine about anyone who is doing something besides the usual. They love their Choice 1 and spew venom over anyone challenging their secure but unsuccessful idea.

Get to "Choice 2." Make this how you think. Zig Zag. When everyone else is jumping over the cliff without a parachute, consider a parachute even if they ridicule you.

This is why I am bullish for good performers who practice good marketing. They are a rare breed and have a chance to rise quickly above the plethora of good performers waiting to be discovered.

Getting Jobs with Zig Zag

Zig Zag is the mind set of marketing where you examine what others have been doing, see if it works, take the best, and find ways of doing things differently. Even the best ways can be improved.

You will be criticized for departing from the norm. Some will dismiss your alternatives as "cheesy" marketing. I doubt any of these folks who whimper about the cheese have a better alternative. Nothing they say promotes a better way. The late CJ Williamson, editor of *Classical Singer* magazine, once asked if criticism bothered me. I confessed, "Yes, it does. It bothers me when people are foolish enough to confuse how they feel about marketing with how they think about marketing."

I share this with you because if you attempt to do ANY marketing, someone will be there acting like the bad-boy character Nelson on the TV show, "The Simpsons." He's notorious for watching someone do something different and ridiculing him, "Ha, ha!"

Cheesy marketing is called that because they "feel" it is cheesy. What does that mean? I did an experiment a few months ago. I wrote a "cheesy" promotion for my Marketing Master Workshops and sold out many workshops – 311 sales.

Another singer who teaches marketing told me she thought my work was less than admirable. So I said, "Fine. I do not care who writes our ads, just as long as they work." If she thought my ad was dumpy, unsophisticated and cheesy, then fine. "Please write a grcat ad for me. I'll pay you – on a per-sale basis." She did and was quite proud about how sophisticated and erudite it sounded. Some of the *Classical Singer* staff loved it too.

Mine sold 311. Hers sold four. Hers did not even fill the back row of one of the workshops.

Now, you decide. Which marketer are you going to hire if it was your money on the line?

But wait. What about your image in the long run? In the long run, you will have most of the same customers you have in the short run – if they like your product. And if they are happy with the product you create, then they will tell their friends.

This is not about image. It is Zigging while the others Zag. It is about finding what speaks to customers. Remember that human emotions and needs do not change. They react consistently to emotional cues regardless of culture, income status, age, gender or wisdom. This might seem to contradict previous chapters about how the market is ever changing, but it does not. One is general. One is specific. In general, people all love, hate, laugh and cry. Knowing this, you'll come up with marketing methods that cue into these emotions. But, being astute at behavior, you'll see that people will express their love or joy or anger in ever changing ways. You'll change you techniques to catch those changes and make yourself job opportunities in the process.

Everything you write is marketing. Everything you speak and present is marketing. You have no choice but to market; you only have a choice of doing it well or poorly. If you have been harvesting beans until now, chances are you have been planting beans, or marketing poorly.

If you are doing it the way everyone else is doing it, you will get their results or worse. Zig Zag. When they Zig, you Zag.

Specifically, here are things you do that need Zig Zag thinking:
* A concert or recital brochure should be more than a tombstone listing. Make the reader excited by the cover and want to turn the page. Make the first thing they see interesting, and make sure it leads to the next item and so forth. Insignificant and irrelevant information is just that.
* How you walk on stage for an audition and how you present yourself is marketing. Find a way to be unique.
* The letter of inquiry you write should follow the AIDA code. This applies for any correspondence where you want something from someone else.
* The visit to the opera house or manager's office is all about marketing. Do it right and you have a chance. Do it poorly and you will reduce your chances. Be yourself. Let yourself come out.
* Negotiating is all about marketing. You do not get what you deserve; you get what you negotiate.
* The cover of your CD is marketing.
* Having a website is marketing. Some scoff, "You say we cannot get a job without a website, but I did." In the early 1900s, the buggy whip owner mocked the guy who just bought a Ford. Yes – you can get jobs without a website. But why not increase your chances with better exposure?
(For even more on Zig Zag Theory, see Chapter 15.)

Everything listed here increases your chances of getting more work. Marketing does not guarantee you work, but it does increase your chances, especially in an industry where hardly anyone does it. You are Zig Zagging!

Those who do Zig Zag stand out and are remembered! You have carved out a position in the mind of the consumer – whether a ticket holder, patron or company art director.

Last point. So many performers with whom I have consulted carry terrible emotional baggage. Among the cargo are bales of guilt for something. I am not a psychologist, but I married into a gaggle of them. They confirm what I have seen.

How we think transfers quickly into how we act. Those who believe they can change the way they feel, have a chance. Those who believe they are captive to their feelings, have little chance of change.

So, do not feel bad. Just do something different. Today! In fact, decide to stop feeling bad. After a terrible day, you are allowed a pity party of one hour, but that is it.

One day at a time. One item at a time. Never panic that you are not everything you want to be. Begin by deciding you will expunge the "feel" mindset. You can and will change and in the meantime, you are just fine.

Then change something that needs changing in your paper presentation as a starter. With each change comes more confidence. With more confidence comes more opportunities. With more opportunities come more experience. With more experience comes more success and satisfaction for your life goals.

One step at a time. Zig Zag. Keep smiling. You are worth it.

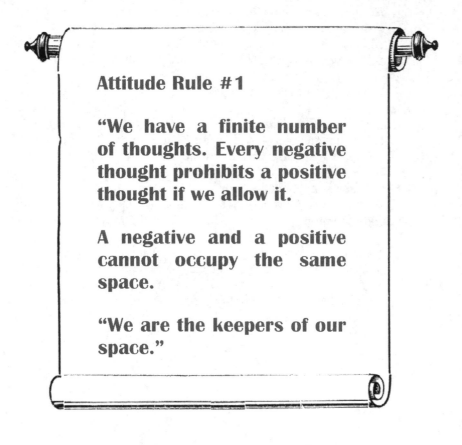

Attitude Rule #1

"We have a finite number of thoughts. Every negative thought prohibits a positive thought if we allow it.

A negative and a positive cannot occupy the same space.

"We are the keepers of our space."

Chapter 14

Identify and Develop an Audience

As previously indicated, the best way to build your customer base is to begin with people who know you – whether you're extending invitations for a concert or theatrical event; selling your latest CD; or in fact, selling anything.

What we have not elaborated on is the underlying psychological reasoning behind this. Let us explore this reasoning; so that once you understand it, you can easily apply the principles repeatedly without giving them another overt thought.

First, a couple of truths about people. People always buy for emotional reasons, not intellectual ones. We use intellectual reasons to gain their Interest (refer to the AIDA code to understand why Interest is so important). We also use intellectual reasons to prevent buyer's remorse.

To illustrate this, suppose you are going to buy a new car at a Toyota/Lexus dealership (Toyota makes Lexus). Once the sales agent ascertains what car you are likely to buy (through asking the right questions, observing carefully, and listening to you), she will then do almost anything to get you to sit in the car. She wants you to feel the leather, hear the music, and smell the aroma – all sensory matters.

Notice how she never tells you about the polymers or the tensile strength of the frame or the incredible alloys used in the creation of the engine. They are all incredible bits of data, but this is the wrong time to mention these items. Instead you will be told how wonderful you look in the car, how it fits your style to drive an RX400, and how the color matches your eyes. You will hear how this car will benefit you with great gas mileage, low maintenance costs, fabulous residual value and on and on.

It is all about you. Enamored, you are ready to give your first born away for this car. You WANT it badly. Soon you sign on the dotted line. For just $2,000 down you get to drive it away. As you leave, a sinking pit in your stomach reminds you of the new $550-a-month payment you will be making for the rest of your life! You can see your spouse's reaction as you announce that this new car costs more than your house. Fortune smiles on you as you recall the final words from the salesman about the high safety features to protect your spouse and children; the tensile strength of the steel; the safety glass and air bags. All the intellectual reasons. And most important, the three-inch thick owner's manual with all the guarantees. That will convince the spouse.

Emotion made you do it. Intellect assuaged buyer's remorse.

Also notice how important the saleswoman was in this whole transaction. She first got to know you before starting to sell and made you feel comfortable. She asked seemingly irrelevant questions to understand you. Notice how she found an opportunity to "press the flesh."

Joe Girard (remember, he is the "World's Greatest Salesman") once told me a story worth repeating. He was hired in the 1970s by a Detroit dealership to come reverse a dismal sales record. Joe saw that the sales lobby was like all other sales lobbies. All along the walls immediately facing the customer were the sales cubicles. Several employees were gathered together, drinking their coffee, smoking and hanging out like vultures awaiting the creation of carrion. A dark, dismal day in Detroit darkened the dank parlor of sales, yet the white-bright cool florescent lighting only cast an eerie cold pall upon the scene. The cars for sale were in the distant horizon. Something was wrong here.

I harp on this notion in this book. If something is wrong and you are doing the same thing you have always been doing, it is time to change the way you're doing things. And if everyone is doing it, it is probably wrong. Zig Zag. It is really that simple. If opera is a great product but not enough people are buying, then look at the way opera is being marketed. It is not working, change it. Either that, or change the product AND the way you market.

Back to Joe. He saw people come in and leave. Potential customers walking out the door is a dreadful sight.

He cleared the cubicles and let whatever natural light was available during a Detroit winter enter the large floor room. He got rid of white-bright cool bulbs and installed warm lights. He put carpet on the floors and moved all the cars to the front so they were the second thing the customers saw. In the distance he placed the cubicles and instructed the sales team never to gather in the sales area.

One salesman was to be walking the car floor at all times, dust cloth in hand to polish the cars. A tender touch to the inanimate objects. As the customers opened the door on the cold, blustery day, the first thing they saw before them was a beautiful formal banquet table, complete with a striking white linen table cloth. An array of shiny silver coffee urns with white china cups and saucers graced the table. He measured the perspective of the customer when he entered the showroom and made sure the table was high enough to have the shiny silver urns in direct eye line.

As the customer entered he was greeted in a new way.

When you enter a store what is it that nearly 99 percent of the clerks say?

That's right, "May I help you?"

And you say . . . ?

Yep, you say, "No thanks, just looking."

Again, insanity is doing the same thing over and over expecting different results.

Joe had the salesmen say, "May I get you a cup of coffee, tea or hot chocolate? It sure is cold outside."

What would you say to that? Especially with the wind nipping at your heels. People were grateful and did not refuse.

But, Joe did not let the salesman step aside and have the person serve himself. No way. The salesman became the servant to the customer – what an idea!

In the process, when the salesman handed the person his cup and saucer, he always made sure to shake hands and then hand the person the cup.

What just happened?

At least four things:

1. The customer received a benefit.
2. The customer just accepted a gift.
3. By pressing the flesh, the giver of the gift suddenly became a human being. It was not Ford selling them a car as they feared when they entered, it was a real human being making contact and bestowing a benefit.
4. The customer just became obligated to listen to the salesman. You can't take his fine cup filled with a warm liquid and walk out the door.

The salesman then told the person his name and added, "And your name?"

As the person started to take a drink, the salesman was instructed to turn and start walking toward the cars, engaging the customer in conversation to better understand the customer, his desires and how all this might relate to buying a car.

Does the customer stand his ground and drink, or does he follow?

Of course he follows as if a rope was tethered between the cup and the salesman's back.

Sales rose dramatically. Customers liked coming in. They liked the service and the way they were treated. The salesmen loved the new atmosphere and adored the increased commissions.

Think about your next concert. How can you incorporate these techniques? This should be a snap for you.

More to the point of this chapter, however, is the concept that people are far more likely to buy from another person than a company. We prefer to deal with fellow human beings.

In your face-to-face meetings, figure out how to make sure you have real human contact and find ways to obligate the customer in doing trade with you. See the chapter on the Monkey's Fist for more ideas.

In your literature, brochures, advertisements or even your recital programs, emulate these principles as well.

None of your work should seem like sales pieces, but a piece of the real you. Remember that the best-selling pieces do not feel or look as if they are sales pieces. Sales pieces hype the seller. They trumpet YOU. The best sales pieces, to the contrary, talk about the customer and how her problems can be solved with clear benefits.

The headline reads, "Global University. The finest name in vocal studies."

Or, "The Marriage of Figaro by Mozart sung in its entirety by ME." Or "AVIS tries harder."

All three are typical of what you will see around you. And all are dismal examples. They are all about the seller and scream "this is an ad," and people do not buy.

Instead we write, "Free tuition and stipend for 12 emerging artists now available." And "You deserve a night out with the one you love." Or "The easiest and fastest way to drive away from the airport is right here."

So far we've discussed ideas on how to identify and develop an audience. We have just shown why people do what they do when buying. It is all about them and how you benefit them.

Now let us understand who these customers are.

As noted in the example of the Law of Concentric Circles, your best customers are those who know you, and then others who know those people.

The trick is to make sure you know as many people as possible, as fast as possible, and to make this customer connection happen (without breaking the bank).

Please take a look at the matrix below. This matrix has been used by many persons to understand that the key to this entire exercise is CREDIBILITY. If you have followed the AIDA code, then the customers are ready to buy - but may be holding back because they do not know if they can trust you to deliver the goods. That's because they have never heard of you.

Examine the Stoddard Credibility Matrix. All marketing takes

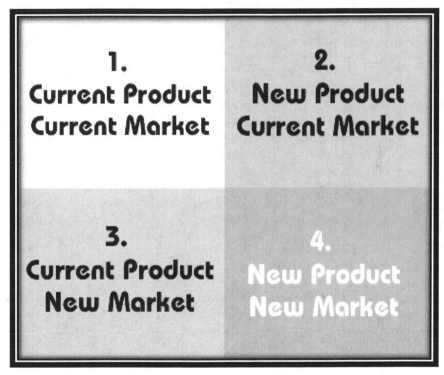

Stoddard Credibility Matrix

place in one of these four boxes. Let us use an example to illustrate. You have just produced a great CD from your last concert. I hope you recorded it. I hope you spent the extra dollars to have a professional mike record and edit you. I hope as well you let the audience know that this concert is "being professionally recorded. For your copy, please use the card in your program. It is my pleasure to sing for you." I hope your card follows the points made in this book, and that you use the card as a convenience to gain each person's name, address, phone number and e-mail address.

Make sure it asks for no money now; but indicates that when the CD is delivered, you will send a notice of the charge. Audience members merely check off how many copies they would like. Have the card read: "Order three and one will be my gift to you."

What box are you in?

These are current customers. They are listening to a current product – your concert. You are in Box One. Now you would like them to buy a new product, but it is not a truly new product, but more of the current product, so you are still in Box One. How likely are they to buy from you? Very likely. Why? They know you. They like the product you just sold them. They believe the next product will be as wonderful as the one they are now hearing – obviously, as it is a recording!

Four months later, it is October and you have produced another CD – this time a beloved collection of sacred music for Christmas. If you have done what is taught in this book, your "house list" includes all the people who came to your concert, all who bought the CD (of course, you found a way to get the contact information of all non-concert-attendees who bought CDs). You send them all a notice of your new CD.

Where are you? You are selling a New Product to a Current Customer. You are in Box Two. How much credibility do you have? A great deal. How likely are they to buy? Very likely.

Now, you get cocky and foolishly decide to do what most do. You take out an ad in Opera News. You are now in Box Three. You are selling a Current Product – the one from your sold-out concert – to a New Customer. You figure since it has sold so well to your house list, and you have garnered great testimonials and reviews and put them in your ad, the CD will sell like hot cakes to these opera lovers. Of course it bombs. You lose your shirt because the few sales you make do not pay for the creation of the ad, let alone the price of the space.

Why? They do not know you. You have no credibility. It will not work even if you have the cleverest ad.

So you do what others do. As mentioned before, you become like the steamboat captain sailing toward Niagara Falls who yells, "Throw more wood in the boiler. Full steam ahead."

You figure the sales were not made because it was a bad CD. So you take the new CD and sell it in Opera News. You are now in Box Four with a New Product being sold to a New Customer.

Alas, you are doomed because you have no credibility *and* your product has no credibility.

But not really, because after studying the principles in this book you would never do such a foolish thing.

The trick then is to find a way to get people to move from either Box Three or Box Four into the box above.

Rather than going to people you do not know, you go to your house list and hold a special concert. You tell them this special concert is strictly for your friends and their friends. It will not be sold to the public. You send them 10 tickets that have a price tag of $40 each and tell them these tickets have been set aside for them as a gift (a $400 gift), providing they will bring eight family or friends. If they need more than that, you will get tickets for them at half price.

You also tell them that if they prefer, you will do the work of inviting their friends. If they will provide you with a list of friends, you will send tickets with a letter saying that "John and Mary Donut thought so highly of you that they insisted I send you these tickets; and it is my pleasure to do so."

These people were in Box Three. They were New Customers receiving a Current Product (you have done concerts before and included reviews).

But here is the magic. You did not have credibility with these people until you borrowed the credibility from John and Mary Donut. Now you have moved the entire selling operation from Box Three to Box One.

How much did it cost you? Hardly anything. A bit of time and some paper and stamps.

How do you now make money? Repeat what we have discussed already.

This, my friend, is how marketing works.

Remember: People prefer to buy from other people. It is credibility. Then make sure that once they are a customer, they have a chance to buy from you again and recommend you to their friends. If you are really quite a good performer and know how to put on a show, you might just sell out not only the first show, but be forced to add another show, and then another. Success begets success, if you know how to develop a house list, move from Boxes Three and Four to One and Two without much money, and borrowing the credibility of others.

Here is one last fact. Once you have customer credibility, you have a chance to sell them just about anything else. It is your credibility at work. If you give them a good product, they will be in line to get the next one as well. Mess up, however, and the upward cycle falls.

What products can you now sell them? Just remember this is the same principle that J.C. Penney and others discovered was the key to making a department store work. If you sell someone a great pair of socks and they love them, when they get ready to buy more socks they will come back to you. And if they trust you with socks, they will trust that you'll take care of them properly on their shoes, and then their shirts and pants and dresses and, get ready for this, their tires and hammers. Credibility is king. Once you have that, protect it but also use it.

Once people know who you are and love your music, sell them on:

1. More concerts, recitals, theatrical performances and CDs. This puts everything in the linear scope.
2. The chance to sponsor you at a competition, university training, special summer program or a series of auditions.
3. The chance to recommend you to others in their circles, including having you sing at their parties, conventions, reunions, etc.
4. Sending students to your voice studio.

If you start a new business that is, for example, a craft and novelty retail store, invite them to the grand opening. If you have written a book, they are a likely customer even if it is on "How to Travel in Europe."

Credibility is the key to developing your customer base. Use the Credibility Matrix to analyze your marketing plans.

Chapter 15

Zig Zag Theory, Self-Promotion & Clarity

To further explore Zig Zag, let's look at a different profession before returning to singing. Carl Sagan once wrote, "In order to make an apple pie from scratch, you must first create the universe." What we will learn in a universe other than the classical singing universe will apply.

Let's select a profession or trade that has been around a long time – one that everyone knows and thinks they understand, yet remains a bit of a mystery. How about ... selling life insurance?

This will work. You are going to sell life insurance. Here is what you will say in your sales pitch: "You need to protect your family in the event you should die. You should take care of their future. Do not leave them destitute. Make sure their memory of you remains positive after you die. Buy term for the best value. Buy whole life for the security and cash value. Get it from a reputable company that will be around long after you."

You can probably add more because you must have heard all the pitches by now, even if you are not in the market for life insurance.

In 30 years I have heard nothing new about life insurance with the possible exception of universal life policies.

So here is the question. If you are going to sell life insurance, how will you stand out from the clutter? Everyone says the same thing. Their advertisements basically look alike. Met has Snoopy, Hartford has a deer or elk or something with antlers. Allstate has good hands. State Farm has some looping logo. Gibraltar has a rock, or is it Prudential? It is all vanilla. Nothing stands out. If everything looks, sounds and acts about the same, then in the consumer's mind, everything is the same. There are distinctions without differences.

So how do you get more business? They are all Zigging, so what is the way to Zag?

You must do something to stand out.

I look at most advertisements and conclude the same. Flip through a woman's magazine. It tends to have more advertising per page than any other type of magazine. The articles get lost in the clutter. And it is so much clutter. Madison Avenue's worst sin is to have a look that is different from the other advertisements of the day – to stand out. They will deny that, but flip through and notice how similar the designs are. Few ads really are unique. Notice how they use similar color schemes, typefaces, models and messages. It is like the automobile manufacturers. Most cars look similar to other cars. At a quick glance you cannot tell a Toyota from a Honda, Mazda, Saturn, BMW, SAAB or whatever. When someone creates a design that sells, everyone follows the leader. In the beginning of the mini-van era, the Dodge Caravan had a look that differed quite a bit from Ford's Aerostar, which looked different from Pontiac's vehicle. Four years later, the Aerostar and Pontiac look were gone and everyone looked like the Caravan. I have a Ford Windstar and it looks nearly identical to a new Caravan. Mine has a rusty bottom, and I refuse to sell it. Other than the rust, it looks the same as all others. I keep the rust so I can find it in the parking lot.

When faced with a blizzard of similar activity, you have a couple of choices if you want to compete in business:

1. Keep a similar look and spend a lot of money on advertising to get people to recognize you. A lot of money means millions of dollars. Rising above image clutter is expensive.

2. Be different in every way. If the rest Zig, you must Zag.

Apply this to singers. The competition is enormous as more than 10,000 singers leave school and attempt the big time only to discover that opera is NOT a growth industry. People are not clamoring to invest in opera companies. I doubt if an opera company is listed on a stock exchange. If someone could make money producing operas, you would see a Time-Warner or Universal jumping in.

Do the math. Opera is a no-growth, non-revenue/profit producing industry on the decline with an overabundant, never-ending supply of singers.

Hollywood has a much larger supply of actors wanting work, but is sometimes so profitable it keeps spawning new production companies.

If this discourages you, good. If reality is all it takes to discourage you, then it is better to get discouraged now than five years from now after your bubble of Utopia has burst.

If this information does not discourage you, then you can embark on the equivalent of C.S. Lewis's Dawn Treader in search of a better world.

Your first stop on this Dawn Treader voyage is to notice how everyone else approaches this singing craft. They take lessons, audition, take more lessons, audition, take some more, get a small role, get illusions of La Scala, take more lessons, settle on a non-theater role to earn some money and say this is just a temporary place, audition, get some coaching, sing some church jobs, get a "real job," get another role that tempts you back into Utopia, audition, win a competition, lose several more, go to a "pay-to-sing" program and get to sing in Europe, hoping it will lead to more work there. It does not, so you take more lessons, and on and on.

This is life for a classical singer; at least how we are told it is.

Bobby Kennedy once paraphrased George Bernard Shaw and said, "Some see things as they are and ask 'Why?' I choose to see things as they never were and ask 'Why not?'"

I like another Shaw quote: "The reasonable man adapts himself to the world; the unreasonable one persists in trying to adapt the world to himself. Therefore all progress depends on the unreasonable man."

Learn how others have done it. That is good. Now figure out that you likely will not and should not do the same things. You must blaze a new trail. Take what is good from this universe, what works in other universes, and emerge with a unique way to pitch your voice (which is your product). If you get criticized for doing it a certain way, you are probably on the right path. If you get called names, take heart. You are onto something.

How can you stand out?

Here are some options to consider:

You are the highest priced.	You charge by the note.
The loudest.	The softest.
The most brash.	The most shy.
The funniest.	The saddest.
The one with the most energy.	The most staid.

You are a one-man opera show.

You have a small group you have put together and you are a packaged team.

You only "do" schools.	You never do schools.

You only sing in English with lyrics you have written.

You sing for children to teach them the beauties of great music.

Figure out your niche and how you like to do things that are different.

For fun and some real education, get a National Enquirer. Get the Wall Street Journal, Christian Science Monitor, Vogue, Guns and Ammo, and any strange magazine you see. Put them in front of you. Find the ads that do not look like the rest. Rip them out. Study them to see what is similar and what is different. See if they are in any other magazine. Call them and see how long they have been running that ad and ask them if they can they track the results to know the success of that particular ad. If they know their stuff, they can tell you EXACTLY how many sales came from that month's edition of the magazine and how many came from another magazine. Why should they tell you? Because you asked, that is why. Get nosy. It is your future.

See who Zigged while others Zagged. Let that permeate your cortex.

Now hit yourself in the head (gently). We all need a good whack on the side of the head from time to time to knock the calcified crap out of our heads that the world fills us with daily.

Then say, "Why would anyone hire me over all these other great singers?" Come up with a reason that does not involve a casting couch. This reason will become your unique selling proposition or USP. You will begin positioning yourself in the minds of consumers as someone they want and to whom they must pay attention.

Easier said than done? Of course. This is a tough profession. You have two choices for success:

ZIG: You have a one in a million chance of being discovered through the usual opera route, or

ZAG: You do things your way, and have a better chance at success as you cast off on your personal "Voyage of the Dawn Treader."

We now enter the dangerous world of self-promotion.

Two seemingly divergent situations converge to make one remarkable point about how best to promote yourself.

About a year ago, one of the hack forums decided to parody *Classical Singer*, but only ended up with sarcasm – the low end of the comedy scale. Your humble correspondent was chided for having loved "Phantom of the Opera." Not being connoisseurs of nuance, I ignored their silliness; but today let us make a point of it. I plead guilty to having written a very favorable review of the movie version of Andrew Lloyd Webber's triumphant stage musical. Was it perfect? Hardly. Was it up to Verdi standards? It pales in comparison.

Then why write a positive review? For a couple of reasons. I do not have to scale the highest mountains to enjoy a view. But more important, ask yourself this question, "When I hear someone give a positive review of Phantom of the Opera, or of Charlotte Church or Josh Groban, does my chest tighten, stomach curl, and righteous indignation seethe from every pore?" If so, you might be part of opera's problem.

Consider a second seemingly unconnected situation. I was advising a singing client about her promotion for her upcoming concert. She was not pleased when I told her the advertisement (for which she had paid substantial money) would not work. It was all about her, all about art, all about snob appeal, and nothing to do with what would benefit her customers.

She was sure I was off my rocker because an advertising professional had prepared it, and it was so graphically stunning the artist should win an award. I assured her I probably was off my rocker and out to lunch, but added that this could benefit her.

So what do these very different situations have in common?

None of us has the luxury of ignoring the obvious: If people do not pay us, we cannot pay our bills – unless we married right or carefully selected our parents. Art without audience is self-indulgent. Everywhere I go I promote better singing. The more that people are exposed to better singing, the more they will enjoy the next level of singing beyond that. It is the nature of positive sensations that once we have experienced and loved one level, we will crave more of it and at a higher level (see marijuana and cocaine use if you have doubts).

Whether I thought the fellow's voice was decent to sing the part of the phantom is irrelevant. The majority of the audience will think it is sufficient and come away with a positive reaction. It is a dramatic story filled with music. Sound familiar? I would have thought the opera world would come rushing to its aid and promote its success. It could then build on the triumph of "Phantom" to foster its own success. But instead they did their usual self-destructive mode of sneering and not believing that a rising tide lifts all boats.

They once again look out and behold a world of unwashed masses.

Such was the nature of my client's graphically beautiful poster advertisement that was all about her. The artist ignored the obvious at her peril. She forgot to "focus on the ONE."

The great operas have great stories, great emotion and the world's greatest music. Nothing that great lies dormant. It will return to great status once its practitioners cease treating their audience as unwashed masses and start focusing on them one at a time. It begins with you. As you begin to market correctly and others follow, you'll be building an audience base that will seek more great productions.

Remember the following two success secrets. They apply to more than singing, but most assuredly apply here as well. The first secret is so obvious, it is a bit embarrassing to even say it – because I am reminded that I'm NOT doing this enough myself.

A program on investing called "7 STEPS TO 7 FIGURES" states, "It is not the stocks you pick that make you rich, it's that you choose to invest in stocks." This premise is correct for long-term, blue chip stock investors. But it contains a much bigger "secret": It's not the specific actions you take that make you successful, but that you take a lot of actions. Marketing is NOT magic, but MOTION!

As liberal arts majors, we love to philosophize and do so at the peril of not getting up and doing something. Do something today – just one thing – that will help you promote yourself. And then e-mail me and tell me what it is (marketingartists@gmail.com).

You see, the first secret is doing MANY things. The second secret is to have someone to report to – this makes you accountable. Do these things today, rather than putting them off until tomorrow – which becomes next week, which ends up never.

So, do something to promote yourself TODAY.

Clarity

As we discuss self-promotion, it is essential to hone your understanding of yourself. I do not want to get too metaphysical, but it is essential that you step aside from your day-to-day trials and understand something about you.

What do you really want? Until that is clear in your mind, self-promotion will be a trial and a drag. It will be a hateful exercise in seeming narcissism.

To expunge these feelings, get down to your clarity of purpose or core values. If you are serving your clear purpose, you will find it easier to promote this purpose than yourself. Tie the two together and you will be on the right path.

A previous chapter discussed the importance of loving what you do, and having that love shine through. The following article from a friend of mine, Dan Kennedy, approaches this from another vantage. He recently pointed out that those who succeed ignore the ladder to success. They never climb it one rung at a time, but begin with a few rungs to get their footing and then have the gumption to take LEAPS. Not steps. Leaps. It is so true. Here is his follow-up thought. It is such an outrageous example that it is great for our minds to consider:

The Awesome Power of Clarity

"In your last Success Marketing Strategy e-mail, I talked about the unhelpful image called 'ladder of success.' Now I want to talk about another image: Las Vegas and its 'Awesome Power of Clarity'.

"I recently spent seven days in Las Vegas ... where construction is going on at rabid pace day and night, and I was told by one construction company owner, 'We cannot get enough workers; we are advertising for them nationwide and bringing them in from anywhere we can find them.' This is where a client of mine bought a home for 1.2 million, had it appraised at 1.4 million by closing, and had an offer for 1.6 million before a month was up.

"This is also where three major conventions were held in the space of 10 days; where the bar at Mandalay Bay did 23 million in sales in '03, and a freestanding steak house earned 21 million. Where money is flowing like water. Why? Well, one reason is zero state income tax. But the other reason, I believe, is simply. . . **The Awesome Power of Clarity.**

"Las Vegas is the only city in America invented, designed, engineered, developed and operated with one and only one purpose: to separate its visitors from as much of their money as possible and have them like it.

"Everyone in its government, everyone in its businesses, every service person, and everyone involved is clear about the mission. Every decision is made with that mission in mind.

"Few city or state government leaders can enunciate their goals with comparable clarity. Few business owners as well. While in Vegas, I spoke to an audience that everyone would consider a 'tough crowd.' It was an audience totally unaccustomed to any speaker selling to them from the platform. An audience never before "pitched" on $1,000.00+ products – in fact, the prior speakers had $15 books and $20 CD sets.

"An audience I had my own doubts about. But with fewer than 150 buying entities (300 people) in the audience, I sold $37,000. Frankly I cannot name five other speakers who might have done as well. I believe the reason is my firm clarity about why I'm there.

"And every day, when I get out of bed, I am very clear about why and about what I intend to accomplish that day. It's also my observation that a lot of people lack this clarity – about their business, even their day ahead. And I wonder just how 'clear you are.'"

Biblically, Isaiah said, "Without a vision the people perish." Paul stated, "Who shall prepare himself to the battle to the sound of an uncertain trumpet?"

Fall in love with a clear purpose and go after it with both barrels blazing.

The toughest job most performers will have is establishing a true clear purpose. Should I try for the opera stage; should I organize my own recitals or world tours or charitable events? Should I plan to be a university teacher or run my own studio? Should I go the audition route that seems so fruitless or persevere?

Find that clear purpose.

I have been assisting one performer lately who really got her act together. She looked at all the jobs she's done, and decided to focus on the ones that not only have the largest potential audience base that can keep her busy for years, but also pay very good money and feature music she loves. She sings a wide variety, including wonderful arias as well as the greater side of Broadway.

We created a marketing strategy that clearly grew out of her core values. We then created a marketing campaign using the techniques that combined excellent personal letters to key directors followed up with phone calls. She is now booking herself and reports a very good schedule of consistent appearances that will create her perpetual job machine.

Do not be afraid to set a course. At the same time, if you set the course and run it - and that course turns out not to be what it seemed to be; or if you find something else, then change.

Singing is what you love, and following these principles may earn you the money and enable you to continue doing what you love.

Chapter 16

An Attitude of Gratitude does Wonders

Imagine opening the mail and finding a non-commercial looking, real-life letter from your mechanic thanking you for coming in and using his service. He expresses thanks for your patience and kindness in working with him. He closes with a sincere statement of gratitude, wishing you the best in life. No gimmicks. No sales pitches. Just a hand-written, genuine expression of gratitude.

You would be shocked and surprised and not likely to forget that letter.

Several things made it work. First, it was a genuine letter of thanks. Second, it looked like a real letter – featuring a believable computer font like Courier or Times New Roman, a hand-written signature in an ink that was not the same color as the body copy font, and a hand-addressed envelope with a real stamp on it. Third, the person obviously meant it.

In our hustle-bustle world such courtesy stands out. In fact, we are floored if someone actually acknowledges we are alive. It does not matter how much money you have, how important you are or how smart you are. When anyone appreciates us, we remember it.

As a performer, what people think of you personally can affect the way they hear you. Talent is only part of the equation of success. True, some pretty weird and awful people hit stardom, but so many more hit stardom with style and class. Others who claw their way through the business often find that the people they stepped on while climbing the success ladder are met again on the descent.

Of course even if rudeness paid, what an awful way to live your life.

Now stop. I am not here to lecture about life skills. I will leave that to your priest, mother or significant other. But understand that politeness can pay off. As soon as I say that, I can hear some performer bemoaning my Byzantine side. Forget it. You ought to be a kind, polite and good person for your own benefit and for the building up of others. But you also ought to be these things to advance your career.

Here is how.

In everything you do professionally, find a way to thank someone. The more the merrier. I watch waitresses struggle to take care of several busy tables, and see other people treat them as second-hand furniture. I often look a waitress straight in the eye and say, "Thank you. Thank you very much." Tips are great, but when I say my thanks, they shine. When I compliment them for the littlest things, they light up. I also find the service increases.

Now apply this to a number of your situations.

1. Auditions. Get the name and address of everyone for whom you audition. Yes, it can be done. Just find out the name of the house they represent and you will have the address. I cannot imagine going to a job interview and not knowing to whom I am speaking. When you apply for the audition, ask the person organizing the audition for whom you will be singing – the name of the person and the house he or she represents. Ask.

Then write the thank-you letter on a nice piece of stationary. Remember, when it comes to your image on paper, be consistent. The top inch or two of your stationary should have the same look as your bio, resume, business cards, etc. It ought to have your name, voice type, contact information and your head shot (one inch size). You probably have much better handwriting than I do, so I can recommend that you hand-write something like:

Dear Johannes Bach,

Thank you for taking the time to come to Century, Iowa, and hear me sing. It meant so much to me to have the chance to perform for you.

I hope we can meet again.

Again, thank you.

Warmly,

Fred

PS. I am starring in The Magic Flute next week and have reserved two complimentary tickets for you. If you cannot attend, I will leave them at "will call" for anyone you would like to invite. My pleasure.

That is it. Nothing more. Write larger than usual. Make it memorable.

Do this BEFORE going to the audition. Have the letters folded and placed in a hand-addressed envelope with a real stamp – the more colorful the better– and ready to be mailed. After your audition – no matter how it goes – drop the letters in the nearest mail box. Do not delay. Do it right away.

Who gets the letters? Everyone you can think of including each person who listened to the audition. At the *Classical Singer* convention, more than 15 houses are likely to listen to the AudComps auditions. That means 15 letters! One or two of the companies at the audition might not interest you. But thank them anyway. Let the word get around that you are a magnanimous, genuine person. Build that image. These people talk to each other. One will mention they got a letter from you last time you auditioned for him, and others who received one as well will say they did, too. Your fame will spread. If someone else also heard you last year and did not get a letter, she will point that out to everyone and now your shame is spreading.

Send a letter of thanks to the organizer, or the assistant to whom you spoke. Spread the wealth around. It only costs you a few minutes and a stamp.

2. **Thank your teacher** after a particularly good session. Same with a coach.

3. **Thank a writer for an article** she wrote that you enjoyed.

4. **Thank anyone who recommends you** or publicly puts in a good word for you.

5. **Here is the kicker**. When you hold a concert or recital – paid or unpaid – find a way to get the name and address of each attendee. Most names came from someone's mailing list. Make obtaining that list a condition of you singing at the recital, so you can thank people for coming. If you do not ask, they likely will not give it. Many will when you tell them, "I am so grateful for the people who came; I want to send them a letter of gratitude for taking the time to come to your concert, and for the chance I had to perform for them." You are making the organizer look good. Some will not do this, but many will.

As you seek people to thank, your capacity for generosity will increase and become easier. Gratitude will be second nature as will the mechanism for expressing that gratitude.

Finally, every person you thank now gets a line in your "house list" spread sheet in your computer or data program. Do not lose this list. Let it grow. Put in a field for the date you performed for them and another for the occasion. For your next concert, play, opera or newly recorded CD, be sure to send your "house list" a notice.

I hope your career is flourishing. Even if things are not going well, do not lose hope. Let the fire for singing that burns within you be channeled into purposeful promotions to advance you and your career.

Do not forget what I keep harping – YOU are the business. Your voice is NOT the business, but one of your products. You have many other products as well.

That might have you stymied for a moment. What other skills do you have? List the many skills you have developed BECAUSE of your singing talent. You'll be amazed. To make it easier, just ask yourself what obstacles or problems you have had to overcome in order to be the person you are right now. The process of overcoming an obstacle is called a skill. To sing Wagner, you needed to learn diction and German. As you overcame these two matters, you developed a skill. I am sure you could teach young students how to improve their diction. That not only requires the skills of diction technique, but teaching skills as well. To learn German requires the skill of linguistics. Once you have learned one foreign language, you can learn a second foreign language with more ease and in less time. That's because you learned the skill of learning languages.

Now, in your journal or in some permanent place, write down every skill you have developed in connection with your singing talent. No doubt at least a few of the following skills will be included. Maybe all of them and many more.

1. Language acquisition
2. Diction
3. Teaching
4. Vocal techniques or voice manipulation
5. Performing
6. Overcoming stage fright and channeling it in a useful way
7. Grooming
8. Stage makeup
9. Dance
10. Stage movement
11. Grace
12. Directing
13. Organization and time management
14. Breathing
15. Discipline or task management
16. Interpersonal skills, working with people
17. Tolerance

18. Dedication to a dream
19. Sword fighting
20. Acting

Keep adding to this Skill Inventory.

One talented conductor was hired to be an associate conductor of a famous orchestra. After a year, he contacted a friend of mine for assistance in earning more income. While the conductor job paid okay, he always found his wants exceeded his income. My friend had him do exactly what I teach: make a Skill Inventory list. The conductor was confused until he was asked, "What has been the biggest problem you've had to overcome?"

"That is easy," he replied. "When I first was notified of my new position, I threw up. Whenever I pictured conducting that wonderful orchestra, I threw up. Before every rehearsal and performance, I threw up. I lost weight and fell into a dire physical condition. I had to change, so I developed a method of focusing my thoughts so it supercharged me. Now I can't wait to perform. My energy is passed on to our musicians who in turn inspire our audience. Energy and passion are contagious."

My friend smiled and said, "What you did to overcome that problem is a skill."

The conductor explained his methods and my friend helped him create a step-by-step method that he could teach anyone.

"But who would need this?" he asked.

That is not the right question. The question should be a double question. "Who needs the skill and can pay you royally?"

Obviously singers and actors would love that skill, but whether they can pay royally is another matter. Focus first on those who can pay well.

They made a list. Hopefully you are doing the same right now. Who needs to be able to appear professional and enthused even if the world is falling down around them, and would gladly pay you for teaching them such a skill?

How about trial lawyers? Better yet, how about CEOs who must stand before a potentially hostile group of investors and explain, without fear, why this past year's dividends evaporated.

My friend helped the conductor create a letter and find a list of CEOs. Within a month the conductor was holding personal seminars with CEOs at $5,000 for a half day.

What is in your Skill Inventory, and who can use it and pay you for it?

Be grateful for all the skills and talents you have, and let them begin to help you achieve your dreams.

Write and tell *Classical Singer* magazine how it went. They just might do a full feature story on you. More publicity!

Now go home, curl up in bed and take a long sleep. You deserve it. You have done something wonderful and fulfilling that will not only help your career, but will also help those who are a whole lot less fortunate.

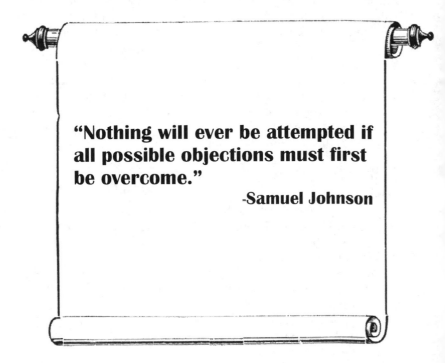

"Nothing will ever be attempted if all possible objections must first be overcome."
-Samuel Johnson

Section II

Advertising

Just for Singers, Musicians

and other Performers

Debbie Wood Ph.D is offering three workshops:

Emotional Resilience
Relationship How-To's
Secrets of High Energy People

Tuesday of Oct 12 – Nov 9 – Dec 7
7:30 – 9:00 p.m.
9948B S⸻
South J⸻
(Between 9⸻
Building just north of McArt⸻

Tuition: $10 per se⸻

Space is⸻
Please reserve y⸻
Phone or Te⸻

Which flyer worked?
What made it work – (and it wasn't the graphics)?
Read these chapters and then evaluate the two again.

Renew your
Enthusiasm & Hope for Life!

- Discover patterns and thoughts keeping you from a happier life
- Learn ways to respond to challenges so you can be happier and healthier

Debbie Wood Ph.D will teach you how in these three workshops:

Emotional Resilience
Tuesday, Oct 12

Relationship How-to's
Tuesday, Nov 9

Secrets of High Energy People
Tuesday, Dec 7

7:00 - 9:30 p.m.
9948 B So. Redwood Rd.
South Jordan, Utah
(Between 9800 and 10600 So)

$10 per session or $25 for all three

Space is Very LIMITED
Please reserve your spot by October 5
Phone or Text: 801.879.2222

Chapter 17

Advertising without Advertising

Let us address a practical matter that seems to consume so many singers.

As previously discussed, marketing means different things to different people. Too often marketing, selling and advertising are mistakenly considered synonymous.

Think of it this way. Marketing is the big picture, the broad strokes and the strategy of getting what you want. Advertising is the means or techniques applied using various mediums. Selling is a term I reserve for face-to-face efforts.

Previous chapters have discussed general marketing, so this chapter will discuss general advertising; and, more to the point, alternatives to paid advertising. I recognize that performers spend a great deal of money honing their talent; thus finding low-cost ways to promote your message and help you find work are no doubt critical.

Actually, buying ads is easy. Anyone will take your money. So it is important to decide whether advertising is really the right thing to do. (Side note – be careful how you decide what an ad is. I define it broadly. You are constantly creating ads. Many performers regularly create brochures for performances. The same principles are going to apply).

The first question to ask is why are you bothering to advertise? The worst response is, "I need to be recognized." In the trade we call this branding and name ID (as discussed in previous chapters). Thinking you need recognition leads to a plethora of marketing errors.

Fame is vastly overrated, and the poor house is filled with once-famous people. Build wealth first and then manage fame. To build wealth, as a person or a company, begin by discovering who your next customer will be – who will pay money for your product or service.

This sounds simplistic. It is, but accurate. The first thing an entrepreneur must know is his first customer; followed by the next and the next. Then he can tailor his message and product to the needs and wants of these customers.

<u>So, how do you get a customer</u>? Harvey MacKay of MacKay Envelopes, and now a famous marketing author, requires every

one of his employees to know "MacKay's 66." These are 66 facts about a real live customer. Name, address, approximate age, education and so forth down to children, grandchildren, birth place, etc. He wants his employees to know everything they can about a customer; so when any employee speaks to a customer, this information comes up on a computer screen. Instantly they know about whom they are speaking. They may also find one of the 66 questions that had not yet been discovered, and can speak to the customer about that. Suddenly the employees begin caring about the one person.

There is an old saying, "No one cares how much you know until they know how much you care." Knowing a person leads us to care about them.

Knowing about a customer – one customer – can help you develop a marketing plan that focuses on how your product can benefit that person.

In addition, by focusing on the one, we can overcome his objections by showing him how our product does indeed solve his problems, or we can change our product to fit his needs.

Remember that human emotions and needs are immutable, so you can generalize to the larger population using the things you discover about this customer.

That's why we must figure out how to approach that one customer. It is wrong to think general media advertising will ever do the trick. It can send some people your way; but until you get to know the customer, it will do you little long-term good.

Right now, think of the name of one person who needs you. Write that name down. Begin creating your own version of a MacKay's 66.

Rather than buying an advertisement, consider some alternative methods to advertising. Each method will help you understand your potential customer base by getting to know real customers.

Method 1: Face-to-Face Contact

Take your product door-to-door (or the 21st-century equivalents). This is a killer hurdle for most people. But then, most people do not truly wish to succeed at business. They just want to be adored and rich. This seemingly humiliating approach will teach the average businessman more about his product, and himself, than just about any other approach. Keep in mind that "door-to-door" is not what it was before the 1970s.

Prior to 1970, a salesman could find someone home during the day. More than 50 percent of women now work outside the home. Door-to-door sales have become a terrible business. But the need is still there for you to come literally face-to-face with a customer, and see if this customer can be persuaded that she cannot live without your product.

Businesses have adapted to the changing times. The following face-to-face contacts have become more popular, and are a more effective and efficient way for you to speak directly with your potential customers:

1. Consumer-friendly trade shows and exhibitions. Salesmen and smart marketing executives purchase a booth where they meet potential customers. The ink for a sales pitch on paper begins to disappear when the salesman talks and then watches the eyes of the potential client.

For performers, this is a very sympathetic means to your ends. A countertenor once asked how he could possibly sell CDs and get more singing jobs. I asked, "Who likes your kind of music?" He began to describe a few of his general audiences. I got specific: "Tell me the name of one of your customers and then tell me about him." He did. One thing that came out of the customer's interest bank was this customer liked everything Renaissance. I asked if his other customers might like Renaissance things – literature, music, art, poetry and such. He said they did.

"Good," I said, "So where do people who like Renaissance go for fun?"

"Renaissance Fairs," he said with some guarded excitement. Indeed they do go to such fairs, and these fairs are held all over the country. I suggested he buy the cheapest booth he could find, play his CDs and meet his customers eye to eye, and voice to ear. He did. He sold a lot of CDs, and had many requests for a live local concert.

An agile salesman can see the interest flicker or wane in a person's eyes; thus he can quickly employ new tactics or words (or new versions of old words) to better clarify his message and offer benefits, freebies or new offers until the light returns to the client's eyes. The neophyte seller ALSO learns to ask for the sale and collect the money.

All this leads the marketer to listen, learn and recreate while in the booth. This marketer should immediately begin taking notes on customer reactions, and harness this energy to create a holistic ad approach including headlines, slogans and campaign ideas stimulated by these customers.

This does not mean that what a single customer says can always be extrapolated and generalized to the entire world, but it is a great place to start. Speaking directly to customers can often lead to an idea that generalizes to the real audience who wants your product/service. Back in the tranquility of the office, the marketer can coolly consider this new information and synthesize it with other pertinent information from other face-to-face meetings with customers.

From such experiences are great ad campaigns born – campaigns that actually make sales.

2. Cottage meetings. The word "Amway" is death to most people. But the business model they used should not be ignored. It worked long before they adopted it and will work forever. It is simply getting friends to come to your home and experience what your product or service can do for them. The trick is to keep them as your friends – something Amway did not seem to care about! If I hear one more person slyly ask me if I would like to hear of a great business opportunity, I shall pour Amzoil all over me, wipe myself down with AmClothes, and hyperventilate into a Melalucca bag.

Now, dear reader, let us both get over the secretive multi-level mentality and get to the heart of this valid method of selling a product to a real, face-to-face customer. During the Soviet era of Russia, advertising was banned. Private enterprises were officially illegal, but everyone knew the black market and the grey market (government-led version) were the only things keeping the insane system of communism afloat.

The average Sergei could not live on his official salary even with subsidized health, transportation, food and everything else. So, he quietly raised potatoes on his dacha in the country – and nearly everyone had a dacha – and sold them to friends as they dropped by.

Russians were great at having people to their homes for conversations that began in the early evening and went until well past midnight. With a lubricant of vodka, the conversations flowed. Survival forced them to KNOW what people wanted and forced them to find the goods or services customers needed. Ironically, communism turned everyone into capitalists on a small scale.

Cottage meetings can do the same for you, particularly if you have a new product that performers might need, like a machine for cleaning the air of allergy pollen or a vocal breath aide. Have friends come to your home for supper and a quick demonstration - or a high tea or snack night or whatever. Tell them exactly what you have in mind and the honesty will leave them excuse-less. Possibly intrigued.

If you are new to an area and want to create a voice studio, a cottage meeting is a wonderful way to entertain people with your own recital featuring a student or two you have been coaching. Let these people know you are opening a studio here and if they have friends, children, grandchildren or relatives with vocal talent, you would love to hear about them.

3. Demonstrations at civic functions. If it is a general purpose product with a wide audience base, or even if it is a narrow niche product, find a public or civic function such as a PTA, homeowners association, ethnic fair or cultural exhibit. Volunteer to sing for them AND give a free talk on a vital subject linked to your product.

If I am a voice teacher, for example, I would volunteer to address the PTA on the significance of what singing can do for children. I would have a special report summarizing what singing programs do for children's mental faculties. I would have ample information on specifically what I can do for people and invite anyone interested in learning more to contact me. Normally at such functions, potential clients will come to you and want to talk about the subject. Talk, listen and learn.

4. Affinity groups. Find groups that have bonded together to do something, and become their expert on a product or service. If it is the local opera guild, get involved. You will find ample opportunity to find customers. If your service is providing counseling services to performers who deal with stage fright, volunteer your time to offer a group session or some free individual sessions.

The "free sample" approach is timeless (more on that in future sections). With a group of people who are like-minded, your reputation by word of mouth will spread.

Churches are great places to volunteer. Often they have congregational forums where outsiders are welcome to present select information.

All of these face-to-face encounters have multiple benefits as noted. Some performers have tried to circumvent this opportunity with a delusion called the computer. With the advent of the computer and e-mail, many have figured they can hide in anonymity and market, but this is not effective until you first know those who will receive your e-mail. With the huge SPAM problem, e-mailing for anything other than contact between known friends is nearly useless.

Speaking to people face-to-face and following up with phone calls and then e-mails is the best method for really learning why someone is willing to buy your product and advertise it to their friends.

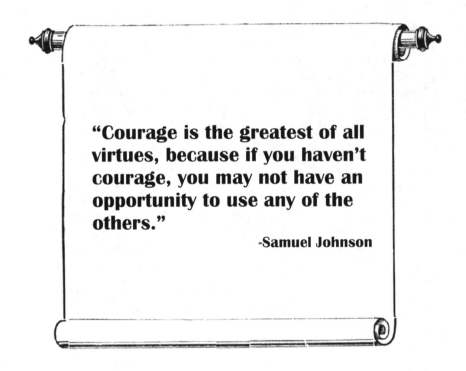

"Courage is the greatest of all virtues, because if you haven't courage, you may not have an opportunity to use any of the others."

-Samuel Johnson

Chapter 18

Methods 2 through 4 of
Advertising without Advertising

In addition to face-to-face encounters, here are other ways to sell your product to real customers before resorting to paid media advertising:

Method 2:   **Free Press**
Go to the local paper. Not the New York Times, but the Pocono Press. Start with the free press and visit the editors. Tell them of your expertise and see if they would like a column written to their general audience. Music is always of interest and if you can apply a local hook – something to get people in the community to actually read the paper – many editors will welcome you (for details, refer to the "Publicity" section of this book).

Of course, give them a sample article free from typos, gross grammatical errors and filled with fascinating insights. When your work is published, you become the local expert. People believe what they read in the papers – no matter what they tell survey researchers on the influence of media.

Method 3:   **Client Lists**
Find a list of highly likely clients. Many list brokerage houses exist throughout the USA, Canada and Mexico. The easiest way to find one is go to the Internet and select a search engine like Google. Specify "mailing lists," and you will find 11 million or more entries. I recommend going to http://www.printvendors.com/rfq_mailing_list.htm.

On these websites, you can provide your key contact information, tell exactly what your product is, and describe your audience. The sites will then examine their lists and recommend one that fits you. With mailing lists, it is possible to obtain an exceptionally narrow list – even down to a list of people who own pink toilets in blue houses on streets named Apple in North America. If you are selling a package of blue exterior wall ornaments with complimentary pink toilet paper holders, you have struck bronze. If the people have purchased blue paint and pink plumbing fixtures through the mail, you have struck gold.

You can get lists of donors to opera houses or to university vocal programs. You can get lists of attendees at Renaissance fairs, or the Wolf Trap.

Avoid a sweepstake mailing list. It is dirt cheap, around five cents a name, but not worth the cost. These sites have obtained names without anyone buying anything in particular, so you know little about the customers' buying habits. When companies start filtering names, they increase the cost per name to make up for the select nature of the list they are creating for you. Usually such a list costs three times more per name. The extra cost is worth it in the postage you save by not mailing to someone with no hope of buying your product.

For more details on direct mail advertising, refer to my book, *Marketing Power of 117*. This book will show you how to write and manage a direct mail program. It provides checklists including making sure the envelope, BRE, letter and enclosures are correct and using the maximum marketing principles (call 1-801-798-6222 to order any of my books or home study courses).

Direct mail is still an extremely powerful marketing method; and for less than the cost of a full page ad, you can effectively test a direct mail project and make money doing so – if you have followed correct principles.

I shall give you one principle right now: the more you write, the more they bite. Do not ever fall victim to the mentality that says, "The shorter the letter the better." Wrong, wrong, wrong, wrong, wrong. Do not say, "I wouldn't read anything more than a one page letter." Nonsense. You read many things longer than 500 words and love them because they are well-written and hold your interest.

It is not the length of a letter, the number of words in a book, or the length of a movie that counts. Rather, it is the quality and ability to hold your interest. People sit through all three "Lord of the Rings" movies again and again.

Create an interesting advertising letter that captivates the imagination and has an offer a person can't refuse, and she will read it. More than 80 years of scientific studies continuously prove this principle. *Marketing Power of 117* provides greater details on how to get people to buy from you through the mail.

Method 4:   Public Relations (PR)

PR is advertising. I've had PR pros try to convince me otherwise, but they are wrong. Michael Baybeck, one of the top PR guys in Hollywood, strongly objected to me asking him what tangible results he had created for my client. In a very patronizing tone he let me know that I did not understand the value of PR if I asked a question like that.

So I asked him another one, "How can my client measure how effective you are?" He went off for a while on building name recognition, tangential affects, and blah, blah, blah. The bottom line is PR had better pay off. It must have some measurable benefit. If it doesn't, you cannot establish value. If value is not there, then neither should the money be there, either.

PR should be short, to the point and project-directed. A theater company asked me to do the PR for their productions. I agreed if I did not have to watch the show they selected again. I've seen it before and it tires me. They said, "Do what you like."

I was sorry to hear them let go of their PR so blithely; to have so little interest in their Public Relations. However, I did my homework and got to know the cast.

I found all kinds of interesting things about them and wrote feature stories about them. Readers love stories about people. The newspaper was happy to carry the stories. I took the clippings and put together a simple media packet. It was not fancy – just simple so the TV guys could understand it and not have to search for the hooks. In other words, tell them what will make their viewers want to see the story. I never stand by and assume they will figure that out. I do their work for them.

Then I started calling the TV stations and convincing the feature and art directors to come out and write a story on these interesting people who are doing this interesting work with this interesting play about … you get the idea. They loved it. Four television stations, one a night, shot stories at the dress rehearsals for the musical. It helped that the lead was a young black man. Media love politically correct stories. And the guy was great as the lead. But, they never would have come if I had not pointed out to the feature editor, "Wasn't it remarkable to have a black fellow raised in the ghettos of America playing an oppressed Jewish milkman during the pogroms? (I had to explain this one). How topical! How timely for you."

When the newscast led off the program with the tease for our play, guess what they said? "Hear the remarkable story of how an inner-city black actor plays the oppressed Jewish milkman Tevya! Film at 11."

The play sold out all four nights. And the cost for all this advertising was just my time. Playing the PR game is all about how to advertise through the free media. It is not difficult. It just takes a bit of creativity and effort.

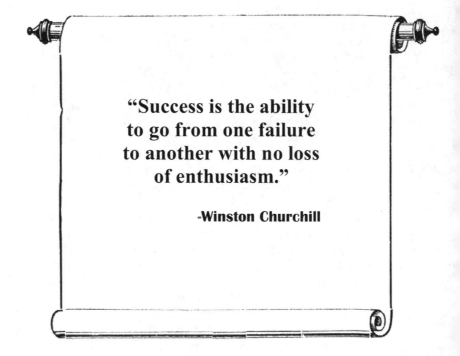

"Success is the ability to go from one failure to another with no loss of enthusiasm."

-Winston Churchill

Chapter 19

Method 5 of Advertising without Advertising

Paying cash to advertise in newspapers, magazines and on TV sounds easy; but far more effective ways exist of communicating your message. We have discussed four methods so far. On to number five.

Method 5:   Get an Award

Do not believe everything you hear about awards shows; how they are given out almost serendipitously to deserving super stars.

You are a star. You deserve an award, because if you do not have an award, how will people know how wonderful you are? Jiminy Cricket was right.

You can win awards all over the place from clubs, associations, civic groups, universities and publications. See what they offer and see if you want it.

In all likelihood, you will actually find your award in a seemingly strange way. Here is what you need to do. Find a group you deeply admire, one you know others admire and that your target customers would find an impressive group from which to receive an award. Chances are, they do NOT give an award. Why? They haven't thought of it.

Then decide if they ought to have an award that just happens to match your area of expertise.

Why will they do this? Because you will show them how good the PR will be for them. When they give an award, they get their name in the paper and the picture of their president presenting the award. Naturally, whoever is going to be pictured is the person to whom you want to pitch this concept.

Producers like to air national awards shows because people like to watch them, thus they're a great medium to sell advertising. The Golden Globe is not some sacred emblem; rather, it was created to give foreign press writers some attention. "American Idol" is not on some altruistic quest to find the best singers. It is trying to find singers that will attract the most viewers. Who wins is the least of their cares. When the show generates 45 million phone calls, producers know they are getting results that will bring huge advertising dollars.

Back to your group. Suppose they do not have an award off the rack in your size? Then call in the tailor.

Here is what I did one time. I was in charge of selling a 120-unit condominium project. The trouble was, the developers came to me *after* they had depleted their marketing funds. Understand that I do not take on hopeless causes, just pathetic ones with great possibilities. These guys had done a good job advertising their condos. In fact, they had nearly sold them all when a financing glitch caused interest rates to rise higher than people could afford. Most of their customers dropped out. The condos were still a good deal and in an ideal location. My job was to advertise without spending a dime in the papers.

One day I was sitting in the developer's office when his worker's compensation insurance agent dropped by. He congratulated the developer for lowering the price of his policy.

The developer wanted to ask, "How much are we saving?" but I asked quickly, "Why did our insurance rate drop and when has that ever happened?"

He reported that the project had more than 100,000 man-hours of work accomplished without so much as a hangnail happening. They had a perfect record of no accidents.

"I think that calls for an award, don't you?" I said.

He rolled his eyes and thought for a second. "It is worthy, but we don't have an award like that."

I said, "You need to give us the Allianz International Safety Award for Outstanding Worker Safety."

"We don't have that award," he said shyly.

"You do now," I said. "Tell your bosses to have their designers take this quick sketch I just drew and create a good-looking award. Here is what it should look like and what it should say."

I handed him a paper on which I had been scribbling furiously. Now, what could he say with the developer sitting there, smiling.

He said, "I'll take care of this."

Of course you will, I thought, or you know we will find an insurance carrier that will.

A few days later he said the plaque was ready and would be dropped off at the office.

"Oh, no," I said, "Not at the office. I would like you to personally come to our job site with a full view of the condos behind you and the local regional director of Allianz presenting the award to the developer and his construction superintendent. I'll get the mayor there as well."

"I can do that. When?"

"I'll call you in an hour." I drafted a quick press release and sent it to the newspapers and TV stations with an announcement that a press conference in five days would announce an award for the ONLY California firm EVER to receive this honor.

I followed up with phone calls to make sure they got the press release and confirm they were coming. They were. I called the agent. Five days later we held the press conference.

That night the project was on TV (with a large sign showing the name of the project, Auburn Woods, and our phone number), and stories with photos appeared in newspapers for the next three days. Within the month, at no cost besides my time, the developers had a shiny plaque on the wall and a deposit for the last condo. Sold out!

PR is creating advertising in the free press.

These methods of "advertising without advertising" provide ways of getting your product into the hands of your customer (the most important ingredient to a successful business) at minimal cost to you. If you have the right mindset and aggressively pursue methods to sell to that FIRST customer, you will succeed.

Of course, this presupposes you are not selling junk. Good advertising can only sell a product once. Reputation creates the second sale.

How to actually write an ad is featured in the next section. Ninety-five percent of ads are wasted because of the penchant for tombstoning. Stay tuned.

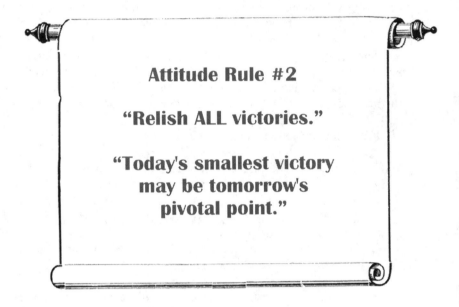

Attitude Rule #2

"Relish ALL victories."

"Today's smallest victory
may be tomorrow's
pivotal point."

Chapter 20

Marketing to Sell Products
Using IRA and AIDA, not DRA

As discussed earlier, all marketing and advertising focuses on either Immediate Response Advertising (IRA) or Delayed Response Advertising (DRA). There is no middle ground. It's either IRA or DRA.

Let us first examine IRA from a practical point of view, as it's most applicable in the world where you must live.

IRA is a skill. There might be some talent involved, but it is primarily about skill. A skill is a learned behavior. That means you can do it. You can learn it.

Because it is so basic, the rules are quite clear. You must do certain things, and you must not do other things. I am going to give you a primer on the 7 Rules of Attraction right now.

7 Rules of Attraction:

Rule One: You have to know what you want. You cannot get what you want unless you know what you want.

Rule Two: You have to know who has what you want.

Rule Three: You have to know why it is in their best interest to give you what you want.

Rule Four: You have to show them how easy it is for them to give you what you want.

Rule Five: You have to know where they are so you can communicate with them.

Rule Six: You have to know when you want it, and let them know when they need to give you what you want.

Rule Seven: You have to use the AIDA principle to complete the Attraction. All promotions follow AIDA. No, it will not leave you up the Nile without an asp. Instead you will be clear, concise, accurate and direct in accomplishing these rules. Here is the AIDA principle:

AIDA is a mnemonic acronym you will never forget, and it will make a difference in how you look at promoting your career. AIDA is an acronym for:

Attention

Interest

Desire

Action

Let's break down the AIDA code and apply it. These words are not listed in accidental, coincidental or haphazard manner. They are listed in the order you must follow and must provide for your potential customer. Whoever you need to give you what you want will require these categories in the order listed.

Attention. Until you have your audience's attention, you are not only a stranger but just more clutter in the blizzard of information. You must cut through the clutter and get their attention. Keep in mind everyone has a short attention span. Eight seconds is all you have. If you cannot convince them in eight seconds to keep reading, they will set you aside.

Outrageous headlines are not necessarily good attention getters, but can be part of the solution. Graphics can be great attention grabbers, too. A well thought out combination of the two can convince audiences to pay attention to your message.

Review the 7 Rules of Attraction.

Notice how all rules begin with YOU. That is because it is your responsibility to do these things. It is not the audience's job to become educated. It is your responsibility to understand what they know and use that information to make you appealing.

A very talented singer once asked a designer for an advertisement. She wasn't pleased with the first one and requested two more versions. The designer complied and then showed the advertisements and asked me, "Which one of these quarter page advertisements is best?"

As with so many clients, 99 percent of the request dealt with how the advertisement made a person feel, and how the advertiser perceived she would be viewed. The question I was asked is about the same question asked in most advertising situations.

I would rather the questions was, "Which advertisement has the greatest chance of making sales?" That is its purpose. Virtually none of the three advertisements had any thought given to how it would help sell the product or service.

So take a look at the following advertisements and determine which is the best.

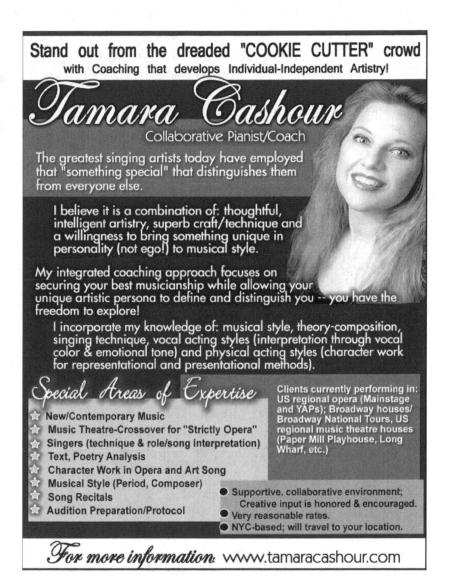

The answer must be NONE of the above, because you don't yet know how these ads performed – how many sales. That is how an advertisement must be judged.

Let us change the question to "Which advertisement has the greatest chance of making sales?" That makes sense.

Too many times people judge advertisements based on their subjective taste and not for sales.

Every singer wants to "feel" an ad is representing his or her best interests ... making them look good. But feeling should not be your criteria for evaluating an advertisement. Feelings must be subordinate to thinking.

Of course it is not just singers. I have watched dozens of business professionals look at an advertisement and make comments like:

"I don't like that font."

"Ewww, the color is awful."

"Could you make my photo and name larger?"

The question is, "Why? Why are you concerned with font, color, picture size and amount of writing?" These feelings are rarely tied to anything to do with sales. Is any thought given as to how these graphic notions can influence sales?

In nearly every case, what the singer wants has something to do with Attraction, but little with the other three parts of AIDA – Interest, Desire and Action.

For most, the question never comes up as to "Will that font help me sell more?" "What else can we do to increase sales?" The changes are typically gut level taste reactions which have NOTHING to do with the sales quality of the ad.

I'm not against graphics. Pictures are terrific for attraction. We look at them. But if a picture is worth a thousand words, and if readers' minds spend too much time on the picture, they might be thinking about words we did not intend them to think. I once showed an ad to a friend. It was selling a car and had a beautiful picture of a Palomino. His first reaction was to turn away. Bizarre. Then he told me about a childhood accident involving his pet Palomino dying. Oh great. That is some emotion to leave him with.

Pictures don't sell. They attract attention. So, immediately place words that focus the attention on the interest, which consists of the benefits that are soon to come the readers' way. Then we have started them along the path of AIDA.

By now you're impatient on wanting an answer so here it is: Ads 1 and 2 are all about the coach. Ad 3 is about the customer. Ad 3 will attract readers more rapidly than 1 or 2 because customers don't care about you, they care about themselves.

As you read on, you'll immediately find ways to analyze your own advertisements in order to find the right focus and have a chance at making sales from your advertising.

Remember, you will have concerts, recitals and many other performances coming up. You want people there. Put them into the advertisement to get them to put themselves in your chairs. What you are about to learn is a mystery to most people and what is worse, they don't care. They believe if they sort of copy what they see the big companies doing they'll be fine. They are also mostly rank amateurs yet believe they know something about how to create an ad. They'll tell you if they confess to having no experience that they "intuitively" know what works. They don't.

This is your career. Guard it jealously. Follow meticulously what you are learning here. It is ALL based upon what actually gets people to buy.

Chapter 21

Your Brochure

Take a look at all your written material and ask yourself the question, "When someone sees this, what are they likely to do?" **If you do not tell them to do something, in bold obvious words, they probably will do nothing.** The worst sin in marketing is to be boring. If your words do not immediately involve them, readers will get bored.

How do you involve your readers? It depends on the printed material. But in nearly all cases their eyes must go somewhere first. Either you design your material so a reader's eyes go there purposefully, or they will wander off and do as they like – and you are no longer in charge of the message.

The first thing a reader sees should be what you want him to see. Using the AIDA code – Attention, Interest, Desire and Action – you must draw attention to your material.

A photo, a pleasing graphic or simply words will do the trick. Once readers' eyes are seeing what you hoped they would see, you then have eight seconds to get them interested enough to read on. That's it. Eight seconds to capture their Attention.

It is NOT just a matter of graphics. Graphics only draw attention. To *keep* attention you have to say something. We call this a headline. When I teach university students how to write academic papers, or teach them how to write an ad, the process is the same. The most important sentence in your paper or ad or brochure is always the headline. A bored teacher may be forced to read your boring text, but that is the way you get a low grade. A great headline grabs the reader by the lapels and says, "Read on!" It compels any reader to want to see what is next.

At least 30 percent of your writing time should be devoted to the headline.

A great headline evokes emotions: curiosity, anger, joy, desperation, inadequacy, superiority, etc. It is not a thinking exercise, but a motivational exercise.

Keep in mind, the world is filled with billions of messages. The clutter is there. You must break through it and the key is one word – relevance.

Is your headline relevant to people? Does it make them wonder what is in it for them?

Behold the typical brochure hoping to get people to attend a concert:

Nicollette Simonson Sings Selections from Tosca
L.A. Civic Center April 14 (with a photo)

Yes, it is cleanly laid out, nice lettering, nice photo and I am so bored. This is like a tombstone:

Here lies Nicollette Simonson, L.A. native
Born June 5, 1980 * Died April 14, 2005

While this is appropriate for a tombstone, what is "in it" for customers?

Why should they attend?

How will this help or benefit them?

How is it relevant to them?

If you are going to create a tombstone at least add the line, "Nicollette didn't smoke, drink or use profound language!" or "I told you I was sick!"

Add something to wake up the reader and keep his attention.

Why don't we do something for Nicollette (whoever she is) and put a headline on her brochure that stirs some emotions?

I will tell you why singers do not do this. They believe "If it is good someone else is already doing it. And if no one else is doing it, I won't do that." Or they consider it beneath them. Or, and this is probably true with you, they just never thought they'd have to worry about advertising, so they never gave it a second thought. Frankly, I wish I didn't have to write an advertisement to get someone to purchase my products. But, that's reality.

The fact that no one else is doing it, however, should be good news for you. The world is so filled with information clutter; the fact that you learn how to advertise while others either don't (and are not getting sales or jobs) or are doing it poorly, leaves you standing on a pinnacle of rarified air, ready to succeed. You are in the world of the Zig Zag theory.

The Zig Zag theory, simply put: if everyone is zigging and you zig, then you are just another lemming in the school. If you zag, you will stand out and be noticed.

Let's TRY some possible headlines for Nicollette.

But what will the perfect headline be? Sorry, you will only learn that as you do something. If you base it on the principles taught here, you'll discover the best headline for your advertisement.

Do not be afraid to fall on your face with this. Just try a couple of different brochure headlines and see which one gets more people to sign up. Then take the best one and send it out. If that does not work too well, try something else. Find the words that will convince people to open the first page of your brochure and devour the rest, followed by a ticket purchase.

Start with my version and create better ones:

**Can TOSCA save her true love with Mario
and escape her plunge from the prison walls?**

**Relive the passion
With Nicollette Simonson's heartfelt renditions**

Experience the world's greatest music as it moves your soul

Scale the walls to grand heights — details within:

****

You are creative. You can do better, but that is the idea. Get some emotion in your written word. And skip worrying about hitting them with all of the details of where and when. Get the emotions going. Get the theater of the mind in full gear, and when they turn the page they will be looking for the details.

A headline is only meant to provoke a customer to read on. Headlines are only the start of the selling process. They must lead the reader to the next benefit, and then to the next.

Now look at *your* brochure. Have you tombstoned it? Have you beaten the life and relevance out of your brochure?

Then change it and get some excitement going. Then track the sales. You must know where every sale comes from in order to know if your brochure is working. It is not enough to "feel" it is working. You must know exactly. And if it is not working, try something else until it does work.

Be sure you create your brochure as if only one person in the world is reading it. Never say, "Everyone is invited." It is always YOU. And only you. Personalize it to make it feel exclusive. After all, if you were standing in front of them telling them about this great program you are putting on, you wouldn't use third party language but second person direct language. Your brochure is just an extension of that conversation, and the brochure written this way is always better.

One final note (until later chapters). Once you grab their attention and raise their interest by showing the relevance of what you can do for their lives, then you can improve the readers' desire to attend by providing some details. It is the most intellectual of the activities, but do not rely too much on logic. Better yet, give them an offer they can't refuse.

One way is to hold six tickets for the customer, and only release these tickets if she calls and says she will not be coming. Tell her two tickets are a special gift from you to her, and ask her to call you with the names of the four special guests she will bring.

Do something to get the old greed glands flowing. Rich people respond to FREE even more than poor people – how do you think they got to be rich?

This final touch is the "call to action" in AIDA. The OFFER is one of the most important parts of any sales piece. It must be simple, uncomplicated, straight-forward and MUST be followed immediately by an easy way for them to respond.

Chapter 22

Let's Apply AIDA

While I prefer to apply marketing principles to performers' real life situations, I purposefully use examples from other paths of life. This method helps you recognize that these are universal principles which can be applied by a creative person to ANY product or service – even singing.

One problem with only using performer examples is that some performers will say, "This doesn't apply to my particular situation in my singing life, so I'll ignore it." By using a construction or real estate example, an astute performer will instantly see it as an allegory that applies to them, and will creatively figure out how to utilize the example in their personal career.

Let us apply AIDA to a very practical situation for many performers. You may never want to be a voice teacher, but enough performers teach that this example will have topical and general applications. So, let us say ...

You are a voice teacher who focuses on teenage students, and you want to fill your studio. You have found a friend living in a good neighborhood where there are many potential students. In discussing the needs of potential clients with those clients and with your friend, you have determined that a good way – not necessarily the ONLY way – to attract these people is to give them a free sample and a chance to meet you. The friend has said she would be happy to let you give a concert in her home one evening three weeks from now. She has a large living room that could seat 30 to 40 people and it has a baby grand. Perfect.

Your friend gives you the names of many parents and their children who fit your voice studio profile. You also scour your "house list" to find the names of people you know in the surrounding area, as well as names of their friends who might be interested. You go to the local church and ask the pastor or bishop or rabbi if he knows of any students in that area who need a good voice teacher. Collect the list, eliminate duplicate names and note when two people invited one person.

Then create two documents.

The first is a letter from you on cream stationary that uses a 10.5 point bold Courier font. You write it to one person, leaving a blank where you can later insert each person's name. You begin the letter with a benefit. You say something like:

"Dear Madge,

_____ *(her teenager's name) has a special talent. To help* _____ *(teen's name) develop this talent, I have reserved in* _____ *name three or four seats at the home of our friend* _____ ."

You did not begin with you. You did not begin with the name of your vocal studio. You did not begin with what was in it for you, nor did you try to sell them something. You began with that person and her needs and what would benefit her. In particular, you began with one of the dearest people she knows – her talented teenager.

Finish the letter by saying:

*"*_____ *told me about your teen's talent and wanted to be sure you were invited. As you know, a university education is extremely expensive.*

Learning to develop your teen's talent could defray $10,000 or more in educational costs. In addition, those who have been blessed with the gift of singing love to share this talent.

Your teen can look forward to wonderful solo performances in some impressive productions, concerts and even CD recordings ..."

Add any words that will increase their Desire to enjoy the benefits of this event.

You have told them "who" is invited, and who referred you. You have told them "why" – because they have a talented teen.

Now briefly describe the event – what, when and where it is, and how to RSVP. Give them your phone number.

Add a postscript (P.S.). National advertising surveys repeatedly find the opening sentence is the first thing read. Then readers flip to the signature line to see who is sending the letter. Naturally their eyes drop down next to the P.S. A P.S. is virtually always read. So, save something special for the P.S., such as mentioning that you're giving them a free ticket.

You are going to use your computer to create a new, personalized letter for each person, which contains all the information. If you know how to merge, this will be easy. If you do not, it is still not that difficult or time consuming.

Now, print this in black ink. In the signature line, hand-sign each one in bright BLUE ink. If your printer is color and you can scan your signature, you can automate this. But remember to use black for the body copy and blue for the signature.

Fold the letter in a lapping letter fold with the greeting as the first thing they will read. The first line contains their teen's name, which will also be visible.

Now you are ready for the flier or brochure. You will use this in several places.

Choose a photo of yourself with students singing at a recital. You can try some other clever photo concept that will cause them to see your flier and want to read more.

You don't need to have each item in your flyer or brochure or ad answer all questions. Just make sure the items lead the reader to want to read more. This is the key.

Write a headline. Any headline to start with.

"An Invitation-Only Recital for Your Singing Star"

Your first headline will likely be lousy. So will your second and third ones. Do not worry. Get the juices flowing and do not edit yourself. Let it flow. Use the headline we just came up with and leave it as a working headline. We will return to it later.

The next line should flow from the headline. It should be all about them and the benefit you are offering.

"At no charge, let your teen singing sensation discover new-to-the area singing techniques. As a parent of a talented performer, you will appreciate the great music selected by Tim Dally, Sarah Parker and Whitney Sorus along with their teacher, Senor Alex Morgan. Senor Morgan will also ask your teen to volunteer to help him demonstrate some wonderful techniques.

Location: Sam and Sarah Smith's home at 2457 Conestoga Drive, Pine Bluff Hollow, CA.

When: 7 p.m., Monday, May 14

RSVP: 809-908-0987. Senor Morgan will be happy to accept your RSVP personally.

If you have anything pertinent that benefits the customer, include it. I do not care how many words are used, just not one more than is necessary.

With a letter-fold that has the brochure/flier on the outside, place it and the letter in a #10 envelope. This is the standard business envelope for most letters. The envelope must match the stationary.

Hand-write the name and address of the person you are inviting. You can run this through your printer as long as it looks personal.

Use at least one real stamp – not a metering label or print. The bigger the stamp, the better. This is personal and you want them to know it. Again, two large colorful stamps are better than one. Hand-write the return address, use a pre-printed label, or run it through your computer. The best font is one that looks as if it is personal yet still a typewriter font. That choice is Courier.

If you send 100 letters, you should receive responses from at least five students and their parents. Typically such personal letters generate a five to ten percent response rate. It might take 200 letters to fill the recital. But, you may be perfectly happy with five to ten prospective students. Check your budget and determine how many students you need.

Now, invite your two best students and one of your beginners to perform at this mini-recital. The beginner will sing his or her best piece to show the skill level where many of your students begin.

Your two best students will knock the audience's socks off and show what a student can achieve. If your voice is still up to it, you should sing at least two, and no more than three, numbers. These numbers had better be crowd pleasers and not esoteric works

Between the pieces, you should stand up front and praise the students. You should also explain why a number was selected, the techniques needed to achieve the quality they heard, and some of the numbers and techniques prospective students will be learning. Be light in your explanations, but spend time in the middle of the program to hold a seemingly impromptu master class on a particular practice or singing technique. Give the audience something to show how valuable you are. Invite the people attending, including the adults, to visit your studio and have a personal session with you. Let them know you would be happy to set up a time; and, of course, there will be no charge.

There is no need to "sell" your studio. You just have. You must, however, have your business cards available for them to take home.

You see, you did what is contained in this book. You first focused on the clients, where they live and what they want. You produced a letter that first got their Attention (personalized and about them). You then raised Interest by letting them know you know about their teen. Interest was also generated by showing how an expensive education can be paid for with a vocal scholarship, which led to a Desire when you described their child singing in an impressive venue.

Finally, the mailer closed with a direct call to Action, complete with your name and phone number. It was also time sensitive because the recital was in three weeks, and was exclusive because you didn't talked generally about "them," but rather about "you" – the individual – and made it "invitation only."

To further use the AIDA Code, study the following example.

A Real World Example

The next page features a blown-up version of part of an advertisement. The full ad is on the following page.

Don't look yet. When you read "Go," you'll have eight seconds to view the ad.

"Go!"

Now, cover the advertisement and answer these questions:

Q 1   What is the first thing you noticed?

Q 2   Where did your eyes go next?

Q 3   What was the benefit for you?

Do not think about it. If you do not know, it was not clear. That is not your fault.

Boston University
School of Music

··

OPERA INSTITUTE

··

Classical Operatic Training for the
Contemporary International Market

A two-year, performance-based intensive program for 12 emerging operatic artists. Full tuition and stipend. Two mainstage productions, fringe festival of significant one-act operas, outreach programs, and an emphasis on career entry networking. Also serves as the center of opera training for degree vocal performance majors.

OPERA INSTITUTE FACULTY

Sharon Daniels, *Director of Opera Programs*

William Lumpkin, *Music Director/Conductor*

Phyllis Curtin, *Artistic Advisor*

Allison Voth, *Principal Coach*

Jeffrey Stevens, *Repertoire Coach*

Laura Raffo, *Italian Conversation*

Claude Corbeil, *French Styles*

Betsy Polatin, *Alexander Technique*

VOICE FACULTY

The benefit should be overwhelmingly obvious and compel you to continue reading.

This advertisement or a variation of it has been run often. Others copy this style or at least use a similar ad.

One would think that because they run it often, they must have a good empirical reason.

Let us analyze the ad further.

What is the first thing you saw? Most people see the picture of the opera scene. That fits the subject matter and the selected audience. For this audience, it's a great Attention grabber. So, the creators started out well. You are a singer and seeing what others are doing is fun. It's also fun to see if you recognize the opera. This is a good involvement technique.

What is the next thing you see? Boston University. Does that do anything for you? You might have warm feelings for the place if you've been there and met the good teachers there. But beyond that, it is not likely that "Boston University" does much else for you. It is a static notion. It means something to them,

but before I lectured there, it meant little to me. That is too bad because they have some good facilities and excellent people like Mark Goodrich.

But Boston University is just a name, so we yawn and go to the next page. It *might* have a meaning and it *might* carry some weight and it *might* get someone's attention.

Would you honestly trust your financial future and singing career to "might?" I hope not.

Now, read through the ad. Force yourself to read it, and tell me one thing that gets your attention.

I bet you found it. "Full stipend for 12 students – we pay for everything ..."

See the advertisement I just cobbled together here. This will work far better. It is all about YOU and not THEM. My final version of this advertisement, should they pay me, would be a bit more polished, but polish doesn't sell. This ad would sell far better than the one on the opposite page, even in its rough state.

Consider the audience for this ad or at least who should be the audience – young students seeking a university vocal education.

What does Boston

University supposedly want? Students to join its vocal program.

Students want an education and Boston wants to give it to them. So, why not say something like that (or something that gives that impression) in the headline. Tell them you have what they want.

Now if, perchance, you have something that could really benefit them – like a free, great vocal education – include this in the headline. "Free" always attracts attention. A reward or a benefit always attracts attention.

NOTE: Include the greatest benefit you offer someone in the headline. Capture their attention by offering them personal benefits. Remember, when you are the reader, advertising must be about YOU, not about THEM. If you can't see or feel yourself in the opening headline, you won't read on.

Now, why didn't they do this? Two reasons. Mark Goodrich is a great fellow and does a yeoman's job at Boston University. And BU is a very good school. But, art directors have a way of ruining a potentially great advertisement by sacrificing the message on the altar of art.

The art director insisted this was a "classy" ad that used an image to demonstrate they were a classy institution. If you listen to an art director talk about selling something, you should simply take your money and dump it in the nearest river. They are trained in art, not sales. Their job is to make art. Most likely, the only sale they ever make is convincing someone to run their art work in place of a sales advertisement.

The second reason is reminiscent of the first. The real reason the art director got his way was that the central point of this ad had nothing to do with attracting students. It was, whether or not he meant it this way, an attempt by those who teach to have others see their names in print. It was a very expensive resume for all those teachers listed.

I asked a director at Boston University how many sales he got off his last ad. He could not say. He did not track the phone calls resulting from the ad. He has no idea whether a call from a prospective student came from this ad, from a referral, or if someone just woke up one morning, pulled out the yellow pages and randomly put a finger on the number.

I hope you learn at least one lesson from this. "Vanity, vanity,' crieth the preacher, 'all is vanity" is a lousy way to run a shop.

Learn also that every marketing and promotion effort you put out is a test. If you fail to track the results, you have just run a very expensive test. You do not know what works and what does not. Test everything and keep track of all results.

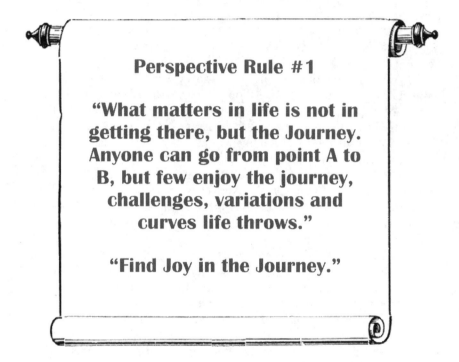

Perspective Rule #1

"What matters in life is not in getting there, but the Journey. Anyone can go from point A to B, but few enjoy the journey, challenges, variations and curves life throws."

"Find Joy in the Journey."

Chapter 23

Get the Most Out of
Your Advertising Dollars

Remember that even though the market place is constantly changing, **human emotions and needs are not**. Most folks I have met believe their product or service category is unique. But advertising igloos or vocal master classes require the same skills, because in the end we're simply presenting a product to a person.

Wouldn't it be nice if we could create an advertisement using a set formula and be assured of getting a set result? Actually, the formulas are there. People have known the formulas for marketing and advertising since who knows when. Long ago, Geoffrey Chaucer suggested that although the formulas for marketing are clear, one piece of the formula – the marketplace – must constantly be studied because its whims and fancies change daily.

To illustrate this idea, consider how many times in the past few years you have liked one thing, and then not liked it too much. Now multiply that by every potential customer. Deciding exactly what people are thinking and exactly how they might react requires vigilance. Do not get discouraged, however, because even though the market is ever changing, there are enough constants that we have a fighting chance.

Again, human emotions and needs are immutable. We love. We sorrow. We laugh and find joy. We love our spouses and find them intolerable at times just as C.S. Lewis suggested in saying we love our neighbors as ourselves – sometimes we are nice and sometimes we don't like them. We learn to understand each other and forgive. We love our children and they drive us crazy. We want more than we can have, long for the impossible and hope for something good.

Important note: These human emotions exist in every culture, in every climate and in every soul. By understanding human emotions it allows us to predict how people will react in any given business climate, regardless of the product or service, and irrespective of the price or purpose of the item being sold.

I have consulted and lectured on marketing and advertising to hundreds of business groups in the U.S., Canada, Australia, England,

Russia, China and Cuba. Following the lectures, I usually have at least one person approach me and say, "That was a great course on Advertising 101." I take this as a compliment with strings attached. While they say they learned a great deal, they also believe there are still so many more principles to learn. They believe that until they understand the more in-depth advertising or marketing principles, they will never succeed in marketing

Wrong. **Advertising principles are fairly simple**. They are not rocket science. Executing the principles, however, can be challenging and test Job's patience.

Most people get into trouble by not following the basics, and then failing to learn something from the advertising experience.

Let me write that again in a positive manner: Follow the basics and learn from the results. Every advertisement you create is a test. If you track the results and test a control ad against a new version, you quickly learn what works.

Too many times, even the best marketers resemble the captain of a steamship who is told a waterfall is ahead. Rather than changing directions he yells, "Throw more coal on the fire. Full steam ahead!" I watch many advertisers run an advertisement they cannot prove will work. Rather than taking the time to alter the ad and track the results, they just create bigger ads with the same concept and run them more frequently.

Sadly most advertisements either do not work or no one can prove that they work, which is the same.

The main reasons advertisements do not work are:

1. We sell the wrong product for the audience. Advertisers often try a shotgun approach by selling a product like opera singing to the New York Times. While a few of the readers are perfect candidates, millions are not and the advertisement is wasted on them.

2. The ad does not capture the reader's attention – it's either too small, the graphics do not lure them in, or the headline does not compel them to read the rest of the ad.

3. The potential clients do not immediately see what is in it for them. Graphics capture attention, but words stating benefits demand that the reader keep reading.

4. There is no call to action.

5.   The ad is not credible. The audience has not heard of the advertiser, or the advertiser makes incredible or unbelievable claims.

With these reasons in mind, here are some tips that will give your ad the best chance of making you money.

Tip #1 – Choose the Right Medium
The single most important decision you will make regarding an advertisement is where it should be placed, or deciding exactly what audience needs your product.

The greatest message to the wrong audience will be outsold by a mediocre message to a great audience.

Selling shotguns in the Sierra Club magazine is probably a waste of money. Selling Country Western Music coaching in Classical Singer Magazine is likely a crazy idea. As obvious as that seems, people still sell cruises for senior citizens in new neighborhoods with young families. That's a waste of money.

Let's illustrate the principle that choosing the right medium is by far the most important decision when advertising. Consider the advertisement on the next page. It's not a terribly good advertisement, although it does have some good things about it.

Examine it first and then come back to this spot.

Notice that it lacks an obvious and immediate benefit to the customer. Visually it is a tombstone ad.

But, it worked. Why? It worked because the ad was in the right magazine at the right time, and it was large enough to be seen and clear enough to be read. The key was selecting the right medium.

Here is what the seminar director wrote to me:

I just wanted to tell you that our ad in the Classical Singer worked beautifully. We totally filled our program and I wanted to say, "Thank you."
All the best for a wonderful Holiday Season,
Julian Rodescu
Florence Voice Seminar

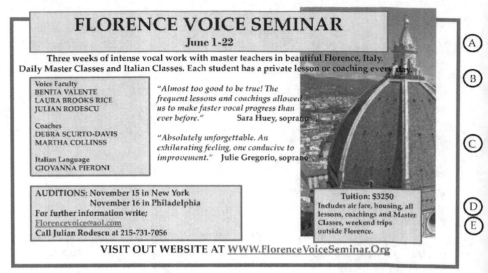

FLORENCE VOICE SEMINAR
June 1-22

Three weeks of intense vocal work with master teachers in beautiful Florence, Italy. Daily Master Classes and Italian Classes. Each student has a private lesson or coaching every day.

Voice Faculty
BENITA VALENTE
LAURA BROOKS RICE
JULIAN RODESCU

Coaches
DEBRA SCURTO-DAVIS
MARTHA COLLINSS

Italian Language
GIOVANNA PIERONI

"Almost too good to be true! The frequent lessons and coachings allowed us to make faster vocal progress than ever before." Sara Huey, soprano

"Absolutely unforgettable. An exhilarating feeling, one conducive to improvement." Julie Gregorio, soprano

AUDITIONS: November 15 in New York
November 16 in Philadelphia
For further information write;
Florencevoice@aol.com
Call Julian Rodescu at 215-731-7056

Tuition: $3250
Includes air fare, housing, all lessons, coachings and Master Classes, weekend trips outside Florence.

VISIT OUT WEBSITE AT WWW.FlorenceVoiceSeminar.Org

The seminar sold out because PRIMARILY BECAUSE 1) they chose the right audience, and 2) they also did some good things. Despite it being a rather uninspiring ad, it was clear, simple and direct.

Here are some specific items they did right:

A. While not a compelling headline, it is at least simple and introduces the product. Simple can sometimes be best. When selling a horse, the ad ought to at least say, "Horse for Sale." This ad made its purpose clear.

B. The ad clearly lays out exactly what is included.

C. Great testimonials. They hit at the benefits and emotions. They are prominently displayed and become the greatest test of credibility for Florence.

D. The ad makes it easy to respond. This is also good.

E. The graphics are not the dominant message, but simply a relevant part of getting your attention. Most people in the classical world understand the Duomo.

With these good things noted, here's a caveat.

In the professional advertising business, we are never satisfied with an advertisement.

We're always trying to find some way to make it work more effectively. With Immediate Response Advertising we can know quickly if our ad is working. Even if it works, as this one did because of the

publication they chose, you can make it better. Here's an advertisement for a similar program that exemplifies some of the good advertisement-writing principles.

A final point on selecting the right audience: I hammer the point of Concentric Circles and the Credibility Matrix (see Section V) because if you follow these principles you can make some errors, take some chances, and still have a dramatically wonderful advertisement – IF you select the right medium filled with real buyers for your product, and write directly to that audience.

In fact, I've seen lousy ads for a great product do wonderfully well to the right audience. I wrote some of those poor ads, but had the good fortune of having an audience that so wanted the product that they saw through my clutter into the heart of a product they needed.

So, pick the right medium to the right people and you've done the thing that will matter the most. As Hamlet said, "That's the rub."

In deciding which

medium to use, follow these guidelines:

1. Select the medium that has the highest percentage of readers, viewers or listeners who would actually buy your product. Because you are in the classical singing business, go where classical singers go.

> **a. Radio** – I rarely recommend radio. It generally works best for those with big enough budgets to constantly run their spot at least twice a day, every weekday, for three months. Only use classical radio stations. However, most are commercial free, so this is probably not an option. One way to get around that is to co-sponsor an event with the radio station where you receive air time. Short air time will not do much good, but a spot featuring you and selections from your CD would be good. Be sure to have a way for someone to contact you immediately or you will have no idea if it worked.

> **b. Television** – Perhaps the Ovation channel on cable might be acceptable, but the rest of the stations have too many non-buyers for your product.

> **c. Magazines** – Opera News can work if you are appealing to opera lovers, not necessarily singers. NATS can have a great pull if the product is selling something to opera teachers. Opera Digest is another possibility. The best performing of all for advertising to classical singers is Classical Singer magazine.

> **d. Newspapers** – Unless it is a trade publication, newspapers are generally such a shotgun approach that you pay large sums to send your message to non-buyers.

> **e. Talk shows** – Many radio stations have general interest talk shows that are apolitical. They are always looking for an energetic guest. I have been on many and have even had my own talk show. This can result in great exposure if the audience meets your product profile. And it costs you nothing. If you have a book or a CD to sell, a good PR agency can arrange these for you. I suggest you pay them on a PIPOP basis – Per Inquiry, Per Order. Few will do it. If they are hungry or confident they might.

> **f. Internet** – Have a website created if you are Web bare. Various programs exist for easy creation. A problem with many programs is while they look cheap to buy, they either stick lots of advertising on your website or have lots of extra charges. You don't want either.

Of all the websites I've seen, the best for classical singers are the websites created entirely for classical singers. Jo and Jeff Isom have put together a myriad of potential websites for you to pick from. And they let you switch versions as often as you like. You're in control of the whole process, including a feature that allows you to easily download pictures, press releases, news stories and voice clips, as well as quickly update your resume, biography, testimonial page, reviews or other things you'd like to have. Jo is my daughter and understands what professional marketers know about proper self-promotion. The Isom's websites have a one-time setup fee of $45. They can also host your site. You'll have a professional site for a fraction of the price others charge. You can reach them at www.ClassicalSinger.com/sites.

Having a website screams to the public that you are serious in the market place and know what is going on, even if they never visit your site. Of course, having the public visit your site can only help you – if the website is decent. websites should be simple, clear, and professional. Do not get too fancy. One performer boasted that her site was so artistic that people would ask her for the Web designer's name. The purpose of the site is to get YOU jobs, not the Web designer. If they are noticing the site design, they are not paying attention to you.

However, using the Web to solicit can be dicey. Never rent a list to send out an e-mail blast. This is SPAM, and it takes millions of hits to get much in the way of results – unless you are selling Viagra, porn or interest rates where the entire sales message can be delivered in the subject line. SPAM filters are becoming much more sophisticated, and some politicians will be making careers of equating SPAM with busting trusts.

Because SPAM is so hated now, be careful how you send e-mails to people. The only way to fly is to gather an e-mail list of people who have responded to you – people who truly know you. Make sure they recognize you in the subject line, otherwise they will think it SPAM and delete you. In the message, do not use many, if any, graphics. Many providers have SPAM filters that eliminate anything with graphics.

Classical Singer used to use a very nice graphics program to send out its newsletter to people who requested it. But many reported never receiving it. If their SPAM filter did not eliminate the message, the reader took one look at the graphic image, assumed it was SPAM and deleted it. When the newsletter began featuring a text-only format, its readership shot up.

2. Tailor the message or advertisement to fit the medium. We have discussed this. One advertisement does not necessarily fit all mediums.

Think about it and see how you can bring elements of the medium into your message.

3. Buy the largest ad for the longest period you can afford. Test it first to see if one approach or another works better. Know that once you find the most appealing message, once you "roll out" for numerous buys, the results will likely increase. Familiarity does breed credibility, which breeds sales.

4. Get to know the ad sales representative. Discuss time and placement with the rep.

a. **Drive times** for radio are the most expensive for a reason – that is when people listen.

b. **In magazines** or newspapers, "thumb" placement is best. It is where the person's thumb goes when holding the publication. Right side is the best, but left is nearly as good.

c. **Find out the most-read portion** and get placed there. Inside covers and back covers always require a premium upgrade fee and can be worth it. Table of contents, letters to the editor and cover stories are well read. But some publications have other unique areas. In Classical Singer, the most read portion of the magazine is the opportunities section where auditions, competitions and classifieds are placed. This is a prime location.

d. **Ask the reps if they give discounts for multiple placements**. Find out if there is an extra fee for changing the ad within the placement time period.

e. **Ask the reps if they ever have "remainder space."** This is space they have not sold that will go empty. Often that is a last minute thing and those on the "remainder space list" will get a shot at the space. You are taking a chance of your ad not running, but if they do run it, you can get 30 to 50 percent savings. However, being on the list does not guarantee they will call you. Getting to know the rep and establishing a firm relationship will keep him thinking of you when a space opens.

Chapter 24

Five Primer Principles

Now comes the big question: "How can I get MY ad to pull, or to work?" How can I get paid?!

Tip #2 – The First Five Primer Principles of Advertising
1. Know your customer. Demographics and psycho graphics.

2. Know the Lifetime Value of the Customer (LVC).

3. Know what problem you are solving in the life of your customer.

4. Know your Unique Selling Proposition (USP).

5. Know that Marketing is not Magic, but Motion.

Here is a closer look at each of these five principles. We've discussed several in previous chapters, but perhaps the repetition will help.

1. Know your customer.
Begin by creating a preliminary customer profile describing who you think the actual buyer will be. Make an exhaustive demographic profile. Gender. Age. Needs and Wants. Buying habits. Create an exhaustive written psycho-graphics profile about what makes them excited, sad, joyful or angry.

We have already discussed Harvey MacKay's "MacKay's 66." You can read more about him in the book, "Swim with the Sharks." Remember that MacKay had his sales force ask each client about himself. As the client told the salesman something about himself, the salesmen recorded that information on MacKay's computer. It included birthdays, anniversaries, favorite foods, hobbies and pet peeves. You should do the same. Record anything that helps you know the wants, needs and desires of those you serve. With computers, keeping track of this is easy.

Now, use the information. Send the client a birthday card or anniversary present. A free ticket to your concert. What, you ask, would a director, dean or president of a musical society or opera house think of getting a card from you? I cannot say for sure, but I do know he or she would have one more positive reason for remembering you. This is good. If a client is worth keeping, this is information worth keeping and using.

In addition, as you evaluate an advertisement, see if the message is one your existing customers would read. Do not hesitate to call a few of them and run the headline past them. People who buy products are most helpful to share their good experiences and their wisdom.

2. Know the Lifetime Value of the Customer (LVC).

This probably needs more explanation. It is quite critical. LVC is how much a customer is worth to your business over that customer's lifetime with your business. It is calculated by examining a typical customer. Add the money the customer will spend with you over her commercial life. Calculate how much profit you will make over the lifetime. This is the lifetime value.

Let us say, for example, a typical customer will do business with you for 10 years. She will spend $300 per year. After expenses you have a pre-tax profit of $200 (margins for services are about 3-1 and for products at least 5-1). Therefore the customer will end up pouring $2,000 into your bottom line over the next ten years.

Now you know how much you can spend getting the customer. If you spend $1,000 in advertising and get 10 customers who each pay you $200 in profit, that is good.

Of course, you must know the "incubation" period. This is the period between when you pay for the marketing to get the customer, and when the customer actually starts paying you. You have got to have the capital to survive the incubation period. If your product and cash flow can survive, it's probably worth spending $1000 to get these customers. It will also tell you that even if you have to give something away free just to attract them, FREE can be very cheap for you.

The person gets the free thing, becomes a customer and buys more.

Let me give you an example: One campaign I worked on used many of the Primer Principles, but it was the LVC that made the difference. We were asked to find a way to sell an analgesic balm. The catch was the company had spent all its funds on massive "awareness" and public relations campaigns. Few sales resulted. The clients needed *cash*. They needed customers. But they needed cash! And they really had a zero budget for advertising. So we focused on radio stations to sell that analgesic balm. We knew enough about the customers who had already purchased the product to calculate the LVC. Armed with that knowledge, we made a proposal to the radio stations that knocked their socks off. We told them they were to sell the balm at $29 a tube but that they got to keep $25! We only got $4. They could not figure out how we could possibly do this at that price. But we told them that before they started selling the balm on the radio, we would deliver a number of boxes of the product to their station. That eased their minds. If for any reason a customer did not get his balm on time, they were free to send one from their emergency stock.

The stations were asked to sell the product for the price we set, but had sole discretion about how much air time they would dedicate to promoting the product. They could also say what they wanted. We gave them key talking points – emotional buttons that showed how the balm solved customers' problems. But they loved the freedom to sell as they wished.

They gave us the name, address and phone number of each client and the $4. We immediately sent out the balm along with some compelling reorder flyers and a letter inside the box.

Now a confession. Five dollars did not cover our costs. We actually lost money on the first sale. But, we had done our homework and knew that 80 percent of the customers would buy more than one tube of balm if we contacted them by phone or mail within two weeks of their first purchase. The "incubation" period was only that two-week period.

Within a month we not only had paid for the income loss from the first sale but had also made many times that back in profits. Because we knew the LVC, we knew that each person who ordered would, on average, buy three tubes. Because we were familiar with the customers, we knew they bought the product either for arthritis or because of soreness from working out or playing sports. Both conditions last a long time and the product was needed almost daily.

Our agreement with the radio stations was that they kept the money from the first sale only, so everything from the next two sales and thereafter was ours. With this system, the reorder process was barely the cost of the paper inserted into the product box.

The station owners were delighted with the large portion of funds they got to keep, and devoted inordinate amounts of air time to selling our balm. The customers loved the product so much, they kept buying.

Through research, we knew how many years our customers would stay with us. With this knowledge, an even larger campaign was born. Today this product is at the top of its field, outselling almost every similar analgesic balm. I would bet you have used it. I wish I had asked for a piece of the action instead of a straight fee.

3. Discover what problem you are solving in the life of your customer, and state it in clear language.

If you are helping a performer find work, say that. If your educational product will help them find work, say that. Performers want to work. They love to perform. This is their problem. If you can help solve their problems and you appear credible, you can get some business.

Telling them your institution or product is wonderful does not lead the performer to know what is in it for them. If they must use two or three steps to finally figure out what you will do for them, you have lost them. In eight seconds, the client must have a clear idea about what problem you are solving. Otherwise, they will turn the page.

4. Find your Unique Selling Proposition (USP).

Why should a customer buy from you, and why buy it now?

I mention this elsewhere in this book, but, it is good for a performer to try and see themselves as a business and their voice is the product of the business. Easier said than done, but if a performer can think that way when their voice is criticized, the performer can more objectively look at the product (voice) and find ways to either correct a problem or ignore the criticism as being not relevant.

When I ran river cruises in Russia, it was a cross between running an X-Games Adventure and a Nightmare on Tverskaya Street. Sometimes the tour bus would show up, sometimes it wouldn't. It wasn't unusual to find the cook on the ship had pocketed the good meat and was feeding my guests virtual shoe leather. Schedules would be changed at a moment's notice and we would be the last to know. Such was a country that lived under communism for 70 plus years. So when people signed up for the trip our materials told them, "If your trip to Russia has no problems we have to solved and you need to be patient for, we apologize – you didn't experienced the real Russia." Some were a bit upset the first day to discover the real Russia led to difficulties, but after they started experiencing the people and events we had planned, they loved the cruise and cried when they had to leave, telling us it was a life-changing event.

After one cruise with about the usual lurches and starts, a person I'd known from other businesses I had asked me if I'd like a critique of the cruise. She was shocked when I said, "No thank you."

"Why don't you want feedback?" she asked incredulously.

"If I didn't know you I would listen to make the person happy. But, because I know you I'm being straight. I already know every little bump and grind in the whole cruise – I was there trying to do something about the problem. You only experience 1/10th of the trials. So, no, I don't want to hear about what I already know."

We talked a bit more and I told her item after item that she was going to say and many more and then she understood.

Sometimes we just don't need one more person trying to help us fix something.

Back to the USP. You are different from every other performer. There is something about you. You need to know what that is. You must stop running down the same ramp as all other performers. You may not be cut out to be a Broadway, La Scala, Met star. You may find you have a greater talent for up close and personal singing in very different venues. The happiest performers are those who sing where they are uniquely qualified. That becomes your Unique Selling Proposition.

Here's an example from the non-singing world to make the point:

In the mid-1980s I helped a veterinarian think through this problem. He had developed a line of dog food that was actually good for the dogs. He had various formulas for different dogs at different times in their lives. But, so what? Other people did too.

We looked at what was unique. His company was strictly dedicated to dogs and cats. It was run by a veterinarian. It focused on high nutritional needs for dogs and cats. We helped him focus his marketing on other veterinarians and specialty cat and dog stores. He got out of the supermarkets where he was getting killed by the big boys. In short order, his company was selling decent volume to those niche stores. He made a big deal out of the fact you could only get his pet food in special places, thereby enhancing his value as having an exclusive product. That uniqueness led to the success. Of course, his hard work and good quality product had something to do with it, too. But he rode his USP. All his materials emphasized high-quality nutrition available only at special stores and veterinarian offices. You will see his product at grocery stores now. One of the large food companies bought him out. They have managed to keep the "high end" image while selling it in the mass market stores.

To discover your uniqueness, ask what it is about you or your product that people cannot get anywhere else.

Is it better, stronger, faster to use, cheaper, more expensive, creates money for the client, or what? Find what separates you from the pack. Voice teachers may ask, "But I teach voice. So does she. How are we different?" No two voice teachers are alike. No coach is the same. In fact, nothing in this universe is alike. There is always something different.

Maybe you are kinder, tougher, more demanding, have great contacts for jobs, have a convenient location or times, or have students who are successful. Find the difference and ride it.

Then tell your story. Tell what you do. Tell why it makes a difference. You do not need to mention that others do the same thing. It is a fact of advertising that *"He who tells his story first, wins."*

Claude Hopkins, the father of modern advertising, was asked to help a Milwaukee brewery increase its pathetic market share. He was intrigued by the way they washed their kettles, had a spots shop, and had grown multiple strains of grain for their beer. The company president yawned and said, "But every brewery does that."

Hopkins shot back, "But no one knows that. It is a story waiting to be told, and when you tell that story everyone will assume you are the only one who does that. In their minds you will be king."

And that is how Miller Breweries was born. They told their story first. In the minds of the customers, they were the only brewery that swept the floor, double scrubbed the pots and, therefore, must be the epitome of cleanliness compared to the others. In addition, Miller was seen as the industry expert because it shared so much information.

Find what is unique about you or your product. If nothing else, just tell your story. The snowflake principle still applies. We are all different.

5. Marketing is not Magic, but Motion.

We've discussed this one already, but perhaps some additional illustrations will reinforce the point.

This principle separates the serious business folks from the hobbyists. Marketing stories have some spectacular results. Because they nearly always involve increases in money, these stories seem glorious. But for every success, I have had five failures. And in nearly all cases my successes came from slogging it out, day after day, trying to understand the market place.

Beyond the principles of advertising detailed in this book, there is not much else to know until experience takes over as the master teacher. What is needed now is to work advertisements over and over to fine tune them for the best possible results. Marketing is not magic. It is motion.

Only by trying things in advertisements do you ever learn enough about the audience to create a great advertisement. For example, while living in Washington, D.C., I worked with clients who had a thorny national advertising problem. They had tried many things.

I tried to study the results, but they had not tracked the responses. So I had to try a few different approaches. Some things worked and did a little better than break even. We tried new approaches to find a headline that worked best; a compelling offer with such high credibility the customers had to pay attention to us.

After several months, we were sitting in a hotel room at Tyson's Corner with some out-of -town agents, thrashing ideas. Nothing made much sense. Our headlines were no better than what we had already tried. But we were in motion. We were thinking in a focused and energetic manner.

In the midst of this chaos, three things occurred to me separately, each with an emotionally charged word that summarized the ideas. It first hit me that no one in America particularly liked Big religion, Big government, Big business, Big brother, Big taxes, etc. Big was the first word.

Then it hit me that what they really didn't like as well were Big Banks. Banks were a logical second word.

Then the final word hit me. We'd done polling and read other people's polling that said Americans didn't like subsidies. They called them bailouts. The infamous Chrysler Bailout, Savings and Loan Bailout, and the New York City Bailout. That was the third word.

I looked at everyone and said those three words together – Big Bank Bailout. "Let's Stop the Big Bank Bailout!" They stopped and immediately smiled. That was the captivating phrase. It established, in one phrase of three ordinary words, everything we wanted. It resonated because we had been doing our homework; we were in MOTION and we:

1) Knew our audience – what gave them a buzz and what turned them off.

2) Knew our product – knew it could deliver on the promise.

3) Knew our margins

4) Knew our Unique Selling Position.

Therefore, when the proposition came, we knew it as well. We had positioned ourselves in the market place as the prime purveyors of this product. With that credibility we got the most senior people in that general field to become our spokesmen. In the course of nine months we mailed more than 20 million pieces of mail to lists of people who precisely fit the profile we knew would be our customers. We had higher than industry results. One letter I wrote to a particular list generated $110 in net profits for each letter mailed. I am told that is still some sort of record.

We used different letters and print ads for different segments of the market. In addition to direct mail, we used radio spots, magazine and newspaper advertisements, mock-FedEx packages (no one had done that before we tried it), sent people cash in the mail, prepared television spots and volunteered to speak at conferences and conventions. We enhanced our position in everything we did, used our USP and never let up. We tailored our message to the audience, touched their emotional buttons, and they responded. Marketing requires motion to succeed.

Next, let's discuss whether the advertisement the graphics department created – or you wrote yourself – has a chance of working.

Chapter 25

Five Deadly Sins of Advertising

Here are the tips we've already covered:
Tip #1 – Choose the Right Medium

Tip # 2 – Five Primer Principles of Advertising

Now for the next two tips:

Tip #3 – Evaluating an Advertisement (Besides AIDA)

To effectively evaluate an advertisement, you must first put off some popular images. When someone holds up an advertisement and asks "What do you think?" we feel obliged to respond with something like, "I like that," or "It does not do anything for me." Neither answer is terribly helpful. Probably the worst answer is that you like it.

Advertising is not a beauty contest. The most beautiful ads may create the fewest sales. And how we like them may not matter at all, because we are not the audience.

I once prepared a letter designed to mail to a customer list to sell cruises to the University of Minnesota's alumni group called the Golden Gopher Club. An art director looked at it and groaned. That would have been fine, but he then had to tell me what he thought. "It is ugly. It is just a piece of lined paper with a badly typed letter." And when he said typed, he meant it. It was done with an old Royal non-electric typewriter (my kids did not know such a thing existed).

I told the art director to not worry about the ad because it was compelling. The offer was clear, directed to the targeted audience and provided an easy action devise. It was what all good writing should be – Clear, Concise, Accurate and Direct. To his surprise, the targeted list responded. The single mailing sold a bit more than $740,000 in cruises in four weeks!

The secret?

One of the Golden Gopher's prominent members, Bill Goetzinger called me one day. He wanted to invite others to return to Russia with him and needed my help. I just told him some things to say and to be sure to type the letter on his Royal typewriter. I knew it would work because he had credibility with the audience. When he sent me the proposed letter, he thought we would rewrite his letter. I kept the letter in the exact condition he sent it because it looked so personal.

A reset letter would have looked phony. I left in the slightly raised r's, the darker than usual e's, the few typos and the lined, school room paper. But when people saw the letter with his name in the return address, they opened it. They read the letter from their friend. They liked what he said and called us – his endorsed seller.

The point?

Bill's letter was not a thing of beauty. The art director hated it. So asking someone who is not part of the audience what he thinks of the ad is a waste of breath.

Select better questions to ask someone when evaluating an advertisement. Instead of asking "What do you think?" ask:

1. "What's the first thing that catches your eye?" Of course you will have been watching his eyes as he looks, and you will know what he sees first, second and third. Make a note of this. It is reality.
2. "Tell me what you think of when you read the headline."
3. "What does the ad want you to do?" If they can respond immediately, it's a bad ad.
4. "What problem in the customer's life are we solving?" If they do not know, you've got a problem.
5. "Which emotion is generated first in you?"
6. "What was the offer?"
7. "Will you tell me about the customer who would like this?"

The answers to these questions will help you create an ad that will sell. If a graphic designer created the ad, return and help him design an ad that might not win an advertising contest but will likely earn greater profits.

If you are seeking an evaluation of an advertisement you have created, time is a valuable asset. Let the ad sit for a couple of days. Try seeing it from a fresh perspective. Then ask the questions listed above.

Be brutal. No matter how brutal you are in your evaluation, the market place is more brutal.

In the end, it does not matter what anyone THINKS of your ad, only how they respond. Advertisements must be evaluated in the long term on how many sales they generate.

Tip #4 – The Five Deadly Sins of Advertising

The five Deadly Sins of Advertising are classic marketing and advertising errors. Here is the list with a nutshell commentary:

1.   Not trumpeting constantly how the customer benefits.

"You will benefit by . . .?" What is in it for your customer? How will this help him? What problem is this solving in her life?

This note was sent to me recently by a friend:

"Regardless of the glory of your marketing, it is all meaningless to people who have paid no attention to it. Always remember that people do NOT read print ads or brochures. Instead, they read only what interests them, listen only to what interests them and view only what interests them. This means you must do everything in your power to interest them."

You must interest your audience not only with your headline and copy, but all the way until the purchase is complete.

What interests people?

A. Themselves.

B. How your offering benefits them.

C. The importance of those benefits.

D. Not being ripped off.

E. Why they should buy right now.

Your job is simply to address these five areas.

2. Using DRA instead of IRA.

Do not follow the example typified by 95 percent of local and national advertisers who believe the solution to advertising is to get someone to remember them. This is Delayed Response Advertising. Forget these "consciousness raising" strategies and demand immediate response. Of course if your budget allows you to spend one million a year on advertising, go ahead. Raise awareness. But the rest of us must find out where every lead and sale comes from and why.

3. Failing to track results assiduously.

Put codes on any coupon or item the customer returns to you, so you will know where they got the notice. Ask them where they heard about you. Check the results every day and see how many orders come in on a given day or even hour.

4. Using "inside-out" thinking.

The market place changes daily. Do not tell the marketplace what it needs, but discover what real problem you are solving in the life of real people. And say it so they understand the problem and how you will overcome it. Verdi was wonderful. Do something to make him alive again and do not be dragged down by the "inside-out" thinking of the current opera world. They reverence Verdi, Puccini, Mozart and the other greats and put them out of reach of most people today.

Rather than trumpeting the composer's name as if the audience knows him, see what struggles people face and which pieces of music would help them. Then describe a typical problem and how the hero overcame this. They'll make the connection, relate and see themselves. Make the ideas modern even though it is a period piece. How? That's your job if you want them to patronize you.

5. Relying on graphics to sell.

No, no, no! A picture is worth a thousand words that are as difficult to control as herding cats. A photo or drawing does not mean what it says, despite what art directors say. And by the way, why does anyone care if an advertisement won an award? The only award that matters is the sales volume and margin of profit.

6. Selling to the intellect and not the emotions.

People buy from people, not faceless corporations (just ask Betty Crocker). Computers can convey more intellectual information than we can read. But people make sales when they give someone an emotional reason that transforms either a passing interest or a need into a want!

Bonus: Here are some notes I have given large corporations on how to beef up their advertising writing and commercials. Those who follow these precepts succeed. Those who do not, diminish their chances. <u>These precepts apply to you.</u>

> To: CEO of _____
> From: Mark Stoddard
> Date: Constantly
> RE: Creating Advertising that Sells

This is generally the order you will follow for creating an advertisement that works.

1. <u>Product research</u>. Find details from research that capture the imagination, prove benefits and set the tone for the sale. The theater of the mind is the best graphic.
2. <u>Wants, not needs</u>. Use research to understand the audience and the benefits the product can offer. Discover what people really want. They do not want to lose weight, they want to be loved. They do not want the product, they want what it does. One of the primal urges is for people to want to get something before someone else does.
3. <u>Attention causing</u>. Get their attention immediately. There is so much message clutter in the advertising world. Do not be or look like one of many. If everyone Zigs, you Zag.
4. <u>Important looking layout</u> in all portions of the ad. It cannot look like direct mail. It has to compel the reader by first showing how important it looks and then how important it is. Never give away a clue as to what is inside the envelope. Use only letters that look like they are written to your mother. Very personal. This should help get your letter into Pile A – the sort pile that must be read immediately. Pile B goes into the trash.
5. <u>Benefits up front</u> and then throughout. Tell a strong benefit in the headline and in every paragraph. If the benefit comes at the end of the paragraph or sentence, move it to the front. Every word must consider "What is in it for the customer?"
6. <u>Do not sell</u>. It cannot ever look or feel as if you are trying to sell them something. Give them something and use words like "get, deliver, receive" but never "buy."
7. <u>The "non" order form</u>. The order form should not look like an order form. It shouldn't look like the audience is being sold something, but should look like something you'd have a

friend send you back that is simple and non-advertising looking. In the memo portion of the form list the products, more benefits, price, and a place to fill it out. But make the order form very simple. Use a stamp effect on an angle for the payment – do not make it look pre-printed but something you personally stamped on the form, giving them a chance to pay you.

8. Look official. Have places for them to sign where you and others have signed to make it look official.

9. Handwriting. Use handwriting in the upper left of the form that says, "Please complete and return this form."

10. No price confusion. If a large dollar amount is placed that is not your price, people will likely get confused and think that is the price. If it must be there for comparison purposes, have it crossed out.

11. Product focus. Do not have too many choices – usually offer one other thing (besides multiple orders).

12. Exclusivity. Make it personal. Only write to that one person and no one else. Never let them believe another place could have what they need or that anyone else can get what they are getting.

13. Proper voice. If it is an urgent personal letter, then a small degree of conversational tone can work. If it is from an executive, the tone must be more formal.

14. URGENT VOICE, or breathless emergency information that is believable.

15. Problem and solution. Pose the problem and solve it. Protect the customer's self-interest. Provide a sense of you protecting them and their interests and of doing them a favor rather than selling them something.

16. USP. Use a Unique Selling Proposition they will not see elsewhere that does not sound like you are selling.

17. TIME sensitive. Without saying it directly, cultivate an attitude and sense that if they do not act now, the price will increase or the supply will be gone.

18. LEADING. Use a leading quality of writing that logically leads the customer through the ad to the point he can order.

19. Helpful wording and graphics that make it easy to read. Reverse lettering hurts response because it is harder to read. Huge or fancy type is hard to read. Pictures never tell a story, but only set the mood and get attention.

20. <u>No negative wording</u>. Specifically do not use "turmoil " or "calamity," although "unrest" and "unsettled" are acceptable. Negative big words stick with people and leave a negative feeling.

21. <u>Do not use a BRE</u> – a reply envelope where the postage is paid when we get the letter back. This is now old school. Make it personal.

22. <u>Use the words FIRST, LAST, COMPLETE</u> where they apply to the product or offer.

23. <u>Keystones</u>. To pay for itself, the order usually needs to be a keystone markup – charge the customer double what you paid for it. You must make a little off of postage, so never just say "postage" but always add another item like "shipping fee," "handling," etc., so the "postage and handling" can be more than the actual cost of postage.

24. <u>Customer beliefs</u>. Overall, the idea is to bind customers by getting them to think of themselves and how they are benefiting. Use that to enhance emotions and build the benefit. Then the actual item will not seem as if it is a sales job, but rather an add-on benefit. Dazzle them with the pinstriped suit; give them a free carnation for their lapel, paid for from their wallet.

25. <u>Markers</u>. Use yellow highlights as if they have come from a yellow highlighter. Use handwritten notes, underlines in blue to draw attention to some benefit and away from some necessary sales item.

26. <u>Font use</u>. Use a typewriter font for everything that is immediate. This makes your message seem more personal. On the letter you can use Courier in boldface to resemble a new typewriter ribbon. Do not use Times or a type face common to printed material, because it will look mass produced. A condensed Helvetica medium is good for getting the official look.

27. <u>Logo use</u>. Do not use large logos. The customer only wants something small to assure them it is official. Make all the type that is supposed to be non-personal in caps and about 8-9 pt. Use Helvetica Neuve Condensed Thin or Medium.

28. <u>Do not print on the back of letters</u>. Let white space keep up the non-selling look.

29. <u>Provide documentation</u> for every claim you make.

30. <u>Offers that have worked</u> before:

a. Item is free if you complete the set.
b. Item is free if you get the display case.
c. Item is free if you pay a processing fee or something like that.
d. Item is free as a bonus for buying something.
e. You may get it if there are enough to go around.
f. We are giving you something and you have the right to receive it.
g. We are giving it to you as a bonus.

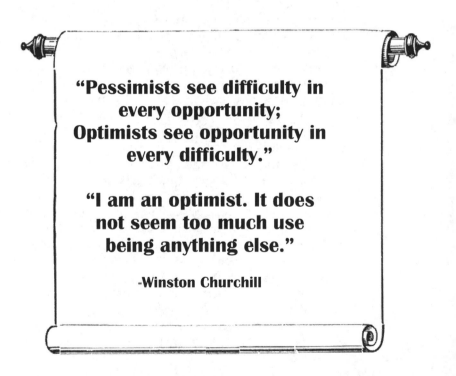

"Pessimists see difficulty in every opportunity; Optimists see opportunity in every difficulty."

"I am an optimist. It does not seem too much use being anything else."

-Winston Churchill

Chapter 26

Writing a Powerful Ad

You want more students in your voice studio, or more people to attend your recital or concert or stage production. You want to find sponsors or clients or more gigs. Regardless, you need a way to introduce them to the benefits you are offering, and convince them to utilize your talent. You need ... an advertisement.

You've read the theory, so now it's time to start writing. When I write an advertisement, here is the prime place I begin.

Speak to me, and me alone.

One ... as in one and only, one life to live, one at a time, and the power of one. Guinness Book of Records called Joe Girard the "world's greatest salesman" for good reason. He sold on average six cars a day His secret for success was simple. He shared it with me one day when he gave me a solid gold lapel pin with just the number "1." By itself. No # sign or anything else, just an unobtrusive "1" about ¼-inch tall. As he pinned it on me he said, "I'm going to give this to you under one condition."

"Sure," said I. "What is the condition?"

"Always remember that it is one person at a time. One conversation. One focus. One sale at a time. One person. Never forget we're all individuals and love to be treated that way. One at a time."

I loved that advice. In marketing and journalism of which I've been heavily involved, we soon begin speaking to "the great unwashed masses." We speak of "all of you out there" or "them." It's dehumanizing. Stop it. Don't do that anymore.

It's always about you. You alone.

When you write an advertisement, think of one person; a real person, not an avatar you create. Talk to that person about your product or negotiating situation. Listen to what she thinks, what she feels and how she reacts. Then write her a letter explaining how your product or service benefits her and only her. Focus on the one.

Don't worry about space. You'll pare it down later to fit the size requirements.

Begin your letter with "You..." Continue with how this will "benefit you..." and what it means for her betterment. Never say "all of you" or "for everyone out there." I see national ads do that, and it's dumb. Don't do it. (And I did use "dumb" precisely.)

Profiling works in certain areas. Personalization in advertising is more effective because humans share so many universal traits. As you address one person you are, in fact, speaking to nearly everyone else.

Have you met a person in a reception line that was shaking your hand but looking over your shoulder to other people? Absurd isn't it? So is speaking to "them" when you should be communicating with me.

The power of you ... the word

Personally, I get bored with certain words. They're used so much they lose their meaning. Words that once were terrific nasty words are long forgotten, their impact diminished from constant repetition.

But certain words ignore my boredom and are still exceptionally effective words. Certainly FREE fits in this category. By now you'd think everyone knows there is no such thing as a free lunch, but put "free" in a headline and everyone's head turns. Rich or poor, free is good.

Another word we never tire of is "you." No matter how often it is used, we still believe it is us they are talking about when they say "you." In all print and especially letters (direct mail letters, business correspondence, emails, etc.), the first words of the first sentence ought to be YOU.

Therefore ... yes, it's painfully obvious. The word YOU is critical to your success.

A tip on writing any letter is to 1) think about the product or purpose or goal of the letter, 2) think about the person to whom you are writing, and then 3) start to write. Do NOT worry about length, grammar, structure, syntax or anything else. Let your writing flow. Make it "breathless writing." Make it so you're out of breath just trying to keep up with all the ideas, and make the reader out of breath in trying to keep up with such great thoughts.

Find something you've written, and look at your first paragraph. I'll bet you dollars to donuts that your first sentence is about you, or your event or your desires. In all likelihood, you're still pawing the ground in the second and third paragraphs. Finally, in the fourth paragraph, perhaps you've written something about your audience and how your product or service is going to benefit them.

Take that fourth paragraph and move it to the front. Now, begin the first sentence with the word *you*. "You were in my thoughts today."

"You must have some great friends because they told me about you."

"You deserve a break today ..."

Follow this up with other ways this person is going to be better off now than they were before getting your message. From there, let the letter flow so it is all about them. You, your product and your event do not matter – except as they relate to the customer gaining the benefits you just told them about.

Be sure to keep your message from becoming an advertisement. The closer the wording is to what you'd tell your mother, the better chance you have of the person actually reading the letter. We're bombarded with messages. Personal notes get through. Ads are trashed.

Here's a quick example of a proposed email from *Classical Singer* magazine to members of an organization. The email offers a free subscription in hopes that the reader will later sign up for a premium membership:

Dear XXXX,

Welcome to the *Classical Singer* Community! ***Organization*** and *Classical Singer* have joined together in efforts to reach more singers and teachers than ever before. For more than 50 years, ***org*** has been THE resource for teachers. And for more than 20 years, *Classical Singer* has been the singer's source for career and life. Now, working together, we are dedicated to helping teachers and singers of all ages and levels in their educational and professional pursuits. Because of your ***org*** membership, you will receive monthly issues of *Classical Singer* magazine for a year at no cost to you. This letter accompanies the first of 12 months of the magazine you will receive.

Who is this about? It's about *Classical Singer* and what it does. Why should I read on? What's in it for me?

Now look at the rewrite that worked like dynamite:

Dear XXXX,

You deserve up-to-the-minute Audition notices. You deserve access to vital career advice from industry experts and stars. You deserve crucial health and vocal technique information. You deserve more for your Singing and Teaching. And Classical Singer magazine is dedicated to providing this and much more for you.

Who is this about? Just you. Some writers get the idea that many people constitute their audience and say, "Many of you ..." You've just lost the audience's fantasy that you're actually addressing that person and that person alone. Never say "many of you" or words to that effect. Write to one person only.

Check out another first draft of a headline:

Final First Round
***Classical Singer*'s High School & University**
Vocal Competitions

My question to the writer was, "Why don't you put ME into the opening line? Why would I care about 'Final First Round'?" The answer was that it brings up an inherent urgency – a final offer. That's true. It does. But that doesn't matter until I am in the scene.

The writer reworked the ad and referred back to basic principles. He came up with:

Your Last Chance to Win $2,300,000
in Scholarships and Cash Prizes

Classical Singer's
High School & University Vocal Competitions

This ad clearly puts YOU right smack dab into the opening of the ad. The subtle "Final" suggesting urgency is replaced by a direct statement. Advertising isn't a great forum for subtleness. Subtle appeals to the artist in me – my plays, stories and music provide great avenues for me to be subtle and gradually lead the audience into discovery. Do that in advertising and you won't sell much.

This new version is all about the audience, urgency, enormous benefits, emotions and specificity. It compels a person to want to know how this applies to them and how they can get it. Free money is always compelling. Sometimes it's not credible, but mostly the allure of free money is irresistible. This headline brings credibility by immediately stating the sponsoring institution, *Classical Singer*, which has a heap of credibility to its audience. The rest of the body copy elaborates on the schools offering the scholarships, thus building credibility as well.

WARNING: Danger ahead.
Five things you must not do in the next five minutes
unless you already have all the money you need.

No matter what kind of marketing you're involved with, you'll need to come up with a headline. So, let's discuss headlines. But first, breathe again. No danger is ahead. I just wanted to get your attention. Hope I did.

Some rules on headlines:

1. The purpose of a headline is to convince the reader to read the next line. Therefore, the headline is the most important sentence in your announcement, advertisement, flyer, etc. Can you guess the second most important sentence? Right. The second sentence. And what is its purpose? Yes, you're right. To get you to read the third sentence and so on.

2. Never write a headline with space in mind. If you think you have cramped space, you'll start parsing your words before you start. Bad idea. The best idea is to write out, without regard to space, whatever you think is the MOST important thing that will benefit your customer and compel him to read on.

Sub point: Don't limit your headline to a few words. One of the best-selling headlines was:

"THEY LAUGHED WHEN I SAT DOWN AT THE PIANO – BUT THEN I STARTED TO PLAY!"

But, that's not long enough to prove my point.
Try this one:
As you can see, I have attached a nice, crisp $1.00 bill to the top of this letter. Why have I done this?

Actually, there are two reasons:

1) This letter is very important and I needed some way to make sure it would catch your attention.

2) Secondly, I wanted to give you your first dollar that you can give a man who really needs your help. And ...

This Is Going To Be The Most Important Message You Will Ever Read!

As you can see, this headline is six sentences long. It started off a letter with a dollar bill attached. I did this in 1981, when I was asked to do my first direct mail piece. I had seen offers that attached a penny and even a nickel to a mail package, so I figured, "Why not put in a dollar bill?" Everyone thought I was nuts except my immediate boss. He loved doing strange things because he understood the principle of "Zig Zag." When everyone else is zigging, you'd better zag. He also understood that if the headline didn't make you a little queasy or sick to your stomach when you were deciding if it was good, the ad was probably too ordinary and thus bad.

So, he took a chance on me. Keep in mind, I knew practically nothing about direct mail except that I knew I could write and sell. Advertising is merely salesmanship in print, so you'd better follow sales rules.

After telling people about Orrin Hatch I closed with, "Remember the $1 bill I gave you. Would you please write Orrin Hatch a check for $24, and include the $1 bill I gave you so you can get credit for a $25 donation."

The checks flew in, and so did our original dollar bills. Some with very nice words written on them. A few wrote nasty words (nasty for Provo, Utah – something like, "Oh my heck I can't believe you sent me this freakin' letter").

Back to my ignorance. I mailed the phone book. Yep. I pulled 1000 names out of the phone book in Provo, Utah, and mailed a nice personal fund-raising letter for a guy running for the Senate for the first time – a tall lanky lawyer named Orrin Hatch. We raised a ton of money and had no business doing so because it was such an unqualified list. But, I wrote a great letter and had a great headline and eye catcher that compelled people to read on.

I went on to use that headline in various forms along with a dollar bill attached in more than a couple dozen campaigns. One campaign raised $120 for every letter we sent out. It also broke a lot of silly rules people create. The letter was 18 pages long. But, it raised $120 for every letter we mailed and we mailed more than 100,000 letters. You do the math.

Like all good ideas, this one got copied. Others started taking credit for it. I didn't care about credit, I just cared that others were using it so much that it began to lose its effectiveness. I had zagged and then they zagged with me, so it was now too much clutter. I stopped using it.

Take the little rules I've given you, and now go create your own new headline with one thing in mind: make it so compelling that readers *have* to read the next line and so forth until they're lined up begging you to take their money.

One last word. I am not a slave to writing long headlines. Just effective ones. I once wrote this headline advertising a one-week adult education course.

"We Don't Sell Fish"

That was it. We had lots of space, but that was the headline. As a result, we sold a course to more than 5000 people that required them to leave their homes and fly to Salt Lake City, Utah. These people would then spend a week with me and my educators learning either investment strategies or entrepreneurship and marketing. These customers paid between $2,000 and $5,000 for each course. We varied the headline from time to time, but essentially this was the theme: We Don't Sell Fish.

3. Don't worry about what people tell you is "the right way to do it." Make it work. One of my biggest errors in headline writing was when I listened to people tell me what an awful headline this was:

"Come visit the country that's been trying to kill you!"

I ran it one time in one newspaper. My staff objected. Thought it was too crass or offensive or something. I got hateful letters published in the Letters to the Editor for that newspaper. Like a cheap tent, I folded. Even after we sold the highest number of trips to visit the Soviet Union from people reading this headline and calling to buy our tours, I didn't use the headline again. Dumb. Stupid. Makes me mad right now to think I let my staff and some mentally constipated people influence me. And to think people wrote Letters to the Editor and re-publicized my advertisement FOR FREE and I didn't run it again. OHHHH it hurts to remember that.

So, write a headline that gives you butterflies and weak knees and if it works ... do it again and again and again until it stops working.

Free is still a head turner
As discussed in earlier chapters, "free" is always a head turner.

Guarantees are just another form of free. They reverse the risk and give the consumer confidence that you might be worth trying.

Many years ago, a couple of motels in the San Francisco Bay area experimented. This was the era when TV in a motel room was often paid for by inserting coins into a slot to turn on the TV – and then you'd only get three or four channels. That aside, one motel advertised its rooms for 17 dollars. TV was just three dollars more. The other advertised 20 dollar rooms with FREE TV. By a 2-1 margin, FREE TV won. Customers paid the same price, but wanted "free."

Free turns heads. One firm with whom I worked made its living off of "free." Just call to get their product free. Only pay for postage and handling. They made their money on postage and handling. Then they made more because no one wanted just one. The second item was expensive, but because the first item was free it seemed like the second item was 50 percent off. Of course, the company featured other products, and many customers bought the add-on, up-grade or follow-on products.

It all began with FREE.

It doesn't have to be a giveaway of your product. Give away something else just for trying your product. As a general contractor, we gave away a free dinner for two when a customer closed the sale of his home. The dinner cost us $50 in today's money. The home cost $300,000. But you'd think the customer had just won the lottery when we gave him a gift certificate for a night out. We didn't advertise the free dinner. That would just be silly – "Buy our house and get a free dinner." Nonsense. We didn't even tell customers anywhere that they were getting the free dinner. We just found out when they were planning to move in and had a courier delivery the gift certificates for dinner to the couple just before moving in.

When the dishes are still in the dish packs and the couple is exhausted from moving, what could be better than an excuse to get away and relax while someone else serves. People loved it. Happy customers are good for business.

Free can also be stated in terms of "Buy one, get one FREE." I'd rather say it: "Choose one and get one FREE." Anytime I can eliminate the sense of customers having to spend money, the more I can focus on what they get. They know they're buying. No need to remind them of that. Focus instead on what is free.

"Formula 409" got started this way. It was selling okay in a region, and the company wanted to go national. Because the Formula 409 company was selling its cleaning product effectively, competitor

Johnson and Johnson (J&J) figured this was a good time to introduce their new cleaning product.

When selling a new product, it's always best to sell to people who already appreciate what the product can do. Once competitors have done the work of educating, you offer something better, faster, cheaper, longer-lasting, etc. You piggy back on their work. Burger King got its start by locating near a McDonalds. Line too long at MickeyDees? There's another fast food alternative.

Back to Formula 409. J&J let the word out to the supermarket chains that they were going to have a major test in one of the cities in the region where 409 was located. The 409 guys quickly got the word.

Rather than panic, they got smart. They stopped refilling orders to the test city. They pulled their product off the market. If orders came in, they got ignored. If a supermarket buyer called from that city, they got put on hold. Soon there was no Formula 409 to be found in that city. When J&J brought in their cleaner, they had no competition. Sales went through the roof. J&J knew they had a winner.

J&J began preparation for the next test phase to the whole region. 409 guys waited until just before J&J would be shipping. They ran a region wide special. Get one spray bottle of 409 and we'll give you the huge refill bottle that would last three months ... FREE.

When J&J's cleaner arrived, it sat on the shelves. Everyone had their cleaner. Wouldn't need a refill for three months. J&J executives were furious. Heads rolled. All product was recalled. The cleaner was dubbed a failure and dropped from the line. Formula 409 had clear sailing.

Free is powerful. Use it wisely.

Special Note to Performers:

Give a free concert. Invite the shakers and movers. Or ask only that they donate to some wonderful cause. Be sure to have a way to capture all of the names of those who attend.

Follow up with them and volunteer to hold a holiday concert in their home. They'll pay you nicely for that. Sell your CDs to everyone who attends. Put everyone on your "house list." You're building a Perpetual Job Machine.

And, you never know. The shakers and movers know the right people in the theater. They're likely patrons. Have them help you get noticed by the opera companies or theater owners. Everyone loves a winner. It all begins with FREE.

Here's a fun advertising idea:

While the heyday of direct mail marketing is quickly receding into the ethernet, perhaps it is just reseeding. The principles will sprout up in use elsewhere.

Take this idea: I used to put into direct mail letters a return envelope. Usually it would be a Business Reply Envelope or BRE that had the bar code indicia so no stamp was needed to send us a reply. This made it easier for a customer to respond.

But, whenever I could get the budget, I would put "live" or real stamps on the envelope. Why?

1. They were colorful and got noticed.

2. I never put one stamp but always at least three ... if one gets noticed, three receive thrice the notice. And one stamp is easy for someone to peel off and use elsewhere. Then they throw your envelope away. But three smaller denomination stamps are just not worth the effort.

3. Put a picture of the product or a selling line boldly on the face of that envelope. We humans are bizarre, and hate to throw away a good stamp. By putting three hard to remove, impossible to throw away stamps on a blatant piece of advertising, I had just bought advertising space in a potential customer's desk or drawer. Every time she sees that envelope, it calls to her: "Use the envelope so you don't waste the stamp."

Sure enough, the live stamps always increased sales immediately, but they also put a long tail on further responses. Months later I'd get responses. My envelope had nagged them into responding. They just couldn't throw me away.

When you send a resume, an inquiry letter, or use a direct mail format, try the live stamps. The allure is more than people can bear.

Chapter 27

Steps to Creating an Ad that Works

Let's write. Here are the steps:

1. Firmly establish in your mind the ideal customer's profile.
2. Find one of these ideal customers and speak with them, face to face, about what you do. See what "turns them on." Listen. Ask questions about what they would like. What would compel them to come to you for this service? What bothers them about the last product like yours they tried? What are the final results they want from you? Listen, ask, listen, ask and listen some more. Never tell them what they need or disagree with their expectations.
3. In a quiet, tranquil place and time, write that person a letter. Begin by saying,

    "You want _____ ... and you want _____.
    Your goal is _____. You like _____ and love _____ and desire to have _____.
    Here is how I can help you get what you want ... _____.

    Tell me if you think I can help you. Please call me (write, email or let me come by and talk to you) so I can better understand if I can be of assistance to you."
4. Put this letter aside and repeat step 2 and then step 3. Repeat this process several times. If you have a sales force, get them to do the same thing.
5. Once you've repeated this enough, you should be ready to sit down and examine the letters and see what customer benefits keep coming up, and which come up with the most passion from your customers. You've now found the universal desires.

    You've discovered that no one wants your product; they only want what your product does for them. You may have also discovered how you must change your product to fit what the customer needs it to do for them. Change your product so it now fits the universal demands from people. They have to buy it because it is exactly what they want.

6. Armed with this marketing intelligence report, you're ready to ask for the sale. Write it down in a letter. Write to ONE person. Think of just that one client. Begin as you did in step three. Begin at the beginning – with the greatest benefit they have demanded. Then go to the next until you've gotten them so excited with what you are doing for them. Notice we don't begin by talking about YOU, but about THEM. And we keep focusing on THEM until they are so enraptured, they're demanding to know who's going to provide all of this and how they can get your product.

Notice price is not part of the discussion. It will come, but don't be too anxious to discuss pricing. Establish the VALUE over and over. At some point price will be mentioned. The less you focus on price, the better. It should be a natural conclusion that is accepted as a matter of course. If they're hung up on price, you haven't established the value or the overwhelming benefits. People will afford what they want. Value is about what they want. They will then trade value for value.

7. Once you've written – and I mean written, not spoken, discussed or thought about – this logical letter that gets your reader feeling emotional and demanding to have your product, NOW you can begin to think about what vehicle would best carry your message. Today you have many choices, but face to face discussion is usually the most effective. Telephone is next. Emails and letters follow. Space ads in "affinity" publications where you rifle-shot your pitch are next. At the bottom as a last resort are broadcast media or general advertising.

Making Your Advertising Work

Advertising is a pain. We see so many advertisements every day that the thought of adding to the congestion and information overload is nauseating. But, if no one knows you have something to benefit them, then you'll stay where you are -- business wise.

The trick is to somehow create advertising that doesn't look, feel or seem like advertising. This is counter-intuitive, because we see all the ads and figure we've got to be like them. But no one wants to be sold something. They want what you have and you just need to let them know how you can benefit them. Keep it simple.

It's not easy. Begin making a thorough list of every way you or your product can help someone else. Even the most trivial sounding benefit might be used. This is all about letting someone get what he wants, and making his life better. In turn, you get what you want. Put the customer first.

How many words should an advertisement contain?

When I throw that question out to groups, I hear some interesting first responses:

1. Groups of people hoping to create their first ads say: I never read long letters or ads with lots of words.
2. Groups of experienced marketers who really haven't written an ad themselves, but have approved many say: That will depend on the media, the space available, and blah, blah, blah.
3. Groups of copywriters say: The longer the better. The more you write the more they bite.

To the amateurs I say: Be a little more humble. Just because you don't think you'd respond, you have, in all likelihood, bought something after getting 700 words or more. Chances are a short ad didn't persuade you to buy.

To the marketing executives I say: Be a lot more humble. The space available is a function of your ability to sell. It also avoids the basic question.

To the copywriters I say: No. Nonsensical. You're missing the point. The point is to make a sale.

If you have limited space then you must have such a powerful message that it compels the potential buyers to seek information someplace else. The remaining words of the sales pitch will be delivered there. One of the most successful ads ever, and the silliest, was in a classified ad in a New York City newspaper. It just said, "Send $1" and gave an address. Dollar bills flowed in. The kooks at the post office or some government bureau who purport to protect people from themselves deemed it a con and shut the guy down, taking his money (they put it in the government coffers as if it was better used or safer there). The space demanded he get pithy and he did. But the action required an address where the curious dupe thought he'd get more information on something bigger. On a less silly front, a lawn sign read, "I'll pay cash for your home" and gave a phone number. The first person who tried this, supposedly in St. Louis, got swamped with phone calls. The ad worked – it achieved its objective.

The length of an ad is strictly based upon its purpose. And you should only use enough words to accomplish that purpose. Not a word more or less. Sometimes it takes many words. Remember, advertising is simply salesmanship in print (or another medium).

Determine your purpose and write as many words as it takes to close the sale. Don't limit yourself when writing to the physical constraints of the ad space or cost. You'll edit later. Get the message out there in a free flowing logical progression first. Don't be constrained by what others will think either. Someone will always be there to utter the foolish words, "That's too long." No. It's either effective or ineffective.

Does all of this apply to what you're doing? It does. At least, it applies in all of the ads I've created in the following areas: 1) non-profit fund raising; 2) construction and real estate development, US or abroad; 3) consumer goods like books, pearls, investment grade numismatics and philately, flags; 4) concerts, recitals, stage productions, voice studios, compositions; 5) Internet and computer products; 6) educational courses (live, taped, printed); 7) franchises; 8) billion dollar transmission project -- currently nearing completion; 9) international tours; and 10) health and diet products. I've left stuff out. But, in all of these, the steps listed in this chapter for creating an advertisement apply.

Chapter 28

Publish or Perish Applied

At some point in your singing career, you ought to get some free newspaper advertising. This is what a press release does for you. But if you simply send an announcement to the newspapers, your chances of getting published at all – let alone in a decent spot – are the same odds a butterfly has when heading into a hurricane.

In order to be published, a press release must:

1. Be newsworthy.
2. Be easy for the editor to understand, and even easier for him to find a place for the press release.
3. Include an action photo of you.

Let us explore each briefly.

1. Be newsworthy.

Do not discount your newsworthiness, but be sure you are approaching the right newspaper. If you live in Swamp Hollow, Arkansas, forget about getting into the New York Times, unless you do something bizarre in New York City – and to be noticed there, it must be magnificently bizarre. But you are newsworthy in the Swamp Gazette.

Hardly seems fitting for a diva, but it is a great place to start because local newspapers make their money selling newspapers to local people. Local folks like reading about themselves and other locals who make good. Traditionally we like to say bad news sells, but with local papers good news sells, too.

Regardless of the size of the publication, the press release will be printed on newsprint and the public is crazy about newsprint. We criticize the papers, but believe everything in them. If you land a story in the paper, post it on your website. You now have credentials. The more stories you have, the more impressive.

What is newsworthy? Do not lose sight of the fact that your talent put to use is way outside the norm. If you are starring in, producing, judging or even reviewing a production, that is news. If you get a job singing outside of the community, a special award or any recognition, that is news.

Your press release will be about ONE of these events. Focus on the single event or honor and leave other things to other releases. Of course, you will lead with the honor. The first two paragraphs will tell who, what, where, when, why and how. After that, you can start including some biographical information about yourself and nice things people have said about you. A published quote can later be blown up as a headline on your website. Self-created news works. PR is all about that.

2. Make it easy to understand.

Make sure the editor immediately knows what this release is about. If you write it properly, you have a great chance that the editor will publish everything you say and keep it intact; AND when you return with another story, she will help you more readily. Editors of local papers are exceptionally overworked. The easier it is to understand, the stronger the chance that your story will edge out better stories that are poorly written, poorly prepared and sloppily delivered.

The easiest thing to do is to take your article to the local paper and meet the editor. She will not give you much time, if any, but will be impressed you took the time to meet her. Find out the deadline for sending the paper to press and show up a half hour later. The editor will not be so rushed and will be ready to be complimented. You showing up is a compliment.

3. Include an action photo.

Newspapers love great photos. If you think a picture is worth a thousand words, double that thought. The average picture can take up the space of 2,000 words – and the editor does not have to edit a single one. But, the shot cannot be a head shot. It needs to have action. An image showing you doing something – meeting a celebrity or singing – is much more interesting.

It has to be clear and easy to see. Do not use Polaroids, distance shots, or groups where you do not dominate. Pictures must be 100 percent in focus. Black and white is often preferred, but color is fine, too. If they want to run it in black and white, they can convert a color image.

Catherine Franz of the Virtual Marketing Newsletter recently created a nice outline for writing a press release. Some of the following ideas come from that story. This is basic stuff, which is exactly what you should use when putting together a press release.

Layout

1. Make your story 1-2 pages in length using Times New Roman 12-point type.
2. Double-space the copy.
3. Use 1.5 to 2 inch margins.
4. Use blank white paper. If you have personal stationery with your one-inch head shot, use it. Avoid bright- or dark-colored paper.
5. Center "News Release" at the top.
6. Place a release date under "News Release."
7. On the second page, type "page 2" and be sure your name and phone number are at the top.
8. At the end of the press release, type -30-.

Format

1. Write in inverted pyramid style with the biggest point or major message listed first, and all other materials listed in descending order.
2. Avoid fluff. Do not paw the ground. Get to it. Devote the first and second paragraphs to your main message.
3. Secondary information comes AFTER the main message.
4. If you have a story to tell, be pithy and cogent. Stories are great, but do not go on and on.
5. Overtly tell who you are, how to contact you, and the action you want people to follow. For instance, "Buy a ticket at this box office by calling this number." Do not be shy.
6. Another effective format besides story is to use a problem/solution format.
7. Proof read carefully. Check all facts, spelling and grammar.
8. Use only one news release per e-mail or envelope.
9. After you have finished writing, rewrite your headline a dozen times to get the most power out of your words, conveying the benefit to the reader.
10. Do not use a cover letter, binder, folder, etc. Just submit the sheet(s) flat.

Distribution

1. Do not send a press release in a mass e-mailing.
2. Take the release in person to the editor the first few times so you learn more about the press operation. Once you submit it,

do not pester contacts. They will either run it or they won't. Chances are, they will.

3. Mail future releases by first-class mail.
4. Do not use any type of labels, including your return address.
5. Add "PRESS RELEASE" and "Release Date: [Insert Date]" to the outside envelope.
6. Places to send press releases include: writers@[magazines]; writers@[newspapers]; trade journals in your industry; print magazines on the topic; and online agencies that distribute news releases.

Happy writing and publishing. Do not wait another week to begin doing this for your career.

"Action expresses priorities."

-Gandhi

Chapter 29

And the Winner for Publicity is . . . You

I came across several good articles recently written by public relation advisors to the stars. Of course, I do not care too much about those they have advised. I care instead if the advice follows principles of human behavior and solid marketing concepts. These folks I am quoting, however, are true blue; so I thought I'd compile their thoughts and pass them on to you.

As you prepare your publicity, know that the media is interested in at least one of these eight angles. These are not the only ones, but this is a fairly exhaustive list. Examine the list and see if whatever event you are trying to promote could be made to fit one of these. If so, it will probably be seen as newsworthy, and you may receive some free press from the event.

Once you receive free press, do not forget to include the clipping on your website. Everyone says they do not trust the media; but if it is in the paper, they automatically figure it is a big deal and true. Get mileage from that.

If you are a managed singer, discuss the publicity you are getting with your manager by using these principles. Do not listen to people who say, "That is the manager's job." It is YOUR career, and if your manager is not following these points, he or she should. Manage your manager.

Eight Powerful, Compelling News Angles

1. **David vs. Goliath** – It is you against the world. You are staging a concert that is against all odds. You are the little guy helping a big cause. You did a concert or got a role no one could have predicted.

2. **Rags to Riches** – You did not have much growing up. You struggled through school, and paid your own way. You walked to school in three feet of snow uphill, both directions. Whenever you show the media you have overcome a tough situation, it is a newsworthy feature. Use it.

3. **Anything.com** – You have a hi-tech way of doing something. You are a performer with a website. That might not be the big angle, but it has some cache'. You are sending out free recordings via the Internet, and that can get attention.

4. **First, Fastest, Biggest** – You are one or all of these and that is newsworthy, although being the biggest weight-wise probably is not great news. You are the tallest performer and that might be a good angle. That you are the first in your community to sing in the "big city" is a great angle for local papers. You are doing some performance at an age that is different. You are holding a concert that is the biggest draw in years, or raises the largest amount of money, or is the first of its kind. These are all newsworthy angles.

5. **Celebrity Affiliation/Association** – You know someone with a celebrity moniker, and he is going to attend your concert. Get him the publicity and get you some as well. Almost everyone in the public spotlight can use some more. Why do you think the National Enquirer is still in business with all the scurrilous things they say about celebrities? Because it is free publicity.

    Rarely – hardly ever – does anyone sue, because deep down they are loving it. Get them some pub and get carried along the coat tails. If you belong to an association and are doing something for them, say that you are part of the formal association (if it is reputable).

    Even if the press has not heard of the association, just naming it raises their eyebrows because they figure their readers might have heard of it and will be impressed with the specificity of the article. If you have become an Accredited Classical Singer, use that. Some nabobs pooh-poohed the idea as they stood afar at the convention. That is to their detriment. If you have such a designation from anyone, trumpet it. The media will say "wow" and you will receive some publicity.

6. **Stir it up** – If you have the stomach for it, do something weird. Something bizarre. Every time you stir up the norm, you are newsworthy. You might recall the story of how I found an award for a construction company by telling their insurance company that the company's "zero accidents" rate was worth an award. The insurance company said they did not have awards. I told

them to make one up. They did that at our request; and the local television, radio stations and newspapers blared it to everyone.

I once created an entire write-in marketing plan for a congressional candidate. The hopelessness of the cause attracted the media because no one had ever won a congressional seat as a write-in congressman. The media attention gave him more exposure. Then we pointed out that the president and leaders from both parties objected to the write-in candidacy. We got more exposure. He was the talk of his SoCal district. And he won! First time ever. He served forever until he retired.

Another time, I had the dubious distinction of participating in a coalition with Ralph Nader to stop the U.S. congress from giving our tax dollars to big banks to bail them out for bad loans they had made to third world countries. We thought the request for $8.4 billion in tax payer funds was outrageous. So we took on the Republican White House, the Democratic House and Senate, and both political party machines; and held up the bill for nine months. They finally bought off some congressmen with a housing bill for their districts in exchange for their votes to push the big bank subsidy bill through. But, they haven't been back for years lest we smite them again. How did we do it? By stirring it up. I created a slogan, "Stop the Big Bank Bailout." We did not have much money, so I created radio commercials filled with some outrageous humor. We only ran them in the congressman's district when we knew his policy advisor would be listening and simultaneously ran them in D.C. at a time and a station we knew the congressman would be listening. In the radio spot in his district I gave his name as the bum who was bailing out the big banks. In DC we just said an unnamed congressman was the bad guy. When the congressman got to his office and heard from his advisor back home, he superimposed on his memory his own name for the unnamed DC congressman and figured the whole nation knew of his duplicitous behavior. One congressman even stood on the floor of the House and shouted, "I am NOT supporting a Big Bank Bailout because this is NOT a Big Bank Bailout." The newspapers and television quoted him verbatim, and the whole world got to read and hear about my slogan. Thanks for being free carriers of our message. We captured the agenda. They were arguing on our turf. This is how you accomplish "stirring it up" ventures.

If it fits your circumstance (and it likely will at some point if you are out doing something worthwhile), do not be afraid to mount a "stir it up" campaign. It offers lots of news angles to manage. Just make sure they spell your name right. Be ready to have some people thumbing their noses at you, but if that fits what you need, do it.

7.   **Seasonal tie-in** – Christmas Concerts, Easter, Hanukkah, Running of the Bulls for the Festival of San Cristobal or whatever. If there is a tie-in, there is a story.

8.   **Problem/Solution** – Tsunamis and hurricanes are, obviously, huge problems. If you can provide a solution by either going there and singing to soothe the victims, or holding a fund raiser, or helping performers in the area, that is newsworthy.

These are just eight ideas. Once you get the hang of this, you will see your life through these prisms and gain the reflection for doing even better things. If you do not get publicity, someone will.

If not now, when?

Most of this marketing game is thinking. Think about how to get publicity, market yourself and apply these principles, and you will create wonderful new ways to further your career.

Have fun.

Section III

Performing Venues

Negotiating

How to...

What to Do Next

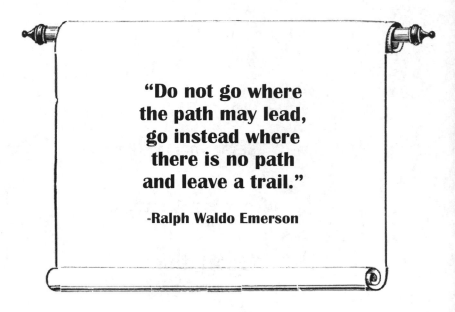

"Do not go where
the path may lead,
go instead where
there is no path
and leave a trail."

-Ralph Waldo Emerson

Chapter 30

Can't Buy Me Love – But Cash is King

Charging for your voice is the performer's toughest job. The entire industry is set up to discourage you from charging for your work. The philosophical bent of the liberal arts world is poised to jump on anyone daring to charge money and, heaven forbid, do it in a new way.

With such a stacked deck, what performer can deal with this? Just the strong individualists who could care less what the psychic vampires say.

But, it is argued, what about the Golden Rule – namely "He who has the gold makes the Rules." If it is their money, how can we go against the grain they have set up?

Yada, yada, yada. Such is the clatter around this sensitive subject.

Let us cut through it. It is your career. You must make the rules, and the simplest rule is, "If it is working, use it. If it is not working, try something else." Sensibilities come into play, but today's outrageous behavior is tomorrow's norm. Being a little outrageous without being obscene can get you noticed and help you stand out from the herd. If that bothers you, skip the rest of this chapter.

When discussing payment, the first thing that comes to every performer's mind is money. This is wrong on at least two levels:

Level One

We are incorrect to think that earning money is evil for performers. The love of money can ruin us, but a proper pursuit of money is essential. Money is best defined, traditionally, as

    A) A medium of exchange

and

    B) A store of value.

You have something of value, your home, which belongs to the bank. The bank officer wants payment, but wants something of value he can use. You might like to pay in leaves or rocks, but that is not the medium of exchange the bank officer will accept. He wants dollars.

Because the U.S. Treasury backs money, we accept this as a store of value. It is not likely that our money will be devalued tomorrow, and we will need to use a wheelbarrow full of money to buy a loaf of bread. Historically, this has happened many times. Solomon brought in so much silver that the silver became worth the value of stones. During the post-World War I period in the Weimar Republic in Germany, the currency was not backed well by the government. They printed too much and thus had too much money chasing too few goods. Inflation resulted. Soon it *did* take a wheel barrow of currency to purchase a loaf of bread. One person reported that, while standing in line, he left his wheel barrow of money outside. When he came out, the money was piled neatly on the ground, and the wheel barrow was stolen. Our greenback has a little inflation, but it is a reasonable store of Value.

Consider, however, one other effect of money. It is a store of time. While it will not guarantee you will live to 65, if you do make it there and you have accumulated proper retirement money, it will now buy you free time.

On this level, we must consider that getting paid is a good and natural thing. You have something of value that you are exchanging for something they have of value. Too many performers enter into a Never Land that finds not getting paid acceptable. You should NEVER find it acceptable to exchange what you have of value with someone else without getting something of value in return. This is theft, albeit allowed theft.

Let us consider whether or not cash is always the preferred value.

Level Two

We can effectively get paid in more ways than money, although whoever said money was not everything knew it was still way ahead of whatever placed second. Until bankers, governments and grocers accept good feelings in lieu of cash, cash will be king. But sometimes non-cash can actually be more valuable, because the non-cash payments may lead to more cash than you originally were going to receive.

Besides cash, here are three things you can accept that could lead to even better things:

1. **The names, addresses, phone numbers and e-mail addresses** of your audience members. The event organizer usually sells tickets. Chances are he obtains the names of invitees from a previously compiled customer list. These are well-scrubbed prime lists (bad addresses gone) that include consistent

advocates of your profession. If organizers do not have a list, their benefactor or sponsor probably does. Exchanging your voice for their list can be highly profitable. Often their desire to secure a non-red-ink bottom line will allow them to trade some words on paper for cash.

Notice I keep saying "often" and "chances are." <u>Few sure things exist in marketing</u>. We try things. We ask. We probe and experiment. They might say "no," but if they do, you are noted as being savvy and astute, and what they end up paying could be of a higher value because of it.

2.   **Extensive PR**. Do not accept the normal for this. I mean extensive PR, not just the required or pro forma expectation of listing your name, biography and photo in both the program and press releases. That should be a given. If you are not getting at least the basics, then this is just a hobby.

By extensive PR I mean the organizers need to hold a press conference in a beautiful place, be it the opera house, a gallery, a natural setting, etc. It should be some special event such as a casting party or grand opening of the organization. If they have anyone with PR savvy, they will find something amazing to do that will attract their donors (and a chance to rub their wallets); and, given that free food and drink will be flowing, the press will come. If you do not understand the juxtaposition of free food and the press, now is the time. As free money attracts politicians, free food attracts the press.

At this setting, you should be one of the main courses. You must be featured and perform well.

If done correctly, this will lead to other work. This means you get the name of every person there - something the organizers already have. You want to send a thank you letter to every attendee, and add a special invitation from you to attend the performance. This is vital to you and to the organization. You come off gracious and ubiquitous.

As a result, the organizers enjoy even more press and circulation.

Keep in mind, I am giving ONE example. Let this lead you to other ideas founded on the same principles.

3.   **In lieu of not getting your full value** in cash, accept a lesser amount with an agreement that you will have a major role in a

certain number of productions they do in a specified amount of time. Do not be ambiguous. Specify the size of the role and the time limits in which they must perform. And insert a penalty clause (do not call it that) that says if for any reason they are not able to either cast you in that role or in the agreed time limit, the remainder of your fee will be paid by a certain date.

4.   **Referrals**. This could be more valuable than cash. Ask the prominent person in the organization to give you the names of other people who can introduce you to the right people who can pay you.

5.   **Letters of recommendation and positive reviews**. Get these no matter what you earn in cash. Make it part of a contract. Get them, publish them and post them on your website.

In the end, cash is still king. Remember this rule: In running a business, never confuse profits with cash. And never run out of cash.

Chapter 31

The Monkey Fist and Vanilla Ice Cream

Let us look at another line of work and see how it applies to your career. Observe a large ocean liner pulling up to a dock. The ropes required to moor a great ship to the dock are tremendous. They are very long and as thick as a man's thigh. How can any seaman, no matter how strong, ever lift such a thick rope, let alone hurl it so that it will reach the pier?

He does not hurl the heavy rope, known as a "hawser." And he does not use twenty beefy guys or use anything hi-tech to send the monster rope to the pier, nor anything low-tech like a crane to hoist it. Instead, a solitary crewman hurls a little iron ball, called a "monkey's fist," which is attached to a thin rope about the size of a clothesline.

He tosses this monkey's fist to a longshoreman standing on the pier, waiting to receive it. When the longshoreman catches the little iron ball, he starts to haul in the thin rope attached to it. This thin rope, in turn, is attached to the huge hawser, which moves through the water as the fellow on the dock hauls it in. And that is how the big, unwieldy hawser gets tied to the moorings on the pier. Throwing the hawser is too big a first step for any sailor.

How can you as a performer apply the Principle of the Monkey's Fist?

Here's a simple illustration. Suppose you wanted to hold a neighborhood concert, but getting people to know about you might be time consuming. Why not go to the local PTA and volunteer to hold a special patriotic music recital with great music about honor and country. Let them sell tickets, and you donate your services. Let them know there will be plenty of entertainment for families with children. All proceeds will go to a PTA project. They always need money.

Chances are they will be surprised and pleased. Convince them to use one of their committees to organize it. Make it modern and upbeat and fun-sounding. Bring in other performers as needed.

Tell them you'll simply want the list of everyone who attends so that you can send them a "thank you" note and a certificate for you newest CD. The PTA will get $5 for each CD sold at the program and thereafter.

Your "hawser," or big rope, would be holding this on your own. By tying into another organization, you're tossing the Monkey's Fist instead. They do most of the work, and they use their credibility and their motivation to raise money. You get noticed, have potentially hundreds of new people exposed to your talent, and a chance to sell your CDs. As discussed previously, if you pick a school district in an affluent area, you'll also have dozens of homes that just might love to have you put on a personal "parlor concert" during the holidays for their important friends.

This Monkey's Fist concept can also be applied to your entire career.

If this business was just about following a set of instructions where you put tab A into slot A, B into B, and so forth; then sure, you would get your undergraduate degree, star in a few university productions, go on to get your post grad degree, get into a YAP, win a competition or two, start in a chorus at a regional house, get better roles, move to the next level and so forth until you have taken the prescribed steps to reach the top level, get your star on the door, sing your heart out, make lots of money, put all the madness behind you and retire and teach someone else this pathway to step-by-step success.

Sounds great? Forget it. It does not happen smoothly like that for anyone. Life is messy and meant to be that way. Every step of life requires some element of faith, or as Soren Kierkegaard once said, "Life takes a leap of faith."

If this sounds depressing, buck up. It is, but so what? It is simply life. No profession has an elevator to the top floor. You'll be taking the stairs. We are here to grow, and we do not grow without flexing our muscles on the barbells of reality. The very process of marketing is what is going to make us better than we were before.

What are the chances your next role will be at La Scala or the MET or wherever you consider to be the pinnacle of success? The chances are probably zero. That is your "hawser." You need to figure that "hawser" or big job will only come if you first get the Monkey's Fist in motion.

Which Monkey's Fist technique you use must be determined by master strategies emanating from your core values. Using an e-mail campaign, website, or a direct mail approach will not automatically get you that job. Trying an e-mail campaign for anything without addressing the overall marketing and career strategies for you is violating your values. That would be like meeting someone for the first time and asking them to marry you. Bad approach.

To determine your Monkey's Fist, decide what thing you want next. Then figure out exactly who your audience is. If you want a role in a regional theater, know who the casting director is. Know who the other players are in the production side of things. Find out how much they pay, if they pay, and the hours you will be responsible to work. See what their fund raising needs are. Learn everything you can about them.

If you still want the role, determine the most-important person who decides which actor gets the part. The artistic director is often the person, but many times he or she is the voice of the company, not the person who ultimately decides.

Know what they want. Casting is often about a "look" they want. Suddenly we are into the cattle-car mode, and this is a fatal location. Suddenly we are doing the normal, and your chances of succeeding are drastically reduced when you become normal, average, same-old-same-old, ordinary, and one of many where nothing stands out. The competition is going to kill you because there are so many, and you have become another vanilla. You must be Rocky Road or Moose Tracks.

But how? Monkey's Fist. Do something that will make you rise above the herd. In some disciplines we would give away something. If I were a voice teacher needing students, I would invite people to have a complimentary voice lesson. Let them get a feel for what I do. If I were a composer I would give the key decision makers a chance to hear my music for free and even offer them a royalty-free use, one time. I did that for a composer, and in three weeks he had six contracts. That was 20 years ago and I understand he is still composing for major motion picture studios.

Everyone else does the usual: audition, bow, smile, say "hello" just right, and sing wonderfully. The casting directors then nod and in deep-browed Homer fashion, narrow it down and yadda, yadda, yadda.

If that is the path you are determined to follow, you will probably get the same results you get now. Remember the insanity definition.

Try other ideas to get you started. Do not merely copy these techniques, as they are techniques I have heard others use and some I have ginned up. They have not come from your reservoir of strategies and values. Come up with a better list that focuses on you. But the principle is still real – you must rise above the herd or you will just be another cow or bull. Avoid being vanilla – be Rocky Road. Where everyone else is Zigging, you Zag.

Here is one kooky idea to get you thinking of better ideas:

Find out where the decision makers go to eat. Many people live in patterns. They go to a certain restaurant on Fridays at 6 p.m. Convince the manager that you want to sing for his restaurant. Offer to sing for free at first. Choose a lilting piece that will not break the glassware or scare the customers. Tell the owner to experiment with you to see if the customers love having dinner music and see if they stay longer, order desert and drink more.

Be persuasive and seductive without being sexual. Make them an offer they can't refuse. Bribe them! I do not care. Get this gig. Volunteer to sing an entire evening concert at his or her home just to be able to sing three numbers at the restaurant two nights. Yes, two nights. Tell the owner your experiment needs to be this Thursday AND Friday.

Use Thursday as your warm up to calm your nerves. Then Friday, no matter where the owner positions you in the restaurant, wander. Entertain. Sing to one person. Do not be a statue. Give them a dose of your personality. Make love with your eyes and voice to members of the opposite sex on a date. It flatters the companion and seduces the recipient. Be about personality.

If the restaurant has several sections, ignore the other sections where the decision maker is not. Do it all within full view of the table where the decision maker is seated. Have two friends seated in the restaurant, one near the table of the decision maker and one at the opposite end of this section. After each number, their job is to applaud and encourage or shame the others around them into doing the same. Get some excitement in the room.

If you are good and have selected music right for the occasion (kill the esoteric numbers, please!) – perhaps a popular piece (it is always good to begin with an Andrew Lloyd Webber winner), leading into a short well-known classical love piece, and concluding with an aria that will be loved by the director. Choose only numbers that build to a climax so you can be on top of your emotion's game.

Provided you have done this a short time before your scheduled audition, ask this: Is it possible that when you walk in for your audition, you will be remembered BEFORE you sing and long after?

It just might be that you are exactly the person they are looking for because they have seen you before and you have filtered through their subconscious mind as an audience pleaser. You helped set the criteria for what they are looking for. If not, have you really hurt your chances? Probably not.

You are now Rocky Road. Everyone else has gone the traditional route. You have dared to be different.

One last thing. Find out when the audition ends. Be there when the decision makers walk out. Go to them and say, "Thank you for listening to me." Shake hands and then leave. Be brief and be like the wind. Leave them wanting more.

So remember the Principle of the Monkey's Fist and the Principle of Vanilla vs. Rocky Road. Make the first step irresistibly easy for your prospect. Offer something that makes it irresistibly easy for your prospect to say yes. Then find ways to be remembered, to stand out.

Please write to me as you try different things and tell me how you are doing.

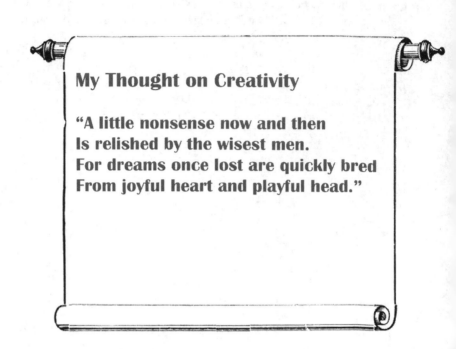

My Thought on Creativity

"A little nonsense now and then
Is relished by the wisest men.
For dreams once lost are quickly bred
From joyful heart and playful head."

Chapter 32

The Only Sure Way to Find an Agent

This is going to be a letdown. It is so obvious. But it is true.

Remember, agents are not machines. They are people with mortgages. If they cannot make money from you they do not need you. In fact, most performers are a liability.

However, the easier time they think they will have making money from you, the more likely they will grab you and want to sign you up with them; and if you can no longer make them money, the faster they will drop you. Unfair? Wouldn't you do the same? You are not a charity and neither are they.

So, how can you make them money? Just prove it. Never say "Trust me," or "I can assure you." They have heard it all before. Only money talks. To have the money to wave in front of them, you must use the Law of Concentric Circles. I have taught you to:

*Build up your house file.

*Increase your number of performances.

*Ever increase the fees you charge.

*Reach a point where you actually become "in demand." At that point you will get two, or better yet, three job offers that pay decent money for a stretch of time.

*DO NOT sign anything when this happens. Take the contracts to the agency you have researched as the best fit for you - which means it's accessible, has friendly agents, finds performers great jobs, and knows how to negotiate.

Take the UNSIGNED contracts to that agency. Say, "I have three contracts for good performance jobs that I'd like to have your agency negotiate. Are you interested?"

Of course they will be interested. It is real money.

Now you are a proven business and they will want to take you on.

From that point on you can mindlessly go about your singing, oblivious to the business cares of the world, right?

Wrong. Instead, you can manage your manager to make sure he is finding the best deals and treating you in the best ways.

No product sells itself. No business sells itself. That is your job.

The manager can be a great help, but you are required to do your part, and that includes more than just being a great talent.

After you build a managed career, the day will come when you are no longer in demand. If you're a soprano used to singing the pretty young heroine roles, no matter your great skill, the day will come when houses don't consider you right for the part. That day bothers many a performer. It can be crushing.

If you remember that YOU are the business and not your voice, you can take an objective look, see where you'll be in demand, and alter your career. Maybe it is time to seek a position at a university. At the top of your career you'll be in greater demand. If you wait until you can't get many roles, your demand as a teacher will drop as well.

Perhaps it is time to open a voice studio. Carol Vaness once told me it was time for her to open a voice studio. She had in her mind that she'd simply announce it and people would line up. I suggested to her it wouldn't quite happen that way; rather, she needed to sit down and think this out carefully. Nothing sells itself.

Maybe you're a free spirit and the thought of being constrained by a university or corralled by a voice studio makes you shiver and quake. Take your Skill Inventory and start asking who needs those skills and will pay you for them royally.

What I'm describing is essential for every career. One day the demand ceases for a product. Every product has a lifetime. Recognize when this happens, and create new products. You are the manager of your career.

Chapter 33

Venues for Performers

If you are a horn player, you have the wonderful chance of getting a job with a symphony, and it may be a job for life. But getting that one job could take years.

As a performer, you have the difficult task of having to find work, then more work, and then more work. The good news is that while horn players have few venues, performers have an enormous selection of venues.

A performer who only wishes to hit the La Scala stage will have to have more than C and D company experience to be ready for the big productions. Nothing can take the place of experience and exposure, except better experiences and better exposure.

As I mentioned in Chapter 7, becoming great at anything takes at least 10,000 hours. For performers that includes lessons, practice time, and, most importantly, performances. You must give a performance of some sort several times a week, every week, 52 weeks a year. You can rest when you finally get your laurels.

Most performers I meet have enough of a voice to please some audience. Find that audience and sing to them.

Most performers I consult with do not put in enough time finding performances. They want the performances to come to them, I guess. It isn't going to happen. You have to make it happen.

If you've gotten this far in the book, you now know more than enough to go out and get the performances you need to earn a living and to prepare you for the next great opportunity.

"To every man, there comes in his lifetime that special moment when he is tapped on the shoulder and offered the chance to do a very special thing; unique, and fitted to his talents. What a tragedy, if that moment finds him unprepared and unqualified for the work that would be his finest hour."   -Winston Churchill

Here is a list of possible venues where you can find work, money-making opportunities, and ways to expand your influence. I am not saying these are for you, but they could be. It will depend on where you are in your career, along with your career goals and values. At the Marketing Master Workshop, we spend quite a bit of time defining these and discussing how your various values and goals will or will not work with some of these venues.

With varying degrees of success, each venue has actually been used by one or more performers. When a performer reports using a venue, we always ask, "How useful or profitable was it?" We have not listed places that have not paid off in a good way for someone.

Here are three reasons you will not choose one or more venues:
1. They do not fit your career goals and rock-core values.
2. It is the wrong exposure or not a good experience (bad location, audience, etc.). The best job may not be worthwhile if the physical facilities make it so you do not sound good. Bad exposure is deadly.
3. You have something better.

I'm not too impressed with excuses 1 and 2. Usually they are stall statics.

If you have had a good experience at any of these venues, please write and tell me about them (mark@vmt-tech.com).

Here are venue ideas for performers – exposure, fund-raising and performance ideas, starting with the most obvious ones:

1) Theater and opera companies
2) Patrons – find one and new venues will emerge
3) Wealthy home concerts – parlor or salon concerts
   I write about this extensively on the Auditions Plus blog. I have sample advertising flyers, programs and ways to pre-sell a CD you are going to make and how to get $400-$800 in contributions to you. You should do 6 home concerts in November, 6 in December, four in February, two in May, and six in July. You'll love it and you'll make at least $12,000 for 24 performances. Go to: http://www.auditionsplus.com/blog.php
4) Friends of wealthy home concerts (use the Law of Concentric Circles to perpetuate this)
5) People of influence – recitals
6) Group concert – being part of a production
7) Retreats – corporate
8) Retreats– religious

9) Conventions and conferences
10) Corporate parties – summer, seasonal
11) Christmas and religious parties
12) Businesses – you can help draw attention to them at an event they create – be a musical spokesperson.
13) Schools – assemblies and specialty programs
14) Events and festivals
15) Create a talent agency that sells to all of the above
16) Community happenings, i.e. festivals, carnivals, street scenes or any gathering of the community. Become known.
17) Trade shows
18) Non-profit television (leads)
19) Start your own radio program (leads)
20) Create your own competition – unique!
21) Specialty catering companies
22) Specialty restaurants
23) Fund raisers – charitable events you or others host
24) Fairs – Renaissance
25) Grand openings of malls, corporate centers
26) Church jobs (call Gregory Scime, the expert on church jobs at 908-217-6464)
27) Recording, voice-overs for ad agencies and TV, radio and film companies
28) Private operas
29) Street work? (Don't discount this one too quickly)
30) Travel groups
31) Symphonies and orchestras (star and warm-up acts)
32) Long term care facilities
33) Senior centers
34) Retirement communities (these aren't old-folks homes, but great places for repeat business)
35) Day care centers
36) Do something unique – hybrid of several of these
37) Unions and other affinity groups (AFL-CIO, PTA, 12-step meetings, etc.)
38) Weddings
39) Funerals
40) Religious functions (blessings, baptisms, bar mitzvahs, church parties, etc.)

41) Large political rallies (Republican gatherings pay better and want you more, because more artists tend to be Democrats so there is an oversupply)
42) Small political group gatherings
43) Baseball, basketball and other sporting events
44) YouTube and your website
45) Facebook and MySpace (use Twitter to help with your viral marketing)
46) High School singing competitions as a guest
47) Libraries – many have recitals
48) Cruise lines – you must have an act
49) Chambers of Commerce, business groups
50) Stores selling CDs and music

All of these carry varying degrees of opportunity. Each experience builds upon the others, making you more prepared for better, more lucrative opportunities.

Chapter 34

Simply Negotiate

Musicians are not anxious to answer this question posed by most potential buyers: "How much do you charge?"

No doubt you've been asked that. Often we are quite sure of the price we want, but just saying it causes palpitations because we really fear losing the sale because we think we're overpricing ourselves.

To start off our negotiating discussion, here's a tip on how to make this less painful and more profitable.

Remember that prices are just numbers and with numbers there is no such thing as a big number. No such thing as "priced too high." It's a matter of establishing value. If you value high, and the customer highly values you or the product, then a high price is just the right price.

One way to get there from here is to use "the big number." Here's an example:

A singer sang her heart out every day in the subways of New York. Not a very glamorous place, but she had a spot the subway system reserved for her. People came to listen and they left paper money, not coins, in her tip box. She was making pretty darn good money and the experience helped her in many ways. But that's beside the point. The point begins when a rather dapper fellow who'd been listening through a number of arias introduced himself. He was the personal executive secretary for a wealthy gentleman out of Boca Raton, Florida. One of his many duties on this trip to New York for his boss was to find a wonderful singer who could organize and produce a production of La Boheme at his home in Florida.

The singer said she'd staged operas and would have no trouble. Then he asked, "How much do you charge?" Fortunately this singer had learned some of the things I teach on negotiating and made sure she 1) established her value, 2) asked lots of questions about what would be expected, and 3) didn't say a price but instead stated, "Operas are not cheap to stage. You know the Metropolitan's budget for an opera begins at $4 million." She then stopped and allowed for a poignant pause.

"Oh," he said, "I can't spend nearly that much."

Of course not, and the performer had no intention of getting that much. But what she did was determine how high "high up" is. Everyone has a price in mind when they're negotiating to buy something. Your job is to break that ceiling and establish a new ceiling. She had taken a ceiling of probably $20,000 or so and raised it to $4 million. NO, it doesn't mean the person thinks the price is going to be in that neighborhood; but, in his mind the ceiling was $4 million and everything he was now going to pay would be less than that. Now you're discussing value on your terms.

Someone asked my brother how much it would cost to buy a corporate jet. I know the person who asked had in mind that $3 million would be a high price, but could accept a price of $2 million. My brother began by saying a new jet, fully loaded could exceed $10 million. "Ouch. Wow. Whew. That's a lot of money," said my friend. But in saying so his ceiling of $3 million was broken. When my brother showed the guy a plane for $8 million he still thought it was too much for him, but he understood the ceiling. When my brother showed him a very good jet the company was selling for less than $2 million (due to a bad economy), the friend thought it was a steal. In a matter of minutes the price he considered unreasonable had become reasonable by using a high ceiling.

If you figure a 50-50 split is reasonable and desirable, begin with an example of someone who did well with a 90-10 split (you get the 90 and they get the 10). Chances are the person will be very thrilled with a 50-50 split when all is said and done.

It's a matter of understanding the human mind. Wal-Mart understands it perfectly. They advertise "cutting prices" and show a number like $9.57 and slash the price to $5.01. Wow. What a slash. Our price perception had changed so we, as the consumer, believe we're getting a value. And you probably are. But now you're leaving the store with the product, and feeling very good about it because the high ceiling price was smashed.

Keys to negotiating are flung around like dough in a pizza factory. We flung a few in the opening chapters. So many of the keys are excellent, but sometimes they are hard to remember on the spur of the moment.

Utilizing negotiating skills simply comes with practice. But let us examine a prime key. Just about every negotiating expert agrees that the first line of your defense is doing your homework. Know everything you can about the person with whom you are negotiating. Learn what she needs now and in the future, not only as it relates to your immediate concern of getting a singing contract, but other matters as well. The more you know, the more chance you have of making the right decision during the negotiations.

You also need to understand what they know about you. That takes some effort and some luck – which usually results from the effort.

In the early 1990s I found myself on the Volga River and in Moscow, Russia, negotiating with Soviet opera singers. Over the next 10 years I employed more than 200 such performers in my productions for American and other foreign tourists.

When I first began, I did my homework. I knew these performers were lucky to make the equivalent of $100 a month. I also knew that the Soviet anti-market system said if a person could sing, they had the right to have lessons and perform. The better they got, the better the forum. As mentioned before, opera theaters were packed because Verdi, Puccini, Mozart and Wagner were all sung in Russian. People understood what was happening on stage. But just as important, the price of admission was within the budget of even the poorest Russian – tickets would be a few rubles, or less than $1 at the Stanislavski or Kremlin Palace theaters. The Bolshoi was a bit more, but still within reach of most people before 1991.

This non-market system, or command economy system, produced a glut of opera singers. Under the system, these singers usually found enough money to live on (the same amount most Soviets lived on as well). Except for the "apparatchik" or "nomenclature" – the privileged leaders and upper bureaucrats – everyone lived in a pathetic economic condition.

So when these opera singers came to me – and the lines were enormous – I knew I could get them for a "song," and have a never-ending supply of reasonably good talent. I could be picky to say the least.

But I also knew enough about the market to know that paying people as little as possible is not the best way to go.

However, they did not know that about me. I knew they typecast me as a capitalist and that they had better knuckle-under or not get a job. If they had done their homework, they would have felt more comfortable in the negotiations.

Because I knew of their situation, and I knew exactly what I needed, I selected the basses, baritones, tenors, mezzos and sopranos that would work best together. Also the pianists, violinists and other musicians. They knew our performance schedules, accommodations, meals, etc. Once the quality was assured, I sat with them as a group to discuss the hard-core money. They were so nervous I felt bad for them.

I asked them how much they would like to make each month. They were a little startled. One lady who seemed to have a little more commissar than the others said they "must have at least an honorable wage," and then added meekly, "if that can be arranged."

I could not stand it any longer. I knew that if I drove a hard bargain I could get whatever I wanted. I knew the market better than they did. I knew I had all the advantages. But I also knew that because they understood the markets so poorly, they would say "yes" to something that would not make them happy.

So, I told them the terms of the contract and how much they would get paid – about double what they were thinking would be the most they could make. I then told them the final term: "You cannot be employed here until you have at least one CD filled with popular music, and one filled with the greatest and most beloved arias for your Fach." Again, they were shocked. But by this time they had loosened up and were enjoying themselves. I could tell they felt comfortable that they were getting into something good.

The commissar asked, "What shall we do with these CDs?"

"You are to sell on the ship." I stated. "During lunch, one of you will be performing. During dinner, three of you will perform. At the evening performances, all will perform. And then, after each of these events, you will stand by a table and thank people for coming. Your CDs will be in front of you. There will be no cashier. Just you. Accept their money and autograph the CD."

Now everyone was in total shock. "Do we give you the money afterward?" asked the commissar, now very humble (she was always very nice, just a little more confident). "No," I said. And to their further shock I said, "You keep it all. You share it with no one. It is yours. You get whatever they give you; and trust me, they will give you more than the price of the CD, which, by your standards will be an obscene $10 per CD." I knew that they sold their CDs for just a few dollars in the metro area when allowed to do so.

I did not try to explain why because I knew they would not understand and would not believe it if they did.

Again, if you want to get what you need and want, you had better know the lay of the land, what the product will do for you, what you need, what they are thinking and expecting, and what they can do. Low price is usually not the final end of negotiations. Usually it is good finances but workable agreements.

Because of the Soviets' lack of understanding, I had to do the work for both of us.

Now, can you figure out why I would make them a better deal than they wanted? Why I insisted they have two distinctly different CDs? That they sell them themselves and accept the money themselves? And of what value is it to me for them to sell foreigners CDs?

Here are the answers:

1.   Why would I make them a better deal than they wanted?

Because I knew their lives, and knew that if I paid them what they would accept, they would eke by. Eking people are not contented and happy people. They do not portray Russia the way I would like my clients to see Russia. I paid them well so they could also brag to the other singers. Those singers would soon come to me and want a job. My performers would know that and would work even harder to keep the visitors happy. They actually went out of their way to entertain the Americans on their own. They knew (because I told them) that the happier the Americans were, the more likely they would come back or send their friends. They did. Most of our customers came from referrals.

Henry Ford saw that paying the prevailing wage in the early 1900s meant his workers could not buy the cars they built. To increase his market share, he over paid his workers so they could, and did, buy the Model A and T. His workers showed others their cars, and his sales grew exponentially.

2.   Why did I insist that each performer sell not only two CDs, but two distinctly different CDs?

I wanted our customers to know what truly gifted performers I had hired. It made me look good.

3.   Why did I insist that they personally sell their CDs, and accept the money themselves?

Soviets did not trust anyone. For good reason. I did not want to get in the middle of that. If we sold 10 CDs for $20 each and gave the performer $200, somehow someone would have said over a vodka that we must have kept some of the money, or overcharged and kept the difference, or charged people back in America more, or made illegal copies of their CDs and sold them. They thought this way because many had done that themselves in the Soviet survival economy.

And, I wanted them to feel the money going into their hands. There is nothing quite like doing a good job and getting paid directly. I built the performers' confidence. They performed even better and LOVED selling their CDs. It was a great source of personal victory and satisfaction.

Plus, the Americans loved paying the Russians. Here is a little secret I knew and did not tell the performers. I knew Americans are generous. If they paid me for the CD, they would either try to get a better deal or at best, just pay the $20. If they paid the Russians, the Americans got great satisfaction of giving the performer an extra $10 as a tip. That blew the performers' minds. It also let the Americans get to know the Russians and enjoy them even more. Many Americans later organized concerts and invited the Russians to come to America and sing for their friends. Some paid the full college tuition to have some of the younger performers or the children of the performers come to their favorite university.

This accomplished another goal in setting up the tours, which was to get Americans and Russians working together. The greatest source of world peace comes when people come to know each other. Fear is gone and trust is built. Commerce allows people a quick chance to get to know each other. I predicted in a 1983 speech at the Heritage Foundation in D.C. that as soon as McDonalds opened a restaurant in Russia, the fall of communism would not be far behind. I was right.

4.   What value do I gain from the performers selling CDs to foreigners?

Why, I knew that travelers love to tell friends back home what a wonderful time they had. I knew if they bought the CDs, the travelers would play them for their friends. We had people who had no interest in visiting Russia suddenly become excited when their friends showed their souvenirs, their pictures and played their CDs. And that form of marketing did not cost me a dime.

There are other keys to negotiating, but knowing your audience, what they need and what you need are the most important.

Someday I will write an entire book just on negotiating because I have learned by sad experience how not to negotiate, and also how to do it well.

Let me give you one story and then a few key points, and call it good for now.

A partner asked me if I would like to explore getting T-shirts made in the USSR. He had all the contacts in the American and European rock concert venues. T-shirts are a huge business at concerts. I bought one at a concert just to cover my ears, so I thought that was a good market.

He wanted me to open doors in the USSR. As my partner in the travel business, he knew I had counseled with the president of Moldova, and figured that would be a good place to make T-shirts. Moldova provided cheap labor that needed our money to enrich the workers. It featured a port nearby and a sea lane close to Egyptian cotton. And it was a pathetic, crumbling communist system that demanded an infusion of capitalism.

I found a textile factory that already made shirts. When I told them I needed 125,000 shirts a month, they fainted. Literally. The president of the newly autonomous factory (that means they are government owned but privately run with profits going to the factory management and maybe the workers) was a lady in her 50s with classic red-dyed Russian hair. When they told her the amount, she fainted. Or so they said.

We were invited to discuss the terms.

My partner and I headed to Kishenyov, the capital, and then took the long drive north to Beltsi. It was not really that far, but on those roads it seemed forever.

We were greeted warmly and soon were head long into negotiations. I first wanted to know their capacity and how able they were to produce 125,000 T-shirts. We delved into quality control and shipping issues. Once it was established that they could deliver the quantity and quality, we discussed price. I will not give the exact amounts because I do not recall them precisely. But use these amounts for illustration purposes only. We figured if we could get the shirts made, shipped and landed in New York, London or San Francisco for $ 0.45 per shirt, we would be fine.

Naturally, I carefully avoided telling the factory managers any price. They tried to get me to reveal a price. We both knew that **whoever gives the price first, loses**. I had more practice in negotiating, and had done my homework. I knew how much they were selling shirts for. A favor here or there loosens lips.

The managers finally said they could do the job for $0.28 a shirt. I pointed out that this was a dramatic increase. You never accept the first price. They came down two cents. That means they could come down twice that or even more. I pointed out that such a price would be appropriate for 25,000 shirts a month, and did so by doing the math while they were spending gobs of time telling me why it would hurt them. You never listen too closely to the bleating of the lambs. Do the math instead.

I then wrote on the board the following numbers: 7,560,000 rubles per year. $0.24 per shirt.

I then subtracted the going rate for cotton. I did not show their costs because that would be insulting to tell them their business.

I said, "This is how much you will gross each year. But I will be paying in hard currency (dollars). Tell me now if this will reward you for your efforts."

The implication was that 1) I had done my homework, 2) I knew they were making more off of this deal than any factory in either Moldova or Ukraine, 3) I would take the business elsewhere if they were not reasonable, and 4) they were about to make an obscene amount of money off of this deal.

I suggested they could make my job easier to conclude the deal if the price was $0.24 per shirt.

They again went into the perfunctory yet mandatory bleating of the lambs. We all do it. Finally the president motioned for her economist (CPA) to write on the board. He crossed out my $.24 and wrote in $0.26. I moaned and complained and stood up and said, "Let us split the difference in good faith. I'll accept no more than $0.25, or I'll leave. I have had enough!" I had to make an emphatic show to let them know this was killing me. Until they knew I was bleeding, they believed there was money on the table.

They asked for an hour to decide. I gave them five minutes. They took 15 and finally came back in after actually having a tea and smoke break. We used their frightfully smelly toilets.

They agreed.

We shook hands and signed a Letter of Protocol as is their custom. In the agreement, I told them I wanted one more thing. I said if they kept the contract and met their quota for three months in a row, then at the conclusion of that three months and every three-month period after that, I would authorize a bonus of $.05 cents a shirt. They were thrilled. I thought myself quite clever for giving them some juice to make sure they kept their quota coming.

After the necessary niceties of concluding an agreement (with plenty of me telling them how tough to negotiate they were), we left.

We left with a potential profit of about $.30 per shirt. That is huge.

The next day we were celebrating in Moscow when I received word from the hotel manager that we had a phone call from Beltsi, Moldova. I did not speak enough Russian to carry on the full conversation, so I had my translator take over. The color drained from his face. He reported that, "They had looked over their numbers and found errors in their accounting, and they would lose money at the $.25 cent price. They had to have more."

I made another error when I asked, "How much more?"

My first error had been in offering the $.05 cents per shirt bonus. I was trying to be a good guy and make it a real "win-win" deal. STUPID!!! You do not know what win truly is for people. They are responsible for themselves. Your job is to get the best deal you can.

For Russians, they believe in "win-lose." If you win, they must be losing. That is equally foolish as win-win.

Because I had allowed for more money – 5 cents per shirt more – they figured I must be making 10 times that in profit. That meant I was winning and, thus, they were losing.

Because I foolishly added insult to my self-imposed injury and asked how much more they wanted, they added on even more. Sergei shook his head and said, "They want $0.75 cents per T-shirt."

I was furious. The third error on my part. I let emotion rule. Terrible idea. I then made my fourth error and told him to tell them the deal was dead. I killed the deal.

A month later, Sergei (my translator) mentioned he had gotten a call from the economist. They were still in shock that I had killed the deal. They figured I would counter with another figure and waited two days for me to continue the negotiations. He said they wanted more, but would have settled on the bonus as the entire extra amount, figuring that was where my real price was.

I am still angry at myself for ruining that deal.

Now it is time to put some of these principles to use in a performer's world.

Here is a letter I received from one performer after she had attended one of my Marketing Master classes.

Mark,

I have been meaning to send you an e-mail for several weeks and I just haven't slowed down long enough to send you a quick thank you. I had a terrific gig on Valentine's Day and I know the principles I learned from your class really made the difference.

I approached an elegant four star restaurant with a business plan. I asked the manager if she would be interested in providing her patrons with the "Ultimate Romantic Evening" for Valentine's Day. She had heard about me as a singer and was very interested in my proposal.

I presented her with an elegant layout of the following information: The Ultimate Romantic Evening, A Valentine Serenade, the world's greatest love duets, romantic violin, decadent chocolate, etc. I remembered to keep my mouth shut and let her talk price first.

She paid me far more than I would have asked. The evening was wonderful. She had a long waiting list for reservations and had to turn many folks away. We performed to a most appreciative audience in a gorgeous ball room, and enjoyed a wonderful four star meal at the end of the evening. I was able to get a nice check for myself, my husband (violinist), a tenor friend and a pianist.

When I was putting the wording together, I remembered to avoid tombstone marketing and most importantly, "He who talks price first, loses." The owner was very pleased and she is very interested in having us back again.

Thanks for sharing your tips and insights with me and many other singers. I thought of you all the way to the bank.

Toni Crowder (a.k.a. Tessitura)

No explanation needed.

Here's another example. See if you can help her. Her e-mail letters are unedited and are in italics. My answers are in a normal font. The singer is Elizabeth Liu from Taiwan, living in Miami.

To: mark@classicalsinger.com
Subject: Negotiating a gig

Hello Mr. Stoddard:
How are you? I have a question in regards of negotiating a price.
I just got a phone call from a company asking me to sing for their "President Club Dinner" for about 50-60 people. The coordinator mentioned that this is pretty upscale event and they will invite me for dinner and sing something nice (2-3 songs) for about 15-30 mins.
The location is in a 4 stars restaurant (private room). They also wanted to know my setup in terms of sound, backgrounds ... etc.
I've asked her to send me details via email and we can go from there, and she did!
What I should do now?
I'll give her a lot of adding value in hiring me, also and want to suggest a harpist for accompaniment, if she agrees ...
Thank you!
Isabel Liu

What should you say?   What should you NOT say? What's the worst answer?

I e-mailed Elizabeth and suggested she write, in her own words, a letter that went something like this.

Dear Kila,

I would thoroughly enjoy being with your group, meeting them and singing some great music that will inspire them. For such an upscale group, it is wonderful to provide them with the music they identify readily as the "best of the best."

I don't charge by the hour because each group is different. I'll prepare your concert so that it really fits this group. That takes extra preparation time. I want to be sure it is the best for you.

I also will be using the entire evening for you -- I won't be able to perform elsewhere that evening.

Perhaps the best thing is for you to let me know what your budget is, and I'll try to find a way to work into that budget.

Don't hesitate to call me. This sounds like a fantastic event and I know few people are as capable of making it a special night to remember as you are.

Warmly,
Isabella Liu

I also asked her how much she expected to make that night. She then wrote back:

THANK YOU SO MUCH! I shall edit the message and send it her.
According to the market price in South Miami, price starts from $125.00/hr and up.
I'd like to get paid at least $125.00 and possibly get more so I can hire a harpist, say another $100.00.
Thank you!!
Isabel

Singers have such low expectations. The next day she wrote me this e-mail:

Hello Mr. Stoddard,
I just got a reply from her. She said the budget was $500 plus more for the harpist and they agreed the price and will book me for the event.
They would like to know how is the procedure in order to book me.

I should reply with a "Thank you for booking me..." and also send them a
simple contract, right? (Just like the one you sent me last week).
I couldn't close that deal without you, thank you so much!
Isabel

You too can do much better. Apply the principles, use strategies and techniques that emanate from your values, and keep working at it. Skills take practice.

Let me quickly give you a summary of negotiating principles to cultivate and develop:

1. He who states the price first, loses.
2. Do your homework. Know how much is being paid, how much they can pay, and why they need you.
3. Never talk price. Talk value. When they bring up price, discuss your value. Discuss their value as well, but make sure that you (as a performer) find out why someone values you. Drive the value high.
4. Ask questions. Often. Incessantly. But ask good questions that tell you about them, tells them you already know a great deal about them, and questions that establish your value.
5. Take your time, but urge them to be quick in their decisions.
6. Never talk nonsense. Be to the point and respectful.
7. Conclude the deal with a written contract. For most single performances, a simple e-mail Letter of Understanding will be sufficient. But every deal must be written down for clarity's sake.
8. Be able to walk away from every deal, but not from emotion. Mean it for logical purposes.
9. Practice this skill. Negotiating is a learned behavior. It is a skill. Everyone negotiates. Some just do it better because they practice and are determined to get better. Practice asking questions with friends. Let the friend be the opera house owner. Try asking questions until you feel comfortable with this approach.

As you put these principles into practice, you will be taking charge of your career and your life.

Let me know how you do.

Chapter 35

How to Organize a Benefit Concert

Every day, people with worthy causes look for something they desperately need; and they believe that without it, their cause will die. They are searching for money. Non-profits rely heavily on benefit concerts and fund raising events to fill their financial coffers.

Recent natural disasters such as Hurricane Katrina and the tsunami disaster in the Indian Ocean areas add to the already long line of worthy causes needing your help in raising funds. This chapter will feature ideas on how to create a benefit concert, including what you need, what actions to take, and what to do with the funds you raise (this could be a problem for some because of tax implications).

Keep in mind, the American public (and the rest of the world outside of the disaster area) will soon tire of hearing about relief needs for a given disaster. The fickle public and media will simply race off to watch the next train wreck. But our attention-deficit does not mean the need to help disappears. For YEARS, the millions of people displaced by hurricanes, tornadoes, earthquakes and tidal waves will find life difficult as they rebuild everything.

Disease will be their major hindrance. Lack of education in how to prevent these diseases can be overcome with the right organizations going to Banda Aceh, Sri Lanka, Phuket and other places. Education can make a lifesaving difference.

For others, the lifesaving difference will be learning how to create a business. Disaster-hit areas are often rich areas for tourism, so jobs can be created by entrepreneurs. Some organizations specializing in this type of education and setting up low-cost financing can help.

As you see, rebuilding is not simply buying food, dropping it on an island and leaving; rather, it is a process that takes several years. We are likely to see indigent people on the news for many months to come.

You can take part in fundraising events as an organizer and driving force, but where do you begin organizing such a large event? Just like all 500-pound marshmallows, they are eaten one bite at a time.

Step One – Sponsorship

Very little can be done efficiently without an umbrella organization.

It's possible to create your own non-profit organization with a non-profit, tax-deductible foundation called a 501(c)3 foundation (named after its section in the IRS code). Before deciding whether or not to set up your own non-profit organization, consider a few things reported by other individuals setting up non-profit organizations. (Please remember, these are general guidelines that must be confirmed with sponsoring organizations, your tax accountant and lawyer.)

1. **Non-profits are run virtually the same** as a regular corporation with sound business practices. The major difference is the non-profit is the sole owner of shares, so when a non-profit makes money, all profits pass through the shares back into the non-profit.

    Non-profits can pay competitive salaries, meaning you can hold fund-raisers, benefit concerts, recitals and concerts for schools and pay yourself a performing fee.

    The non-profit can charge another non-profit a fee for setting up a benefit concert. It can also charge fees to schools and other venues for a program.

    There are some restrictions; but as you educate yourself, you will find "profitable" ways to bring in money for the non-profit that can fund relief efforts and other purposes of your non-profit. Plus, you get paid for your efforts.

2. **It takes two years** from the day you set up your non-profit until the IRS decides whether it is a qualifying organization. During that time, you can operate fully and all donations are tax-deductible. If you are rejected, the donations received to date still qualify and you are not penalized provided you have carried out a proper organization.

3. **Setting up a non-profit is fairly simple** – at least easier than rocket science. Usually the forms can be retrieved online at your state's Secretary of State website.

    Better yet, go to the Secretary of State's office and let the personnel help you fill it all out. Many report that the entire process began and ended there quickly. Try it. It might be far simpler than you imagine.

4. **You will need a name and a purpose statement** such as: "This non-profit is dedicated to raising funds through music to assist in disaster relief." Add other things you would like to do such as: teaching music in schools, educating the public on the benefits of great music, etc.

   You will also need a board of directors. Your directors can be friends, family members, fellow performers and patrons. They do NOT need to donate a dime of money; they simply act on the board by attending yearly board meetings to approve past actions and future plans.

5. By creating a non-profit organization, **funds collected must be placed in the non-profit bank account**. If you place collected funds in your private account, it could not only lead to people asking questions about dubious transactions, but could also result in significant tax problems.

6. By creating a non-profit, **you will find far greater credibility** when working with other non-profit organizations. Non-profits rarely work with individuals, but often work with other non-profits. Affinity breeds credibility.

7. By creating a non-profit, **you will be able to reach potential patrons for your art**. Many patrons who love helping starving artists would prefer to give a tax-deductible donation to the artist's non-profit, knowing the artist is not only being supported, but noble works are being achieved.

   Frankly, this is a potentially enormous benefit to artistic performers. Non-profit musicians not only have patrons who support them financially, but also the leading performer of the foundation gains tremendous amounts of credibility by having prestigious patrons on his or her letterhead as members of the foundation's board of directors.

   And nothing begets success like being aligned with successful people and their friends.

   These are just a few notes on creating a non-profit. It might be right for you.

   If you do not want to go this route, it is likely that you will need to find a non-profit that will let you organize a benefit. Often a strong patron will refer you to the non-profit organization of his or her choice. Such a recommendation carries considerable weight and will open doors to the nonprofit so they will give your benefit proposal a fair audience.

Step Two – Date and Venue

Select the venue before the date. Why go to all the work of finding a date when the venue you wish to use is already booked? With the advice of cooperating non-profit groups, select the venue, making sure it is conducive to the benefit concert theme. "Joe's Beer Bar" might not attract the crowd you need.

It should hold about 250 people to achieve a moderate success. Listen to the acoustics yourself. Know that it is a good venue. It is critical that you put forth your best sound, and that the other artists can enjoy the setting. Failure to do this will cost you future work.

Once the venue is selected, get a couple of back-ups – second and third choices. Bargain with the first one to see if they will give you the hall without charge as a donation to the Katrina Relief Effort (for simplicity, I will use the relief efforts for victims of Hurricane Katrina; but, of course, you can substitute your own charitable cause). Make sure the venue managers know they will get a full-page ad thanking them in the benefit's program, and that they will also be mentioned in your press releases for their generosity. Many venues will consider at least a steep discount or some other help.

Sometimes locating a venue will not be necessary, as the sponsoring institution or government body will provide that. Once you have established the venue, set a date. Before confirming the date, do the following:

1. Call the local Chamber of Commerce for a list of conflicting events (like a professional athletic or theater production).
2. Call the two or three most prominent churches in the area where potential patrons might be attending and see if they have conflicts.
3. Call the mayor's office and see if they know of any conflicts.
4. Call the local university and see if it has conflicts.

Step Three – Establish a Theme

Determine the positioning of this benefit, which is how you will be seen by past, current and future patrons. Keep in mind that although you will be doing something wonderful for others, you had better be doing something wonderful for your future as well. Do both.

Begin by setting a theme that captures imaginations and sets your tone. Since you are an expert in classical music, you would likely focus on a classical music theme such as, "The Greatest Music for the Greatest Need – Katrina Relief Effort Benefit Concert."

Be big and bold and verbally assertive to stake your claim to their imaginations and aspirations. Do not sell the benefit short with a humble theme and title.

Step Four – Design the Concert

Keeping in mind the audience you wish to attract, pull together the cast you wish to use that will:

1.   Attract the most people,
and
2. Do the most memorable job within the theme.

When lining up performers, do not be shy about who you ask. You are engaged in a noble endeavor, and are giving them a chance to be a part of it with the attendant publicity and notoriety.

Find a variety of performers. Although you might love a certain side of classical music, think of what will please the audience most. This is no time to be the curator of the Opera Preservation Museum.

Of course you will have some opera buffs, some opera critics and aficionados, and some others who just love great music; but define the concert more broadly than your tastes alone. Have something for them all – don't worry about being accused of selling out (unless, of course, you are "selling-out" all the tickets to the benefit!).

Write a script tying the disparate elements together that centers on your theme. This requires an artistic leadership that focuses on the audience and the intent of the program. In doing all of this you will probably have some bass, baritone, tenor, contralto, mezzo, countertenor and soprano musicians singing in solo and group settings. Egos need to be cast aside, but they will be considered.

A great ensemble performing wonderful music has an opening effect on wallets. This is its purpose. Keep this in mind. Do what you can to get everyone in the ensemble to respect that BEFORE they sign on. Prepare a Letter of Understanding expressly stating the "who, what, where, why, when and how" of the event and his or her participation. As soon as possible, get publicity out with new ensemble members' names to both partially cement them into place and gain some good publicity for the event and the performers. Publicity for the performers can be a huge incentive for them as well. New ensemble members are news.

Be sure to ask the members of the sponsoring organization or of your non-profit for their recommendations on participating performers, and try to get their ideas to gel with your initial vision. Do this by helping those who would give you their opinions to buy into the vision of the theme.

Respecting coworkers' opinions builds the organization for future events and gets them more tightly involved – so they will be more apt to actively sell tickets, promote the benefit and come up with some terrific guest performers.

Stage Five – Obtain Corporate Sponsors

People love to be associated with good things. They love being associated with winners even more. And at the pinnacle they love to be associated with good things that are done well and bring attention to their interests.

Corporations are figments of industrialized economies designed to raise capital and provide various protections in raising capital. Keep that in mind. Corporations have zero responsibility to do anything else except make a profit for their shareholders. Despite the silly phrase, "corporate responsibility," or a corporation being a "member of the community," the first statement of this paragraph is the only truth to this matter, and the sooner you approach the subject of fund raising with this in mind, the more likely you are to raise funds from corporations.

Keep in mind as well that corporations are neither moral nor immoral. They only exist as a legal creation. They are run by people and rely on people for the morality.

People are in a corporation for one reason: to earn a living.

Their secondary reason is to "get something done in an organized fashion."

Now that you know what a corporation really is, you can begin to make corporate appeals that work.

The best way to get a corporation's money is to provide them with beneficial exposure. Think how your concert will benefit the corporation and its leaders. This includes calling them a sponsor because they have paid for the venue, the program or the advertising, and in return have their name and products proportionately presented to the public.

The more positive exposure they will receive, the more they'll be likely to support you. Many have established nonprofit organizations to which they donate (and get suppliers to donate to) so they can select community projects that will serve their corporate purposes.

If you find a corporation that has had serious PR problems, yet still has good products or services, they will likely be interested in the positive press gained from associating with your concert. Your goodness rubs off on them and presents cognitive dissonance in the minds of people who thought poorly of them.

However, they will only want to be associated with you if you have sufficient credibility. If you lack significant name recognition, then put people on your board who have that recognition and credibility.

Have your board members – the whole group of them – sign the sponsorship request letter. By looking at the board of directors list, prospective corporate sponsors should believe that aligning with you means they will be with a program that demands quality.

Finally, sponsors will want to know how much you plan to raise.

Tell them your direct ticket sale plans and how you will gather other donations. Give them credit for being the ones to help raise that much money for charity. There is enough glory and praise to go around and let everyone take full credit.

The corporation will expect a professional presentation to involve them, even if they are a small firm. The presentation does not need to be expensive but must be a well put together executive summary of what you are doing, and how the money will be used. Identify the parties already aligned, and communicate exactly what you would like the potential sponsor to do.

Do not shoot low. Aim high. Aim with an aggressive air generated from intelligent knowledge about your project.

Give the corporations five different levels from which to choose, such as Diamond, Platinum, Gold, Titanium and Sterling levels. They all sound good but will be on a downward scale depending on the contribution. It is also good to use softer names, such as Humanitarian, World Citizen, Vigilance, Lighthouse and Brotherhood Levels.

Each level must spell out exactly how the money will be used. Often, the money will pay a specific cost or carry out a certain project. For example, a corporation might agree to handle all public relations and promotions, guaranteeing a certain number of tickets sold. They will then turn the project over to their PR department and promote it in a way that benefits them.

The corporation will also want to see what you are going to do for them. How many mentions, how many signs, how prominent a location, where they are on the concert program, etc.

Your corporate sponsors are often willing to tackle challenges that include:

1. Public relations (as mentioned), and
2. Purchasing blocks of tickets to give to suppliers.

They will also often refer you to suppliers who buy their own blocks of tickets. Sometimes corporations will distribute ticket blocks (like NBA basketball tickets) to star employees and VIP clients.

What better way to treat a great client than with tickets to the greatest music in the world for the world's greatest cause?

Never look past the little guys, either. Give them a chance to sponsor. They may be light in their up-front contributions, but can become heavy weights in rallying the community around your cause. They also have long memories of good deeds and kind actions. Let them get others they know to contribute to their contribution.

Step Six – Make the Booking

Armed with a cooperating entity (such as another nonprofit, a government agency or a corporate sponsor), a date, a viable venue and, we hope, other corporate sponsors to front the money needed to promote this event, you should now be ready to book the venue. Of course, this and every other arrangement you make in this effort MUST be reduced to writing. Artists sometimes have trouble with this concept, preferring to "trust" everyone. It is better to see most people as honest, hard-working people struggling with the onset of Alzheimer's.

Write down every arrangement. Send them an e-mail, fax or letter spelling out the agreement. They will keep this as their instruction manual on what they are supposed to do.

Most conflicts come from differing expectations. Writing down the expectations keeps peoples' memories aligned with one another.

With that, it is time to sell the tickets.

Step Seven – Sell Tickets

The least effective way to sell tickets is to buy space on the radio, television or in the print media. It is a shotgun form of advertising that mostly broadcasts to those who would never come, in hopes of getting a few that might.

Instead, here are the most effective ways to sell tickets:

1. Have your board members and corporate sponsors buy all the tickets and distribute them.

    One of your corporate sponsors could specifically buy blocks of tickets for less advantaged people who might also be future customers for their company. The corporation may also need to make a favorable overall public impression, or a good impression on some city fathers for an upcoming project.

    Rarely will the sponsors and patrons fill more than 25 percent of the house, but try to get more.

2. By now you should have an overall committee including many, if not all, of the performers. Give each 10 tickets to sell to their friends.

3. Go to radio and television stations and offer to be on their programs to discuss the latest news – which you need to make sure you are solidly armed with – on how the survivors of Katrina are doing.

    Emphasize the local angle – how local people are doing something specific to help, and how coming to the concert will help a great deal.

4. Talk to the Chamber of Commerce, Rotary Club and other service organizations about making a presentation to their boards asking them to help you sell tickets to raise money. Volunteer to sing (get some publicity for your voice, too!) at one of their luncheons and then ask each member to buy 10 tickets and bring their friends and family members.

5. Obtain mailing lists (just ask for them) from these groups or have them mail, at their expense, a special invitation that you will write. Previous chapters have outlined patterns and suggestions on how to write a sales letter. If you need more details, check out my book, "The Power of 117," which provides detailed check lists on what to include in a sales letter.

    Meet with several other cultural organizations, and your city, county and state's arts councils. Ask them to promote the event. Mail your sales letter to them.

6. Visit every local university's vocal program and offer the students a special donation rate. Convince their vocal program to

sell tickets on and off campus, and offer a prize to the person who sells the most tickets.

Go through the chairman of the vocal program for suggestions on how best to involve the students. If you can add a chorus of performers from the school to the benefit's program, you instantly have more people who will buy tickets to see them.

7. Go to the local newspaper with a well-written article using the who, what, where, when, why and how inverted pyramid formula, emphasizing the local angle of this benefit concert.

Take good head shots of the local performers. Meet with the feature editor and arts editor to explain your purpose, sponsors and patrons, so they can see it is a legitimate operation.

Armed with these seven tips, you will discover even better methods. All seven are maximum leverage types of selling because they are focused, rifle-shot strategies rather than shotgun blasts to the broadcast media.

Step Eight – Bank the Money

As the money comes in, make sure every expense is well-documented and every donation carefully noted. Make sure you get the name, address, phone number and e-mail address of every ticket holder. This will become an invaluable asset for later use. Put all cash and checks into the bank immediately and never hold back any cash for "emergencies." This is bad form and potentially a smoking gun for gossip-mongers.

Step Nine – Rehearse the Entire Program Several Times

Even though it is a concert of parts, get the parts together and run through the pace and timing of the program. Add or cut where needed to enhance the program's flow. You may have to cut several people back one number. Do not cut yourself back, however. You must perform. You have earned it.

Step Ten – Have an Emcee

Ask someone else to emcee, preferably a local celebrity, dignitary, radio or TV personality. Give them careful guidelines on what you want them to say, and what the tenor of the program must be. Give them a brief bio on you so they can introduce the producer of this event.

Let them prepare to praise you – and you will use this praise later to enhance your credibility.

Step Eleven – Arrive Early, Give a Great Show and Hold a VIP Reception

You should have thought through every detail of the night, including seating, ushers, vendors, sponsor introductions, bios for other performers, a full printed program (perhaps donated by a print shop?) and a VIP reception. During the show, have the emcee introduce you to speak about how the funds will be used.

The more specific, the more captivating.

The more unusual and creative, the more they will want to help out.

You must paint a clear picture of the need, complete with names of victims and how you are going to help them.

Photos would be great in the program. ASK for more donations right now.

Do NOT be afraid to ask; the audience came to help. Let them know how much money you need to raise, and then ask them to make out a check, enclose it in the pink envelope they found on their chair, and drop it in the barrels at intermission.

After the concert, have a special room backstage, if possible, where the performers can greet your VIP guests. Be the social host and graciously make introductions.

Step Twelve – Follow up

For every name, address and e-mail, send a thank-you letter. Tell them what the goal was and how you did, and then ask for another donation. Do not think that they have been asked enough. Ask. You will be floored with the post-concert donations that come in if you held a good concert.

Thank your sponsors. Again, ask them for more donations. Thank your board and make sure you ask them who else you should thank. Thank the service organizations and government agencies that helped in any way.

And then send the money, after deducting expenses (including your expenses!), to the promised organization. Certainly the American Red Cross (not the International Red Cross, which has become a more political organization), Catholic Charities, LDS Foundation, Doctors without Borders and other great charities could use your help. Get letters from them confirming the donation and praising your efforts.

Write a story for the press telling how much money you raised, and a review of the night's performers. See if you can get quotes from dignitaries and VIP guests about the event, and especially about the quality of performers – so those performers can use the reviews in future biographies and on their websites and press-packets.

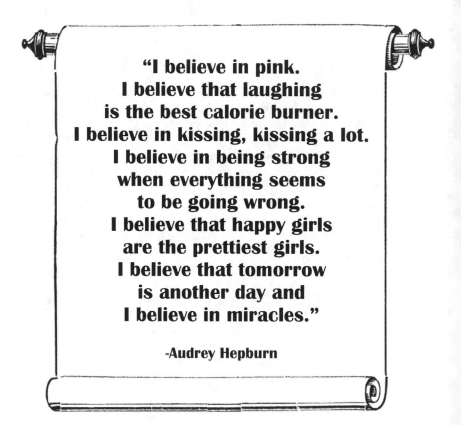

"I believe in pink.
I believe that laughing
is the best calorie burner.
I believe in kissing, kissing a lot.
I believe in being strong
when everything seems
to be going wrong.
I believe that happy girls
are the prettiest girls.
I believe that tomorrow
is another day and
I believe in miracles."

-Audrey Hepburn

Chapter 36

I Can't See You, But I Hear You Great!

Would you rather have live performances or sell a bunch of recordings?

Not too long ago, recording artists supported the free downloading of their songs on such sights as Napster. The recording companies hated Napster. Why would artists like free downloads of their songs, and why did composers and record companies start filing law suits?

Follow the money to know why. Recording artists only receive a tiny income from each record. Recording companies get the rest. Artists make their money from live performances, so they were thrilled to have thousands of new fans in cities where they would perform. Ticket sales increased as their fan base increased. The fan base increased as their music became known, even if people only heard it from downloading a free recording. What we like, we buy. What we buy, we buy more of.

The opera world continues to think the rules of human nature do not apply and, and as a result, they do not understand how rap artists, Frank Sinatra or Tower of Power earning money has anything to do with them. Remember that smart artists find similarities in different universes, and soon realize that all universes are not that different.

If you want to develop a music career, watch what recording artists do. First and foremost they perform live, and then do it repeatedly. (The next chapter shows you how to hold a live concert that pays you.)

If they cannot get paid initially, they do it for free - at YMCA dances or in a rented booth at the county fair - until they start to build demand. The greater the demand, the more jobs they receive; and the more the jobs, the more they can charge. Remember: ALL markets are psychological. Nothing is inherent. Value must always be created in consumers.

The good news for classical singers is that their type of music demands a higher premium than folk singers, because people who like classical music think it is better if they pay more. So, you are starting on the inside lap of this race with a downhill slope if you are astute in pressing this advantage.

In chapter 33, you found a list of 50 places you can sing. Select the ones that fit you best. Do not get too up-itty or consider some beneath you. Perform. And perform often.

Wherever you perform, get your CD up front. Normally I would advise selling it; do not give it away. A sure way of selling it is to announce "My CD is in the back. Profits from the CD will help the XYZ charity." People who like classical music tend to love charitable work. Notice I said profits. Sell it for $20. Pay the recording company the hard costs and their costs for the artist. About 20 percent can be the profit. Of course, you are the recording company. If that bothers you, stop letting it bother you. You deserve to be paid and the profits are going to go to charity. Frankly a 20 percent profit is exorbitant. Most businesses run at a less than 10 percent profit basis. You are being generous.

What songs should be on the CD? Certainly not the ones opera singers say they enjoy while sitting in the coffee shop schmoozing with other performers.

Record what people will buy. This is a democracy. People will vote with their pocket books, and if you do not sell them what they like and what inspires them, they will buy from someone else. Have a variety of CDs to test the market, and you'll soon find what sells best.

Recording something unique does not contradict this. It can be fresh while seeming familiar or within the comfort zone.

Record something for children. Write your own lyrics to the great songs so kids can enjoy the music. Make the words about something they like. Get creative. Consider turning the Ring Trilogy music into the Lord of the Rings with words that fit certain songs. How about the music from La Boehme with English words to Narnia or Spiderman? Does it make your blood curdle? Good. You are on the right track.

Speak to whatever audience you attract and can find. Develop your audience. Use great music to teach history, geography, religion, whatever. Make sure they understand the words. Parents are demanding tools to teach their children, so they do not have to spend time with the kids. That is a fact.

Feed the need. ANYTHING set to classical music is better than the crap the radio plays. ANYTHING set to classical music with an educational twist that kids find fun is a great deal more educational than what they are currently getting. GET CREATIVE. My first exposure to classical music came from Daffy Duck singing the Hungarian Rhapsody, and some lovely lady singing Tales of Hoffman about "Far from home my little toy boat is sailing so soft to the sea. . ." Put that music on today and I get misty eyed. I will pay money to hear a couple of great vocalists sing that music. Get kids hooked on the music, and get their parents' attention by teaching them something.

As you develop your audience base, THEN it is time to convince them to hire you for a live performance. September is about the right time to start finding people to hire you at Christmas. During the Christmas season, getting jobs should be like a mezzo hitting middle C. Christmas is also a great time for setting up Easter recitals.

Just remember this quote from Field of Dreams (be glad I am not here to give you my lousy James Earl Jones imitation). At the end of the picture, Jones' character says words to the effect of, "Oh they will come, Ray. They will find themselves in Iowa City, wanting something. They'll hear about this place. It will remind them of everything good. They will come here to look around. You will charge $20, and they will hand it over without giving a thought, for it is money they have and dreams they want."

This is the very essence of marketing. Sell the dream. Be the dream. That is the benefit. People who tend to like classical music fit this to perfection. It is money they have but dreams they want. For Christmas, their hearts are turned to divine thoughts more than at any time of the year. Your music is little 'd' and big 'D' divine. Put on a concert for them in their own home so they can invite their friends, loved ones and business associates. Let them show off their home so they can show off their heart as well.

How do you get to these people?

Begin with who you know. By now you should have a list of people who have purchased your CDs - if you have been doing what I have told you to do.

Employ the Law of Concentric Circles. Start with those who have paid you money for your singing. They will want more.

Next, go to friends and relatives. Do not sell them short. Let them do something for you. Tell them, "I need your help. I must get three paid home performances this year so I can maintain my status as a professional performer. May I give one in your home for your friends?" Flip the tables. Everyone says they have to sing for free as a favor for friends, because they let their friends set the agenda. You set the agenda, and tell them you need help to build your career. Promise them a free gig in the future when you are famous.

If you work in a company, start with the boss. He or she probably has money and is looking for peace more than anyone. Running a business is tough work. MLK Day, Valentine's Day, Easter, Memorial Day, 4th of July, Veteran's Day, Columbus Day, Thanksgiving, Christmas and New Year's will be upon us soon enough. There is no time like now to get your game plan together. Great music sung well is perfect for a home concert during every one of these holidays.

Romance it. Paint them a picture of what it will be like. The theater in their mind is where you must market. Paint the dream of what it will be like to have local royalty grace their home and have friends admire their generosity and good taste.

Make sure the music fits. For MLK Day, choose messages of hope, freedom, struggle and survival. For Easter, choose songs of rebirth and great sacred music. Be original with traditional selections. Add your touches and avoid being an opera automaton. I heard a wonderful rendition of the Messiah – the whole thing – sung by a quartet. Stunning. Original and interesting. Personal.

Can you think of a better and more romantic Valentine's Day event than with the music you have? So much of opera music fits that day.

Sing "The Battle Hymn of the Republic" for EASTER. "In the beauty of the lilies ... " is more for Easter than Independence Day. Explain this to your audience. For Columbus Day, sing in Italian. You get the picture.

At every event, sell your CD. Be sure your first CD is called "The Best of (your name) Part II." You can record Part I later, as they will want to complete the set if they like Part II.

For more jobs, ask your boss or the wealthy people you know for references. People like to help artists. This is a word-of-mouth marketing plan.

No flier is going to work unless it is just a reminder. Create one, but don't feature your photograph, rather feature the host. "J. Jones is pleased to invite you to his home for a personal concert." Place your photo in a lesser position.

This is all part of using the Law of Concentric Circles. Begin inside the closest ring to you, and then expand from 1) people who know you, to 2) people who barely know you but have an affinity for you, then to 3) their friends, and 4) the friends of those who know or have bought your CD or who have heard you sing before.

Again, start with the inner circle of people you know. Expand outward to the people they know. Contact catering companies and volunteer to be part of their package for a small fee; or in the beginning, work for tips and the list of attendees, or a chance to give away your CD if guests will just sign your guest book with name, mailing and e-mail addresses. Later you can contact them about your future performances. Make yourself a star.

Do this, and you will have at least 24 jobs in the next six months that pay you $500 each – maybe not at first, but soon. Eventually you want to be making at least $1,000 for an hour long in-home concert. And the number of jobs should be more than 50 as you ramp up.

As you build your client base, you will have a list of people to invite to larger theater concerts. You will have a following that will buy tickets to the opera you are in, making you more attractive to the promoter. Do not let them lie to you and say that does not make a difference. Someone who can sell 1,000 tickets at $75 a head will get any promoter's attention –even to the point of telling the artistic director exactly who must get that role, or heads will roll.

Can't happen? Think auditioning is the only way? That is the longest of long shots. You might as well play the lottery, which is the investment of choice for the mathematically impaired.

Know this: your career will not happen by itself. It will not happen unless you build it on your terms and ignore all the psychic vampires out there. The principles are clear. Offer a desired product to your inner circle. Follow the Law of Concentric Circles and expand outward from your core friends and fans. Get them to give you referrals. Build a house list. Work the house list and build a career. It has been done repeatedly in this field and many others.

Enjoy the fruits of your labors, and you will have more fruit than you can hold. Follow these tried and true principles to expand your chances of being seen by the right people as you earn money.

Can You Fake Sincerity?

Christmas. I hope every Christmas is sensational for you. It is so easy for this holiday to become just another holiday void of deeper spiritual blessings. For classical performers, it should be a time for literal rejoicing, because you get to sing some of the most majestic, heartfelt music ever written.

What does this have to do with marketing?

I once participated on a televised panel before a gargantuan convention with some famous marketers. The moderator was a rather serious fellow with deep philosophical questions for us. The others were up to the task, but when it came my turn to answer the question du jour, I could not resist. The question was, "What is the key or most important element of good marketing?" I girded my loins, cleared my throat a few times, got my most serious look and said, "Sincerity." The moderator nodded in deep approval. I continued, "If you can fake that, everything else is easy."

The moderator was horrified and the audience burst into laughter. He eventually came around, too. When he composed himself, he asked, "You must tell us more." Keep in mind, he had cut everyone else off to give himself more time to talk, but now, the floor was mine. I simply said, "If you believe it, they'll believe it. If you don't, they won't."

I have never been impressed by performers who go through the motions and sing by the numbers. I have hired dozens of great performers for many parts, and what strikes me in auditions are those who have real stage presence that comes from within. They own the stage because they own the heart. Of course, they had taken the essential steps to perfect their voice, but had never let their voices get in the way of the music. They caressed the words, stroked the notes and loved the audience.

I never let their off-the-stage conduct fully persuade me, but I have yet to hire someone who was not in love with what they were singing. Let me back up. I have watched someone who seemed to have it all, but was missing something. I wanted him for the part, but something nagged at me. He was clearly the best voice, but I was not buying him fully. Sure enough, as I got to meet him later, his sincerity was a mile wide but only an inch thick. Another performer with one of the best baritone voices I have heard was just the opposite. My audiences of rather wealthy people, who had heard about every great Metropolitan opera star, ate him up. As I came to know him, I found he was everything off the stage that he was on the stage.

No, that does not mean when he plays the devil, he is the devil off stage. It means that he loves playing that role and gives it everything he has. He once asked me to sing a song with him during a concert. That is not my forte, but I do enjoy singing. I could not imagine being on the stage with him, but he insisted. I always try to make my performers look good, and the comparison of him singing with me would showcase what a great voice he had, so I did it. We sang "Anthem" from Chess. I have never sounded so good, only because his performance lifted me up. He exuded magnificence at every note, and it was contagious. He made me look and sound far better than I am. Of course, having a Soviet and an American singing that song during the Cold War moved the audience as well.

Great performers love what they are doing, love the music, and love the audience. Sincerity is not faked, but becomes who they are on stage.

A great man named David O. MacKay said that one time as a missionary, he was feeling miserable and did not understand why. While in Scotland, he looked at a nice building and read a scroll in the gable: "What ere thou art, act well they part." He pondered this and thought, "I'm not acting my part very well." He rationalized that he did not fully understand everything he was to do, and he thought acting in this case would be phony. But, the words were emblazoned on his heart and he tried them. He gave his missionary work everything he had. The work was good work, and when he immersed himself in his part, he grew to love everything about his mission.

Others have said, "If you want a virtue, assume you have it and soon it will be yours."

Sometimes we have to fake parts of our sincerity; but if it is a good thing, in a relatively short time that feigned sincerity will turn to genuine love of our mission.

At Christmas time, those who believe in the message of the Messiah and Redeemer can put every fiber of their being into their work. They should be able to touch people as they have never touched anyone before. Ultimately, that is the best marketing.

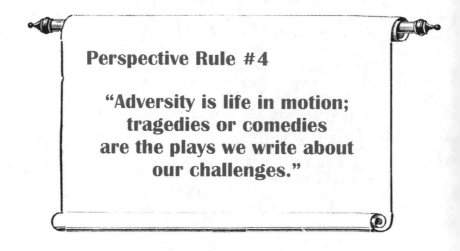

Perspective Rule #4

"Adversity is life in motion;
tragedies or comedies
are the plays we write about
our challenges."

Chapter 37

How to Hold an In-Home Concert

Performers find themselves in the precarious position of waiting – waiting to see if they get the role, the gig, the opportunity...wondering if they should be doing something else and if that something else will ruin their chances at a greater opportunity.

Even when you get the roles you cherish at the A, B, C and D Houses, the dilemma will stay with you, although you'll have an agent at that point to help manage your career. But until then, doing something is the better choice because what performers need is performance experience. The more the better.

This blog begins a series that will go into details on how to create a job that will pay you money, develop your fan base, help you create a CD or DVD and performance blog, and provide a base for many more gigs in the future. Doing the first job isn't that difficult and, once you've done one, the work of creating more simply gets easier. Best of all, this is something every performer can do and is always well within your control.

Let's get started. The performance category idea actually evolved from Jay Meetze of the Opera Company of Brooklyn, at least in my head. I know others were doing this long before Jay and in fact this concept was all the rage during Mozart and Beethoven's time.

Jay found that the four walls of his theater were rather expensive and confining. So he began, as he told CNN and many other news outlets, to "make opera accessible." As he points out, at one time opera was the "pop" culture and in some places still is. The key is to make great music accessible. He did that by taking ensembles into people's homes and entertaining their guests.

About the same time I was consulting with a bunch of performers in the Washington, D.C., area. One performer who sang for the Washington National Opera Company said he needed more income and more performing opportunities. I asked him if it would be beneath his dignity to come to a friend of mine's home in Chevy Chase and hold a concert for 50 of his friends around Christmas. He lit up like a Christmas tree and thought that a wonderful endeavor. I carefully laid out for him what I'm now going to show you. He followed the instructions precisely. He reported back that he was delighted that he had all of the work he could want in November and December as well as other holiday times.

We now call those concerts "In-Home Concerts." Hundreds of performers are catching on to the magic of In-Home Concerts. Some report they make about $400 per concert. Other $700 or more. I helped one family and four performers raise $30,000 for a young expectant mother who had been hit by a stroke, lost her baby and needed funds for therapy and equipment to walk again. More than 300 people showed up to the family's friend's home that backed up on a golf course and dozens more sent in gifts. It's all possible if you know the following steps to take.

How to get people to host you

Here is how to get people to host you, to get them to do most of the work, the program selections and variety that will please you and them, the advertisements to use, the printed program that will help you bring in income painlessly, how to incorporate tastefully selling a CD even if you don't have one, how to parlay one concert into dozens more, and much more.

The big question is where to hold the in-home concert. This could be a deal killer, but don't give up.

First, what you need is a home in the colder months that can hold 50 people comfortably or a backyard in the summer months that can seat at least the same number. The more the merrier. They will also need a good piano. Be sure to test it out.

Most homes of 3,500 square feet or more have such accommodations.

Here are the most obvious candidates:
1. Family and friends
2. Friends of family and friends
3. Parents of your voice students
4. Your boss and work associates
5. Family or friends of fellow performers who may want to join you in holding such a concert
6. Friends or family of professors from your university, either in your vocal program or other university programs
7. Church and community associates

It all goes back to discussions on the Law of Concentric Circles. Your best sources for any marketing begin with those closest to you, with whom you have the most credibility. And then you go to their friends and then their friends. It's always the best past to travel.

How do you ask them? Humbly. "Mrs. Johnson. I've been singing for groups a number of years and wondered if you'd allow me the honor of singing for your friends at your home this Christmas (or whatever occasion)?" The key is "may I be of assistance to you… be of service to you… allow me the honor…" or something along those lines.

They'll never have thought of this, so expect a shocked look. This first one will be the most difficult. Once you've held one concert, this will snowball. Those who attend will gladly hold a concert in their home.

Always ask face to face, never in an email, over the phone or through an emissary. Do it yourself. Let them know your excitement.

Keep this first concert simple and easy for the family. Let them know you'll do all of the work and that they can help you in selecting some of the music. You'll give them some choices and thoughts. Guide them to some great selections and away from Grandma Got Run Over By a Reindeer.

More on that later. But let them know it will be a night of beautiful music, selecting from the best of the best, including stunning arrangements from Broadway and the Met as well as wonderful spirituals and other art songs appropriate for the occasion. Christmas is quite easy. Summer time becomes more diverse and requires more dexterity in planning mixing in not only show tunes with opera arias but some patriotic as well. You are there to entertain and uplift.

Getting People to Come

Anyone can hold a concert. Just like anyone can make any number of products you see or buy in the market place. Making products isn't the problem. Finding buyers is. With the ever increasing snow storm of advertising and information flashing before our eyes, getting to the messages we want is difficult. That means getting your message about your concert to the right people is the challenge.

First, what not to do. Don't advertise to everyone, just to the people who are most likely to come. They are:

1. The friends, neighbors and family of your host. That includes people they know at their place of employment, church, clubs, associations or anywhere else that respects them.

2. Your friends and family. If you're still in school or teaching school, that's a great place to round up bodies. The other people mentioned in item one apply to you as well.

Start making a list of the names, addresses and emails of every person from the possibilities listed above. That is your "house list."

The first photo is from this Kristin Jensen's first home concert. It led to a second home concert, etc. Her greatest asset was her persistence. Of course she had a beautiful voice and was prepared to deliver a great concert, but her persistence & determination made it happen. Notice the very simple set up and equipment. Don't overdo the production values. Keep it simple!

The second photo is from another home concert. Four singers got paid AND raised $30,000 for a young mother and father in the neighborhood for her medical treatment.

You are going to prepare an invitation that will have the following features:

1. It will first tell the person how the concert will benefit that person. The wrong way is to begin by telling how wonderful you are, and that is how most concert and other ads begin. This is about THEM NOT YOU!
2. You'll continue extolling the benefits of coming to the concert and the kindness of the host.
3. You will become a benefit of the concert.
4. Your music will be a great benefit of coming to the concert.
5. You'll clearly let them know where, and when.

Remember the AIDA Code already discussed in this book.

All of this should be accompanied with a social media campaign that you orchestrate. Set up a Facebook page just for this event and get your friends to invite people to it. Use Twitter and other social media to get the word out. Make this a media event.

Decide on the purpose of the concert. It can just be a concert hosted by a family, or it could be:

1. Evaluation or Feedback concert. You're seeking opinions of people about what music you should put on your CD or use for your auditions, or whatever. For this you'll need an evaluation form.

2. Pre-CD launch concert.

3. Benefit concert for a cause your host believes deeply in. (See the chapter about how to hold a benefit concert and get paid twice for doing it.) We held a benefit concert at our backyard that opens out to a golf course and had 400 people attend and we raised our goal of $30,000.

4. Pre-audition tour concert or Summer Program Funding Concert. Let them know you're going on an audition tour to New York or London or wherever you're going for a Summer Program and need to raise funds and donations will be accepted along with feedback.

On the next page is an example of flyer or invitation that worked quite well. It is benefit heavy right from the start and catches people's heart. It's all about THEM and how you can help them. A simple letter accompanied this with the email and email of where to RSVP.

Here is the note I received from this performer and her results are fairly typical:

It went great!!! I sang well, the pianist played well; we had 45 people there in this huge, gorgeous home. The acoustics were

Come Fall In Love –

in a delightful Evening of Broadway,
Opera and Spiritual Songs that will
lift your Heart & Stir your Soul.

Featuring Award-Winning Singer
Kristin Jensen

Selections by Rogers & Hammerstein, Andrew Lloyd Webber,
Lerner & Loew, Meredith Wilson, Puccini, Charpentier,
Mozart, Schubert, Fauré, and fresh arrangements
of the great Negro Spirituals.

8:00 pm
Saturday, October 11, 2008

Decker Home
3516 E. Knoll Street.

New CD Home RSVP Seating is limited—RSVP is required

PERFECT--the room I sang in had a monastery-cloister arched
ceiling. The guests were very happy. I pre-sold 29 CDs.
Donations brought in $610. Not too shabby!
People are talking already about doing a Christmas program there
in a couple of months, and a couple of other people expressed
interest in having entertainment in their homes.

One of the ladies who came was my drycleaner--I met her the
day before when I dropped off my dress to be cleaned. Turns out
she's from CA and loves opera. It was just a lot of fun and everyone
came away w/something.

Thanks for your help! It was a team effort that has paid off
beautifully.

For your concert your reasons for holding will determine your
next actions. If it is just to sing, well, you've sung so there is nothing
more to do. But I'll now assume you're more ambitious. As such, you
want a singing future. Therefore you need to 1) earn money at the
concert, 2) sell CDs, 3) book more concerts or engagements and 4)
gather information to lead to even more engagements.

Here's what to do:

1. Prepare a printed program. You want everyone to have one. Yes, it's nice to have them see the numbers, but what you really want is for them to see the survey. More on that in a moment. I've included a sample. Don't use this one. Create your own, but use the concepts. Notice on the program is a good mixture of music that progresses from the familiar to the more esoteric (for some) that is all great music. Please the fans but uplift them for a thoroughly entertaining night. Don't go too long. A one hour concert is grand plus a ten minute break/intermission. A ten minute break is great as a dramatic pause for you and for your audience to discuss how wonderful you are.

2. The survey is NOT a scientific survey but a leading marketing document. You're leading them down a logical path. You're asking them to recall positive things about your performance and letting them put those down on paper so it sticks in their mind. The more they write the more they'll bite.

"Fall" In Love Tonight!

Decker Home
October 10, 2008

Kristin Jensen, Soprano
Jeremy Peterman, Piano

Think of Me	Andrew Lloyd Webber
Phantom of the Opera	
'Till There Was You	Meredith Wilson
The Music Man	
I Could Have Danced All Night	Frederick Loewe
My Fair Lady	

O mio babbino caro	Giacomo Puccini
Gianni Schicchi	
Quando m'en vo	Giacomo Puccini
La Bohéme	

Depuis le jour	Gustave Charpentier
Louise	

Du bist die Ruh	Franz Schubert
R'tzel	Stephen Richards

Laudate Dominum	Wolfgang Mozart
Come, thou Fount of Every Blessing	Joseph Martin
Were You There	Moses Hogan
Give Me Jesus	Moses Hogan

Kristin would like to thank you for coming this evening, and would like to ask for your feedback as she works to make every performance more memorable and moving for her wonderful audience.

What was your favorite selection tonight?

What selection(s) moved your heart most tonight?

What would you like to hear Kristin sing in the future?

What did you most enjoy about this evening?

Would you come hear Kristin again?

What title do you prefer for Kristin's upcoming CD? Options: "Stir Your Soul," "'Till There Was You," or your personal suggestion:

What can Kristin do in the future to make evenings like this more memorable for you?

Kristin would like to send you a special thank you for coming tonight. Please write down your information below.

Name: _____ Phone: _____

Address: _____

Email/website: _____

Contributions to Kristin's CD fund are being accepted tonight with much gratitude. Please indicate below what you would like to contribute:

$10 ____ $20 ____ $30 ____ $50 ____ Other ____

Thank you, and may God prosper and bless you!

Kristin would like to thank you for coming this evening, and would like to ask for your feedback as she works to make every performance more memorable and moving for her wonderful audience.

What was your favorite selection tonight?

What selection(s) moved your heart most tonight?

What would you like to hear Kristin sing in the future?

What did you most enjoy about this evening?

Would you come hear Kristin again?

What title do you prefer for Kristin's upcoming CD? Options: "Stir Your Soul," "'Till There Was You," or your personal suggestion:

What can Kristin do in the future to make evenings like this more memorable for you?

Kristin would like to send you a special thank you for coming tonight. Please write down your information below:

Name:_____Phone:_____

Address:_____

Email/website:_____

Contributions to Kristin's CD fund are being accepted tonight with much gratitude. Please indicate below what you would like to contribute:

$10____ $20____ $30____ $50____Other_____

Thank you, and may God prosper and bless you!

As you see it leads them to volunteer to contribute or buy a CD or to hold a concert – take some action. In that they enjoyed your singing and they're recalling how much, why wouldn't they want to share you with their friends? And they will. I've yet to find a performer who does this that doesn't make at least $300 to $500 for the night plus book other concerts.

The survey on the right side of this program (the correct place to put it) fit this performer's program and needs. You may have a CD. Change to fit. Don't copy. But follow the logic and don't be shy about asking.

You're providing value so be prepared to ask for value in return. She did quite well. I would add the line about "Would you like to have a concert in your home? ____ Yes (don't put no) Put this after the Email line.

3. Make sure you've gone over all of this with your host. Kindly ask them if they'll emcee the affair. It's their home. Ask them if they'll do the introduction, the intermission announcement and the closing comments.

Ask if they'll introduce you and give them a written introduction. Keep it short and to the point. Don't tell them to read it. Tell them you've jotted down a few ideas that they can use if they like. They'll probably just read it so make sure you write it so it sounds great if read.

After the intermission, have them suggest to the audience that if they would like to have you sing in their home there is a place on the back of the program where they can request you to hold a concert for them.

Work out with the host that at the end of the concert to please read a blurb about the feedback. Write out what they should say, something like,

"We want to thank Fred/Kathleen for being our honored guest tonight and for the beautiful music. She is always looking to improve and would appreciate you opening your programs right now and filling out the brief survey so she can get your feedback. We've provided pencils (make sure you provide them in nice boxes all around during the intermission). And Fred has a CD that you can take home with you as our gift. We'd ask you to make a donation to his audition fund. As you know, to audition for Broadway/ Metropolitan Opera roles it takes quite a bit of money just to get there and Fred could use your support. So make a contribution to that fund and we'll give you his CD."

Something like that. Work it out with the host. Maybe you don't give away the CD. Maybe you sell the CD AND ask for the donation. Feel your way through this. There isn't a right way, although there is a wrong way – not doing or trying something and holding back. Get out there and do something, even if it doesn't work the first time.

4. Have a nice clear ornate classy bowl for people to place their programs with their feedback. Have envelopes there to put the feedback sheets in and the $$$ as well.

5. Mingle, mingle, mingle. Shake hands with everyone. They're likely to hand you $$$ then too. Thank them for coming and say, "I am anxious to read your feedback sheets" to encourage them to fill them out. Bring a Sharpie that you know works so you can sign your CD. When someone buys one immediately say, "Would you like me to sign that?" They'll always say Yes and in doing so people will see that and it encourages others to buy.

6. When you get home, enter all of the names and demographics you've gathered onto your House List spreadsheet before you sleep.

You should have this from the feedback sheets and you should have also gotten the list from the host, telling them you need the emails to thank the people personally for coming. Putting this off is deadly. The next day, be sure to write a Thank You note on a nice card to the host with profuse kind words.

Then email all of the guests, thanking them for coming. If they have asked you to do a concert, begin the discussion. If they haven't, let them know a date you're available and see if they'd like you to come then. NOW is the time. Every day that goes buy the lead grows colder. Offer everyone your CD where appropriate. Don't be shy but be wise.

7. Get someone to video at least one of your best songs along with shots of the audience and home. Get the hosts permission to publish this. Then post this on YouTube, Facebook and Twitter and whatever other social media you can. Get out there with the message that you perform. And provide a contact website, email or phone number.

Following this path can lead to additional home concerts. It can lead, as you'll suggest to the audience, to you singing at their professional functions like office parties, office openings, company conventions, reunions, political functions, church meetings or retreats, and so forth.

Many will live in retirement communities. That's not an old folks home. That's a community with a community center that loves to have events on a regular basis. I know performers who have a regular circuit of these centers that pay them for monthly or quarterly concerts that pay $500 to $750 for the evening. They perform at least three nights a week year around.

At first it takes a great deal of coordination and marketing work to get this piece meal singing career going. Once you get this perpetual job machine in gear, it becomes more and more on autopilot. The more you perform, the better you become and the more exposure leads to better chances.

Once again... marketing is not magic, it's motion.

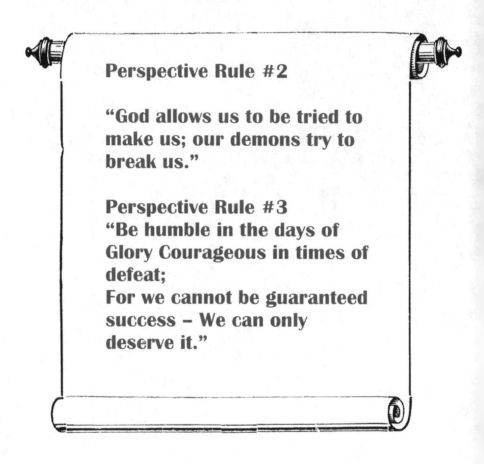

Perspective Rule #2

"God allows us to be tried to make us; our demons try to break us."

Perspective Rule #3
"Be humble in the days of Glory Courageous in times of defeat;
For we cannot be guaranteed success – We can only deserve it."

Chapter 38

Mixing Business with Pleasure

In chapter 33 we discussed different venues. Follow along with me now as I try to help one good performer who is also running a jewelry business. Her situation has been repeated by several performers with whom I have met. Hopefully this real-life example will bring together and clarify a number of principles we've previously discussed.

Rather than printing her letter first (in italics) and then adding my comments, I have simply inserted my comments throughout the letter as they relate to what she said. I have changed her name.

Letter: *Hello, Mark!*

Thank you again and again for the incredibly valuable information and guidance you presented at the Marketing Preview and Workshop the end of last year. Both of my careers (singing and retail) have been benefiting from what you taught me! There are so many things I still need to improve, but I am really rolling now.

I am writing regarding an "added value" snafu I have been experiencing time and time again. My retail business is fine jewelry and arts. I keep my prices low A) so that more people can afford to have the arts in their lives, and B) to keep the profits rolling in so that I can hire musicians to perform at the parties I will shortly start holding regularly (every 4-6 weeks).

My Comment: These are nice thoughts, but not your business. Customers will afford what they want. Spend your time on their "wants," and help them want what you sell. Your altruistic reasons, while good, are problematic. Giving people too many choices confuses and diffuses your efforts. Keep it simple.

Do not keep your prices artificially low for personal reasons. Price is determined by perceived value. If they value it, they will pay for it. Spend time increasing the value, not justifying low prices. People are suspicious of low prices and figure it must be inferior. Jewelry stores always have a few items that are a lesser price and are nice (but not great) products. You do not want junk, nor do they, so they keep it elegant but simple.

Letter: *These parties will be free to the public. Invitations will be sent to my mailing list, and ads will be placed in local papers. The events are designed to expose people to every kind of art, encouraging them to value it and make it a regular part of their lives (that is my overall goal with my store).*

My Comment: Ben and Jerry's started people thinking more about this approach. They weren't, however, the first or anywhere close, just the most famous. What they do not tell you is when they were developing their business, they didn't donate. They focused on their business, and made ice cream that was good with unique combinations and catchy names.

However, they have left in their wake a false concept of "corporate responsibility." Corporations have one purpose and one alone. To make a profit. That's it. The owners, shareholders and human beings directing the company may have "human responsibility," but confusing the two can lead to business disaster. Do not think I believe it's just fine for corporations to rape, pillage and plunder. I do not, but I do not blame non-animate objects. I blame the amoral leaders who hide behind a legal entity. You may not buy what I'm saying, and that is your perfectly acceptable choice. But, your business will struggle when you mix altruism and profit-making. If you want to be a non-profit, form that kind of corporation and run with those rules. If not, follow the rules of business.

Letter: *Of course shopping is encouraged at these events! Ideally, the events will add to the value of everything purchased at Seaside Gems; every time customers pay to enrich their lives with tangible art, they are funding intangible art to enrich everyone's life.*

My Comment: Inviting people to a location to hear great music, sponsored by Seaside Gems is great. Get them there, and then "now a word from our sponsor." That's particularly effective if it does not come from you, but a notable emcee that lauds your generosity and raves about your jewelry. Make sure, of course, they are wearing some of your jewelry.

Letter: *And now for the aforementioned snafu. Each time I tell a customer (or soon-to-be-customer) about these events, no matter how I couch the great news, the result does not vary: whatever they were interested in buying, they immediately put down.*

My Comment: So, do not do that. Let them buy it and then give them the chance to be on the mailing list. Say something like, "With each purchase you receive a ticket, worth $39" – or whatever the concert ticket should be worth, and make sure that same price is on EVERY ticket. Sell them at the store. Only give them away as a premium. Sell them elsewhere. People value what they pay for.

Letter: *Their desire changes from wanting to buy the merchandise to wanting to be on the mailing list. They say, "I will definitely come! That sounds fantastic!" Well, great, but they were about to buy something, and now they are not going to! They act as if their excitement about attending these upcoming events will somehow pay my rent!*

My Comment: That is because you trained them to do this. And no one cares about how you pay your rent when they are buying your product. They buy it based on the perceived value and the relationship it has to the price. On a personal level, they do care what happens to you, but not when they are buying. Do not mix the two together.

Letter: *I always prefer to bring up this aspect of my business when I am trying to wrap up a purchase. This way, the customer is even happier about his/her purchase. But so often, people ask about my prices, or the piano in the room, and so I tell them all about the events. And every time, their focus shifts. No sale is made.*

My Comment: You have done a great job testing your sales pitch. Now, use the results.

Letter: *Mark, I just do not get it. I keep using different words to explain my plan, but the result never changes. They were going to buy, and now they are waiting for the party. And whether they will actually buy at the party remains to be seen.*

My Comment: People who buy at the store will likely buy at the party. People who do not buy at the store will likely NOT buy at the party. The best people to sell to are people who have PURCHASED something from you.

Letter: *I am officially living up to that cliché about insanity: doing the same thing repeatedly, yet expecting a different result. Will you please shed your bright light on my dilemma?*
> *With much gratitude,*
> *Sarah*

My Comment: A patient once said to the doctor: "Doctor, doctor. It hurts when I walk this way." The doctor responded, "Do not walk that way." Business is actually far simpler than people try to make it.

One last word about price. While I ALWAYS complain about price when I buy something – looking to find a discount, a soft spot, an anomaly – I do not begrudge anyone charging whatever they charge. How high is up is impossible to know. The correct price isn't something you can look up on a chart. It's what people value. I whined at the Marriott Marquis this weekend about the $44 dinner at its elegant restaurant. I did the same at the $89 dinner at the Bellagio in Las Vegas. I didn't buy my dinners there, but the places were packed. I couldn't get a reservation at the View if I'd wanted to eat there. Obviously, someone thinks $44 is worth the price of the meal.

How much it costs to put on that dinner is irrelevant. Price is the regulator in the market place. It will go as high as consumers are willing to go.

Remember this when negotiating prices for your singing services as well. Do not spend time justifying your price, spend time building your value.

Hope this helps. It will.

Here is another instructive letter:
Dear Mark,

I would like to share with you a marketing lesson I learned from a fellow performer last night. Both of us performed in a showcase (non-paid) with many others, which included many styles of singers, dancers and a puppeteer.

I sang five art songs and the MC graciously advertised my CD of Art Songs that would be for sale at the intermission.

Following me, my fellow performer took a different approach. At the end of his set of folk songs, he announced that he only had one copy of his CD with him. He did not want to sell it, but at intermission, the first person who made a donation to the presenting group could have it for free.

Well, you can imagine what happened. A gentleman quickly came up and made a $20 donation to the group and grabbed the CD. And many others wanted to do the same.

My CD was for sale for $15, and we did not make any sales. I sang beautifully, so I know that that was not the reason my CD did not sell. My fellow performer created excitement around his CD by presenting it in limited availability, and increased its perceived value by linking it to the group.

I thought you would be interested in this.
All the best,   *Jane F.*

My Comment:

Thanks for sharing. What's the principle here? The emcee endorsement is good, but exclusivity and limited offers with a hook always out sell others. What this really shows is how artists are trained to be sophisticated, gentle and not overbearing. That instantly puts them at a disadvantage in marketing themselves. Modesty and marketing are NOT great companions.

Artists are creative people. Once they start thinking creatively about marketing, get over their hesitance, and forget about what their peers will think (as this fellow did), they make the best marketers. Classical singers are natural performers – the same skill developed by good salesmen. A good performer would normally die before thinking of himself as a salesman, even though a great performer has a keen eye on his audience's reaction and, coupled with his artistic integrity, delivers a memorable show. Applause follows. Ovations then come. And if the artist is savvy in marketing, he parlays this success into new jobs.

The shrinking violet artist stands back and hopes she will be discovered because of her overwhelming talent. It just does not happen. Remember that "overnight successes" are years in the making- they NEVER just happen.

Back to the selling of the CD. Note that the artist set himself apart from all the others. He made a unique appeal. Using the AIDA code, he gained Attention, then generated Interest by saying he only had ONE. The potential consumer became curious: Why is he not letting me have his CD? Why isn't he selling it? How dare he not sell to me? He then generated Desire to buy by aligning himself with the cause de jour, insisting that to qualify for his CD they had to make a donation to that cause.

Keep in mind that the artist could get paid – even though he made a donation. Before the event he could tell the sponsor that he will take 10 dollars (or some figure) for every donation, and the rest will go to the organization. It's done every day. When big name groups hold benefit concerts, nearly every group gets paid BEFORE the donations are counted. They may charge less, but maybe not. Their draw is worth it to the non-profit.

Finally, the performer promoted Action because he went down into the audience. He had people come to him and he would make it easy for them to give up their money. So many artists find this distasteful. So many artists are broke. There is a correlation.

You are a terrific performer and need to simply apply what you are learning about marketing to make this great talent pay off.
Sincerely,
Mark

Dear Mark,
You are right. I am now applying these principles and already I have seen my CD sales rise dramatically. I'll keep you posted.
Thank you,
Jane

Questions and Answers

Here, are some questions I have been asked in e-mails, letters, at conventions, Marketing Master Classes and in private consultations. I keep a running list. Here are the questions and my answers.

Do you consult with performers?

If they are motivated and willing to try what I suggest, absolutely. My rates are simply 50% more than the hourly rate the performer is currently paying for music/voice lessons. I do insist upon a preliminary consultation by phone and follow up emails to establish if I really can help the performer. No charge for the preliminary session.

To start the consultation process just email me at mark@mjstoddard.com

How do you deal with criticism?

The music and art industry, ironically, is filled with people who like to criticize each other. My suggestions:

Knowing your purpose helps you develop a thick skin.

Focusing on that purpose tunes your ears and helps you filter suggestions.

Accentuate the positive and suggest good ideas.

Keep a quiet mouth so you never give criticism.

I don't believe in "constructive" criticism.

What I've learned most from negative criticism is self-loathing and personal despair. Once over that, I stumble forward none the wiser but more cautious. Those who wish to teach using negative criticism only fool themselves into thinking it is teaching en route to learning.

Learning comes mostly from emulation. It's how we learned to walk, talk, sing, and live.

I've heard it said we learn more from our failures than our successes, but I'm not so sure. Failures are filled with angst, depression, cynicism, skepticism, contempt and loss of confidence.

Yes ... Failure is a part of life, but well worth leaving behind as quickly as possible. Visiting the caverns of failure should only be done after positive experiences have led us to understand we are of value. Perhaps in tranquility we can then stop for a moment at the cavern of failure, peek inside and pull out something of use for later.

Should anyone seek to shove us down into that dank cavern of despair through words of criticism (to make sure we learn from our failures), we enter unarmed and at the mercy of the bowels of negativity.

Instead, journey forth to the springs of eternal life and sip from the clear pools surrounding it. Take others with you. Encourage them as if they were already there with kind words and thoughtful encouragement.

A mansion can be built upon a tiny foundation if positive thoughts are the concrete and steel. As those thoughts mature into actions, the foundation magically increases and soon becomes rock solid and a far larger platform than the loftiest mansion may need. As the shingles of positive thoughts are applied to the roof, no longer are the hailstorms of negative criticism allowed to damage the mansion's gossamer draperies and plush carpets.

I've considered criticism, and conclude that I welcome all criticism so long as it is filled with love and adulation.

What are the five most important words in advertising?
Free. You. (The person's) Name. Act Now. And the most important 9 words in a row: Don't let someone inexperienced in business touch your business.

Can singers market themselves and keep their artistic integrity?
Only if their marketing plan is based on their value system. If the marketing plan springs out of a desire for money, then you will follow the money path, which invariably leads away from your values. You need to begin with your values, determine where you want to be, and then create a marketing plan to help you maintain your personal or artistic integrity.

What is the difference between marketing a car and a singer?
The principles are the same. Techniques vary.

Who are my customers?
Whoever has what you want, or whoever wants what you have.

Should I incorporate?
See an attorney or CPA for the final discussion, but consider that a number of business structures exist for you as a singer. The two main reasons for a business structure are 1. Tax implications, and 2. Liability considerations. Another reason is how you are funded or how people invest in a business. These structures include sole proprietorships, partnerships, Limited Liability Company, S-Corporation and C-Corporation.

Let us cut to the chase. I recommend you set up a Limited Liability Company, or LLC. In most states it is a $50 to $100 matter. You go to (name of your state).gov and follow their menus. Call them if you cannot figure it out. No lawyer is usually needed. In fact, I took a nice typed form from our lawyer to the Secretary of State's office, and my friend took a hand-filled out form. The clerk said they preferred the hand-filled-out form, but it did not really matter. She actually helped my friend finish filling out his. It is so easy and simple.

Next you call the IRS and get an Employer ID number. The clerk will give you the phone number. The IRS will issue you the number over the phone and mail you a confirmation.

Once you have these items, you can set up a business bank account. Now you can have all your jobs make out the checks to your new LLC's name. The name can be anything you like that is not already taken. You can change it by filling out a "Doing Business As" (dba) form. Keep it simple regardless. What's in a name.

With the money you have coming in, you can now pay for all related expenses from this account.

If, for any reason during the course of your work, someone is injured (you accidentally trip the lead singer and she breaks her nose), the LLC should give you protection. If you are teaching and a student is harmed, the LLC could give you protection. At least it is designed for these purposes.

Check with your lawyer to make sure this is correct and fits you.

Chapter 39

Make the Moment Matter

In the rush to find ways to get performing jobs, it is good to stop occasionally and assess where you are. A few lines from a poem come to mind:

When I stop to see my roses bloom
Or sing a sacred tune;
Then breathe and feel the air so fresh
And fill my aching breast;
I know I've run too far, too fast
And sacrificed life's best.

Performing, like all serious careers, demands finding the best in you. Lawyers must arduously complete tough college work only to face another three years of sleepless study in law school. This is only the beginning. Many years lie ahead of mind-numbing low level research before they find their niche. Doctors face even more education and even more time in emergency room frenzies, internships and rudiments of practice.

Overnight sensations are years in the making.

Artists paint, sculptors sculpt, and poets write in obscurity most of their lives, hoping their genius might find a home.

Musicians have the same plight as any genius craft. With so many wanting to perform, often without paying the price to practice or perform nearly anywhere for anyone, the percentage of those who succeed in making some kind of a living are low.

This is as it should be. The American political process of electing a president demands that a candidate go through an enormous grind. Nothing is more arduous than the work to gain a major party's nomination – truly the toughest rise to the top. It is always up for debate if they are the best; but then, everyone has a definition of what is "best." "Tough" is a better word. We want a tough president. No shrinking violets going toe to toe with the world's other tough guys and gals. Sex plays no favorites. Margaret Thatcher became known as the Iron Maiden for her grit.

The problem for classical singers is that they're in an unforgiving profession. Cracking on a high note may be justified, but not acceptable to the audience. It can ruin a career. Singers must pass through the gauntlet if they wish to achieve La Scala fame. No amount of marketing can assure that. "Voce, voce, voce" must be there (to quote Rossini).

But this presupposes that successful singing means singing at La Scala. It does not. La Scala is just one avenue. Knowing how to market yourself can help get you to La Scala by perfecting yourself in other avenues. You know the other avenues and, despite the snobs and naysayers, many legitimate avenues exist for singers.

Ten Things You Should, Must and Can Do Right Now to Build Your Singing Career:

1. It is NOT whom you have met or know, but whom you can recall. Start a house list. Get and record business cards.

2. Build the habit of doing favors rather than asking favors. Only do favors in the relevant area – getting coffee is menial. One example: referring a key person to a piece of needed information.

3. Perform everywhere, anytime, constantly. If the conditions are lousy, find a way to make them work for you. Some have said singers can ruin their voice. Yes, if you yell. Do not yell. Sing as you should. If the venue's acoustics are poor and the mikes do not work, the people in the back will give the manager hell. Maybe you will not sing there again; but, maybe the manager will love your effort so much (and everyone else has blown him off) that he will agree to your terms next time including better sound systems. I have heard all the reasons for not doing this. I do not buy any of them. Enrico Caruso often sang in noisy bars and developed a style to tame the wild beasts.

4. Organize other singers' concerts. Be in the mix to network and build performance sensibilities. Know what audiences really want by forcing yourself to take things to them.

5. Create your Foyer. Create a resume with a banner with your name and particulars and a 1"x1" head shot. Keep the banner in your letterhead, cards, and Web sites.

6. Do something unusual to be noticed. Thank everyone with e-mails AND personal notes on your head shot letterhead.

7. Start and maintain a swipe file of effective advertising; benefits, not tomb stones.

8. Audition often and think of it as a command performance. Remember, you are not your voice. Your voice is not your business. You are the business, and your voice is one of your products.

9. Get into the newspapers.

10. Get involved in your community. Be selective. Volunteer to teach a single FREE music class for children in wealthy neighborhoods. Hold an audition for children for a special PTA program.

Now, let us talk about living.

When rushing to get there, we forget life is not about getting to the objective, but the process of becoming. During the process, enjoying daily life is critical. This is far more essential than the final objective; for without the enjoyment of daily life, two things can happen:

1. We can ruin our lives, our health and our friendships – and cut short our lives.

2. Life can cut us short through no fault of our own, and we are left wishing we had stopped to love our spouse, play with the kids, get to know our neighbors, help out in school, volunteer for community actions, teach the younger, serve the needy, or feed and clothe the poor.

Nothing makes this more obvious than what happened several years ago to Carla Wood, known as CJ Williamson to *Classical Singer* magazine. Her life's ambitions were cut short. A brain tumor suddenly developed, and in two days her life was turned upside down. Her career was not what she wanted in singing. She expected more. But on the way to her career goals, she enjoyed a great marriage and raised two excellent young people now in their twenties. Eighteen years ago she started an opera newsletter to help her fellow singers find work, and transformed it into an international magazine. She always wanted to make it better at serving singers, and she did. She wanted a convention and other products that could help singers, and they happened.

Along the way, she discovered teaching others to sing was wonderful. Her church choir members and those who listened found her teaching remarkable. Her voice students loved her technical proficiency and nurturing environment. She kept singing concerts and roles. It was not La Scala never-ending, although she had done the Met and other top venues. Some might question her career – although I will never understand such pusillanimous thinking. **She did something.** She actively sought to enjoy life.

For weeks, her life hung in the balance. Were it her choice, she would have placed weights on the living side of the scale. But, it was not her choice. Death lays its icy hands on princes and paupers with impunity and without respect.

Our choice is to either end life prematurely or live life daily with joy. It is our choice how we look at life. In our silly society, we are constantly pummeled with the nonsense idea that we are victims – we cannot help it. We mouth the axiom "attitude is everything," but live otherwise.

Attitude *is* everything. We can determine how we act and view food, diets, weight, relationships, finances, living conditions, work, practice, determination and on and on.

The great therapist, Victor Frankel spent the prime of his youth in the Nazi concentration camp of Auschwitz. In the midst of those horrible conditions, he saw that some men and women chose to look their persecutors straight in the eye and defy them. Knowing they would likely be killed, they struggled to escape. Others in the same physical surroundings could bear it no more, and went to their bunks, turned to the wall and died. If Victor Frankel could be in Auschwitz, where he saw that some chose to live and some chose to die, given the same terrible conditions, surely we can choose to smell the roses every day and enjoy life while it happens.

I once served a two-year mission for The Church of Jesus Christ of Latter-day Saints in Australia. That is tough work. For a 18-year-old boy who is now an Elder and a 19-year-old girl who is now a Sister, there is no pop music, no dating, no partying, and no goofing off. It is a grind from 6 a.m. until 10 p.m., seven days a week, for 104 weeks or so. Nothing glamorous. Like any human beings, some would find excuses for not doing their best. We would look at those who were soon to head home and feeling "trunky" (bags packed and mentally checked out) and say, "When they finally leave, then we will get something done." I said it myself.

Then it hit me: someone was always going home. Life was always happening. If I waited until conditions were perfect to enjoy the service I was rendering, I would spend two years in vain. I chose to ignore the Elders and Sisters going home and let them do their thing. That changed everything. I did my work. I paid the price. I saw people's lives flourish going from sad and miserable to joyful and purposeful. I saw destitute persons become full of hope. I still communicate with many of those whose lives were changed. I lived life daily, loved the mission daily, and ignored anything keeping me from enjoying the experience. I loved my mission.

That challenge continued in school. Waiting to be happy until I got a degree or two was not acceptable; nor was waiting to love life until I found the love of my life. But once I found her, she made everything easier. We then had children. If only they would get out of cloth diapers, we would be happy. If only they did not have colic we would be happy. If only they did not have dwarfism, or Down's Syndrome, or the tumor. If only they had not been born with three strains of E. Coli, or reflux, or been teased during the awkward years. If only we had not had two of them taken prematurely from us, or had a business failure and lost all our savings, or, or, or. Life goes on. As the cliché goes, "Life is what happens while you are waiting for life."

By all means pay the price for your art. But part of the price is enjoying life every day. Disappointments are here. We cannot avoid them. Pity parties are good. You need the grief time, but only for one hour. That is it. Then learn and lead on. After the hour, do something frivolous and fun. Do it with your best friend or if you are married, your spouse. Rejoice that life goes on.

In the end, we cannot control the environment. We cannot dictate time. But we can dictate our attitude. Begin now to enjoy the great talent you have and share it with a world that desperately needs you. I hope your are properly preparing yourself for your great future.

"Gather ye rosebuds while ye may . . ."

"To every man, there comes in his lifetime that special moment when he is tapped on the shoulder and offered the chance to do a very special thing; unique, and fitted to his talents.

"What a tragedy, if that moment finds him unprepared and unqualified for the work that would be his finest hour."

-Winston Churchill